Religious Faith, Torture, and Our National Soul

RELIGIOUS FAITH, TORTURE, AND OUR NATIONAL SOUL

Edited by
DAVID P. GUSHEE, JILLIAN HICKMAN ZIMMER, AND J. DREW ZIMMER

Mercer University Press | 2010
Macon, Georgia

MERCER
UNIVERSITY PRESS

Endowed by
TOM WATSON BROWN
and
THE WATSON-BROWN FOUNDATION, INC.

MUP/P411

© 2010 Mercer University Press
1400 Coleman Avenue
Macon, Georgia 31207
All rights reserved

First Edition.

Book design by Burt&Burt

Books published by Mercer University Press are printed on acid free paper that meets the requirements
of American National Standard for Information Sciences—Permanence of Paper for Printed Library Materials.

Mercer University Press is a member of Green Press initiative (greenpressinitiative.org),
a nonprofit organization working to help publishers and printers increase their use of recycled paper
and decrease their use of fiber derived from endangered forests. This book is printed on recycled paper.

Library of Congress Cataloging-in-Publication Data

Religious faith, torture, and our national soul / edited by David P. Gushee, J. Drew Zimmer,
and Jillian Hickman Zimmer. — 1st ed.
p. cm.
Proceedings of a conference held Sept. 11-12, 2008 at Mercer University.
Includes bibliographical references (p.   ) and index.

ISBN 978-0-88146-203-6 (pbk.)

1. Torture—Government policy—United States.
2. Torture—United States—Moral and ethical aspects.
3. Torture—United States—Religious aspects.
4. Terrorism—United States—Prevention—Moral and ethical aspects.
5. Human rights—United States—Religious aspects.

I. Gushee, David P., 1962-
II. Zimmer, J. Drew.
III. Zimmer, Jillian Hickman.

HV8599.U6R45 2010
973.931—dc22

2010001572

Preface and Acknowledgments

The papers collected in this volume were initially presented at a national summit on torture hosted by Mercer University, Evangelicals for Human Rights, and the National Religious Campaign Against Torture on September 11–12, 2008.

Dramatic changes have occurred in the political context since these papers were written in summer 2008. In November, Barack Obama was elected president. Two days after his inauguration in January 2009, he signed executive orders reversing the Bush administration policies related to the treatment of detainees that are so sharply criticized by the authors whose work is gathered in this collection.

One might think these executive orders render these papers of mere historical value. But this would be to miss the counterattack proponents of the former policies rendered immediately after Obama's executive orders. And it would fail to take into account the profound split in public opinion that remains on the issue of torture in this country—a split illustrated by the results from a poll of evangelical Christians that we took in August 2008 (see appendix). It is simply true that many millions of Americans have supported and would continue to support torture in the name of national security. And if there is another terrorist attack, President Obama will surely be criticized for having "risked" national security by "tying the hands" of the CIA and others by his executive order on interrogation. The issue of torture is surely not dead. Far from it.

Therefore, we offer the collected papers from our conference on "religious faith, torture, and our national soul." We have allowed the authors to speak in their own voices and at the moment in which their reflections were crafted—summer 2008, during the waning days of the Bush administration, when every effort to force a reversal of that president's detainee policies had proven fruitless. We very much appreciate the excellent work done on the groundbreaking poll about torture attitudes by Robby Jones of Public Religion Research and Katie Paris of Faith in Public Life.

The papers cover the waterfront. They begin with reflections on "how we got here." How did the world's leading proponent of human rights end up embracing cruel, abusive, illegal, and extra-legal policies in relation to detainees captured in the so-called "war on terror"? Karen Greenberg follows the paper trail in her indomitable way; Don Guter and Steve Xenakis offer important glimpses inside the military's response to their new orders; David Gushee and his respondents reflect on reasons for religious complicity or silence as news of torture came to public consciousness.

The impact of torture is outlined in a painful testimony by Sister Dianna Ortiz and in the analysis offered by Doug Johnson, whose Center for Victims of Torture serves thousands who have been on the receiving end of torture around the world. Also, the inside accounts of life inside Guantánamo, and the struggle to represent clients there, as offered by lawyers John Chandler, Mark Denbeaux, Gita Gutierrez, and Thomas Wilner, provide a critically important glimpse into that now infamous symbol of American cruelties in the name of security.

The second half of our collection seeks to focus on "recovering our moral bearings." Writers in this section all attempt to help us discover "where…we go from here," mainly by drawing on religious, moral, and political resources available in American life. A series of sermon-reflections by Cheryl Bridges Johns, Fleming Rutledge, and Tyler Wigg-Stevenson begin this work by digging into the theological-ethical resources available, especially in the Christian faith. Glen Stassen and his respondents emphasize the power and centrality of the religious human rights traditions. Rick Love and Mahan Mirza model the kind of (difficult, sometimes controversial) dialogue required to build bridges across the chasm that divides the Muslim and Christian worlds. George Hunsinger looks at how "violence finds refuge in falsehood," zeroing in especially on the CIA's clandestine role in torture, and not just since 9/11, wondering about whether this largely unaccountable Cold War institution can be brought under citizen control. Doctoral students Michael Peppard, Kathryn Reklis, and Natalie Wigg-Stevenson offer extremely rich insights from the next generation related to, respectively, religious desecration of the Koran by American forces, the suffering torturer/hero motif in American culture, and the moral/theological disaster of the existence of extra-legal, law-free zones like CIA black sites.

The closing chapter by Rachel Laser of Third Way sketches the political context in Washington that must be taken into account if citizen activists want to bring serious change to policies on any kind of national security issue, including torture. Her comments are especially appropriate as those of us still wrestling with these issues realize that congressional action—and not just presidential executive orders—is needed in order to bring lasting change to US counter-terrorism policies.

Those who were present at the conference at Mercer experienced a profound sense of moral unity despite confessional diversity. Muslims, Jews, Protestants, Catholics, conservatives, liberals, skeptics, and secularists found common ground in their belief that the kinds of indignities our nation has visited upon those in our custody must be rejected and repudiated. Searching the resources of their moral, religious, and professional traditions, they found various ways to ground and articulate this visceral conviction. We learned from everyone's effort to find words for a conviction that goes beyond words: *No human being should be treated as we have treated people in our post-9/11 national fear, grief, and anger.* This conviction we shared, and this conviction pulses through this collection of essays.

As editors, we are deeply grateful to each contributor to this volume, as well as to those who spoke at our fall 2008 conference whose work did not end up in this collection. We have been inspired by their moral clarity, conviction, and courage and are so grateful for their willingness to participate in our project. We thank all who participated in planning, sponsoring, and staffing the conference. We are grateful to Peter Otto, a librarian at Mercer University, for his excellent work in compiling the bibliography. We would like to express our special thanks to Mary Head, project administrator for Evangelicals for Human Rights, for her invaluable efforts in planning the conference, relating to speakers and writers, and preparing the groundwork for this edited collection.

David P. Gushee

J. Drew Zimmer

Jillian Hickman Zimmer

June 17, 2009

Part I

TORTURE AND U.S. FOREIGN POLICY: LOOKING BACK

1

＊

Torture after 9/11—The Road to Abu Ghraib

Karen J. Greenberg

Let me begin with a confession. Each and every time I am asked to speak or write about torture and the treatment of suspected terrorists in US custody, each time I am asked to lay out the facts of US detainee policy, each time I mouth the word "torture," I pause. I pause because each time, I find myself in doubt. I think, each time, I must be wrong, I must be exaggerating. I'm just buying the line of those out there who seek to criticize the government. I'm just listening instead of knowing.

And then, I go back to my source material and re-examine it. I read the FBI reports from Guantánamo and Abu Ghraib. I read the memoirs of interrogations for the US military. I study the Pentagon reports on prisoner treatment and interrogation at Guantánamo, Abu Ghraib, and other unnamed prisons or camps. And I learn, all over again each time, that in fact it is the case. Under the auspices of the United States government, individuals were tortured—both physically and psychologically.

So, before I launch into a chronology of how this happened, I thought I would share with you the details of *what* happened—according to the words, not of human rights organizations or others attuned to looking for such abuses, but of those seeking to protect the reputation of the United States. Here's what the government documents tell us.

I.

I begin with al-Qahtani. Al-Qahtani—Saudi, thirty years old at the time of his interrogation—is one of twenty alleged hijackers. He had attempted to enter the United States in August 2001; however, he was detained and deported without making it out of the Florida airport through which he had tried to enter the country. This must have severely disappointed Mohammed Atta, who had reportedly waited outside the airport to pick up al-Qahtani. Al-Qahtani, detainee 063, was discovered, by accident almost, at Guantánamo. Once he was discovered, the US intelligence services decided they needed to get whatever information they could out of him. Their reasoning was that, as the possible twentieth hijacker, he would have knowledge not of follow-on attacks but of the al Qaeda network.[1] He could help us, for example, find bin Laden. (Or Mullah Omar, the person we originally sought in Afghanistan, who is now back in power and once again increasingly powerful.) Al-Qahtani was subjected to 48 days of sleep deprivation, isolation, temperature adjustment, prolonged stress positions, forced standing, hooding, forced nudity, use of dogs to induce fear and stress, forced grooming (which includes cutting the hair and beard of an individual for whom these things are religiously proscribed), sexual contact by a female officer, loud music, control over use of a bathroom to the point where he urinated on himself, and removal of religious items. His hands were cuffed so that he could not pray, he was constipated and dehydrated so that he was subjected to forced enemas and IV fluids, he was forced to behave like a dog, he was forced to look at pictures of women in bikinis, and then made to answer questions about details of the pictures. His cell was flooded with light constantly; when he refused to drink water it was poured over his head.[2]

Here is how he reacted, according to FBI reports. He cried, he began talking to people who weren't there, he crouched "in a corner of the cell covered with a sheet for hours on end." He stated he was hearing voices. The interrogation log, written by his interrogators, stated that he began forgetting things, was dizzy, cried out for Allah. He screamed, woke up without being awakened during the four hours of sleep he was allowed, had pains in his kidneys, trembled uncontrollably, became incoherent. One year later, at Abu Ghraib, similar techniques were used—not by the rogue soldiers we read about—but by interrogators.[3] A former Army interrogator at Abu Ghraib, Tony Lagouranis, has described using dogs, hypothermia, sleep deprivation, isolation, stress positions, and in one case a mock execution on detainees held there. According to his report this was done under the direct instruction of his superiors.[4]

Beyond the government reports, we have other corroborative evidence. One of the leading officials stationed at Guantánamo in summer 2002 told me she saw prisoners shackled for excessive periods of time, so much so that she worried their organs would collapse upon one another. She recalls bringing in the doctor who put an end to the treatment.

By the time the photos from Abu Ghraib came out, astonishing us all, the story had moved on to ghost prisons, or black sites, around the world. In Jordan, in Egypt, apparently in Poland, and other locations known and unknown, detainees were held and interrogated by US personnel as well as agents of other countries, unhampered by the boundaries of morality or United States law.[5] Here, there are no government documents. Instead, there are reports from journalists, from lawyers, from released prisoners. But they are not different.

The most famous example is that of Maher Arar. Arar was stopped while on his way home to Canada. Passing through John F. Kennedy Airport, he was detained, held for thirteen days, and then sent to Syria (stopping temporarily in Jordan on the way).[6] While detained in the United States, he was deprived of food, held in solitary confinement in a cell constantly flooded with light, and denied access to his lawyer. US authorities lied to Arar's lawyer regarding his whereabouts.[7]

In transit to Syria, and for months once he was there, Arar was beaten repeatedly. He was whipped with two-inch-thick electrical cables, as well as punched. He was kept in an underground cell, three feet wide by six feet deep by seven feet high. He was held in isolation, placed where he could hear the screams of other detainees and threatened with electric shocks. Held in his tiny cell, he was given no exercise and lost forty pounds.[8] According to his statements, the questions he was asked in Syria were the same as the questions he was asked by officials in the United States.[9] Under this treatment, Arar confessed to many things, including having trained with terrorists in Afghanistan. Yet Syrian as well as Canadian officials have determined that Arar was never in Afghanistan and was never involved in terrorism.[10]

So, though I distrust it every time, though I try to deny it, it is a fact. Detainees were tortured systematically with similar techniques over thousands of miles of difference beginning in 2002 and lasting until we're not sure when.

These events are not denied by the Bush administration. Officials who supervised the transfer of alleged terrorists have been quoted saying, "If you don't violate someone's human rights some of the time, you probably aren't doing your job;" "I don't think we want to be promoting a view of zero tolerance on this. That was the whole problem for a long time with the CIA;" and "We don't kick the [expletive] out of them. We send them to other countries so they can kick the [expletive] out of them." Cofer Black famously said that "[a]fter 9/11 the gloves come off."[11]

Reporting on questions of rendition, Bart Gellman and Dana Priest stated the following:

> According to Americans with direct knowledge and others who have witnessed the treatment, captives are often "softened up" by MPs and US Army Special Forces troops who beat them up and confine them in tiny rooms. The alleged terrorists are commonly blindfolded and thrown into walls, bound in painful positions, subjected to loud noises and deprived of sleep. The tone of intimidation and fear is the beginning, they said, of a process of piercing a prisoner's resistance.
>
> The takedown teams often "package" prisoners for transport, fitting them with hoods and gags, and binding them to stretchers with duct tape.
>
> Bush administration appointees and career national security officials acknowledged that, as one of them put it, "our guys may kick them around a little bit in the adrenaline of the immediate aftermath." Another said US personnel are scrupulous in providing medical care to captives, adding in a deadpan voice, that "pain control [in wounded patients] is a very subjective thing."

The CIA's participation in the interrogation of rendered terrorist suspects varies from country to country.

"In some cases [involving interrogations in Saudi Arabia], we're able to observe through one-way mirrors the live investigations," said a senior US official involved in Middle East security issues. "In others, we usually get summaries."[12]

II.

Behind these stories, there was a policy. The policy began to some extent with the authorization to use military force. But more importantly, it began with the military order, issued by President Bush on 13 November 2001.[13] In that order, he turned over the matter of detention and trial for prisoners from the war on terror to the secretary of defense. The order was groundbreaking. It sidelined civilian authorities completely, taking a process meant to be one of prosecution and trial, which would normally lie squarely within the expertise of the Department of Justice, and transferred it to the military sector. It took an issue that comprises, almost exactly, the reason for the existence of the Department of Justice, and delivered it instead to an organization developed for the purpose of waging war. The order recognized no oversight, no procedural checks for the executive branch.

The movement to take professional activities away from the professionals who normally engaged in them continued through the congressional hearings attended by Pentagon officials in late November and early December 2001. There, the Judiciary Committee and the Armed Services Committee held hearings on the military order, the use of the military to perform a legal function. In response, one after the other, John Ashcroft, Jim Haynes, Michael Chertoff, Paul Wolfowitz, and Pierre-Richard Prosper each emphasized that the United States was at war, that interrogation was a priority, and that the detention and trial of these prisoners could not be considered a law-enforcement activity.[14]

In late December this policy began to take a more nuanced shape. On December 28, John Yoo and Patrick Philbin of the Office of Legal Counsel wrote a memo explaining that detainees housed at Guantánamo were beyond the bounds of United States law, i.e., out of US jurisdiction, and therefore were not entitled to the Writ of Habeas Corpus. They justified this with the argument that, since the detainees were housed in Cuba in an area where US rights existed only under treaty, the enforcement of Habeas rights by US courts would infringe on Cuban sovereignty. Again, therefore, there would be no checks on executive power.[15]

This memo was followed by a draft memo by John Yoo and Robert Delahunty on 9 January 2002. Having explained that US law would be off limits to Guantánamo detainees due to their presence in Guantánamo, the next memo proceeded to exempt the executive from international law as well. "[N]either the federal War Crimes Act nor the Geneva Conventions would apply to the detention conditions in Guantánamo Bay, Cuba." The reasons for this included that Afghanistan under the Taliban was considered a failed state, that al Qaeda operatives were non-state actors, and that "customary international law has no binding legal effect on either the President or the military because it is not federal law, as recognized by the Constitution."[16]

Secretary of State William Taft failed to be convinced by Yoo's draft. In a response to the draft memo he called Yoo's theory "seriously flawed," "incorrect," "incomplete," and "fundamentally inaccurate" in both its analyses and conclusions. The OLC memo was also "procedurally impossible," "unsound," at points based on arguments that were "completely irrelevant," ignorant about political concepts such as "failed states" and even about the Taliban, as well as about legal protocols such as reciprocity and treaty suspension. It was also weak in its own assertions, especially in passages where it resorted to wimp-ish words such as "probably" and "strongly indicates" rather than basing unequivocal conclusions on argument and conviction, according to Taft's legal team.[17]

Yet on January 22 Jay Bybee, speaking for the OLC, circulated a final memo accepting Yoo's analysis. Under the OLC's interpretation, the War Crimes Act, the Geneva Conventions, and customary international law would have no control over what the president decided to do with the detainees at Guantánamo.[18] On January 25, the OLC determination was adopted by Alberto Gonzales in his own memo to President Bush.[19]

Throughout this period, beginning in December, various officials, including Donald Rumsfeld, had stated that the detainees at Guantánamo were not entitled to protections under the Geneva Conventions, but that they would be treated "consistent with" the Conventions. Combined with the legal wranglings going on behind the scenes, this assertion had the effect of saying at the same time "we are doing the right thing" and "we don't have to do anything." "We are doing the right thing" was combined often, as in a press conference by Donald Rumsfeld on January 22, with warnings against hyperbole by the press or complaints from the human rights community that abuses were ongoing at Guantánamo.[20] "We're doing the right thing" allowed the administration to downplay these complaints and encourage onlookers to look away. "We don't have to do anything" reflected the supposed moral superiority of the United States, giving these rights to individuals who did not deserve it, while at the same time preparing the public to accept the idea that these detainees were not entitled to these rights.

On February 7, President Bush issued a decree formally stating this policy. First, the decree stated specifically, with the weight of presidential authority, OLC's interpretation of the status of the detainees in relation to the Geneva Conventions. Next, the decree stated that "the United States Armed Forces shall continue to treat detainees humanely and, to the extent appropriate and consistent with military necessity, in a manner consistent with the principles of Geneva." Notably, the memo mentioned the nation's armed forces, but no other government actors such as the CIA, one of the agencies that received the memo.[21]

At this point, the groundwork was complete. The Pentagon had created its own legal shield—a set of memos by the Office of Legal Counsel arguing that the president and the executive branch were unbounded in wartime by any domestic or international statutes, even those created specifically for times of war; legal and public argument that in fact this was a time of war; diversion of a process traditionally handled by legal professionals to military officials. The next step, however, would become the most famous.

On the first of August 2002, the Office of Legal Counsel, over the signature of Jay Bybee, the departing head of OLC, issued a memo legalizing what amounted to torture. Attributed to John Yoo as well as to Bybee, the memo redefined the nature of torture. Anything other than "pain...of an intensity akin to that which accompanies serious physical injury such as death or organ failure"[22] fell outside the category and did not constitute torture.

With this memo, a mission and a policy that had begun as a discussion of battlefield detention and military tribunals had officially been transformed into an interrogation mission. And for that mission, the basic rules of conduct had changed. Not surprisingly, there were still no defense attorneys at Guantánamo, nor much discernible progress towards the military commissions. Detention, originally the handmaiden to the battlefield effort, simultaneously the alleged partner of the military commissions, now had the legal backing to become the stepchild for interrogation outside the law.

From there, the step to al-Qahtani was relatively small. On October 11, a new memo appeared over the signature of a military lawyer at Guantánamo, Lt. Col. Diane Beaver. Under increasing pressure to get information from the detainees, and concerned with getting information particularly from Mohammed al-Qahtani—the so-called twentieth hijacker—the memo suggested a list of eighteen new techniques outside of those allowed by the military interrogation manual that could be used during interrogations.[23] Although the techniques were supposedly requested by officers at Guantánamo and first appear in a memo written by an officer at Guantánamo, interviews conducted by Philippe Sands have shown that in fact these techniques were determined by officials throughout the intelligence services, and that the request for their use originated with the Pentagon. Recent revelations on the techniques include the fact that they were largely adapted from Chinese techniques used to extract false confessions in the 1950s, as well as from studies into brainwashing.

These techniques were divided into three sections. The first group, Category I, included yelling and techniques of deception. Category II techniques included sensory deprivation, prolonged isolation for up to thirty days, the use of stress positions and twenty-hour interrogations, hooding, the removal of clothing and the use of phobias, such as fear of dogs, among other things. Many expressly violated the Geneva Conventions. Category III pushed the standards even further towards illegality, including techniques such as waterboarding and the use of death threats against the detainee or his family.[24]

Under tremendous pressure, this Guantánamo military lawyer, Diane Beaver, had been asked to assess these techniques on legal grounds. Her memo concluded that the techniques were legally permissible, even those in Category III.[25] "It was not my job," she said to Philippe Sands in her own defense, "to second guess the President."[26] Her hope, she later claimed at hearings before the Senate Armed Services Committee, was that at SOUTHCOM or somewhere else up the chain, someone would review and annul her work.[27]

The request was approved, finally, famously, by Donald Rumsfeld, on 2 December 2002. His approval included his note in the margins, "I stand for 8–10 hours a day. Why is standing limited to 4 hours?"[28]

III.

But chronicling the memos doesn't tell us how and why this came about, and for this, I'd like to reserve the rest of this essay.

The scandal of Abu Ghraib broke in spring 2004. Immediately, the question became whether Abu Ghraib had been the result of a few bad apples, an isolated group that had gotten out of control, or instead by a policy encouraged if not created by the Pentagon.[29] Weeks after the photos became public, a US Department of Defense paper, the Taguba Report, catalogued countless instances of prisoner mistreatment at Abu Ghraib.[30] The photos, it seemed, hinted at just a small part of a larger policy of coercive interrogation. What we see now, from documentation by Philippe Sands as well as from the similarity in techniques we can see by comparing Tony Lagouranis's description of Abu Ghraib interrogations to the interrogation log of Mohammed al-Qahtani, is that this was about a policy that had been in place from Guantánamo.

So what about Guantánamo, what about the United States led to this policy? If you look at this early period in Guantánamo, there are a few things that jump immediately to the foreground of our explanations. First among these is fear.

This fear was not illogical. Guantánamo became operational in January 2002. This was only four months after the attacks of September 11. As described by Jack Goldsmith, among others, there was a palpable fear throughout the various echelons of government, almost certainty that some new attack was imminent. The Pentagon was desperate to avoid another such catastrophe.[31]

Meanwhile, the country found itself in an entirely new situation. Not having been successfully attacked on our own soil since the bombing of Pearl Harbor, dealing with an enemy apparently entirely different from prior enemies, feeling the urgent need to outline and describe the new situation, policymakers desperately sought to get a handle on the threats and the options and gain information to foil the plot that every person involved felt must be in progress.

Worse yet, the very fact that we were taken so unawares created a pressure outside our need to protect the country. It pointed to a hole in the American national security and intelligence community. It pointed to a failure of government. It pointed to a gap in our knowledge that had grown so large we could not fix it in the time that anybody believed was available. This led to a felt need to go forward with absolutely anything that could possibly fill the information void. Detainees became tools to rectify our own mistakes in the face of our own terror concerning what might be coming.

In September 2006, President Bush attempted to justify use of "alternative procedures" for questioning detainees in a speech on military commissions. He stated that through these procedures, which included waterboarding, the government obtained information that led to the capture of Ramzi bin al Shibh and Khalid Sheikh Mohammed, as well as providing information that led to the prevention of an attack on the United States.[32]

At this point, we had come full circle. First we were desperate for information and came to believe we needed to use torture. Next, as the public and the international community began speaking out on the abuse they heard about, we denied that we were using torture. The final stage brought us back to our first thought—we embraced the fact that we used torture and had gotten information by using it.

The use of torture may have gotten us information. This point is debated. Many have said that the information President Bush bragged about when discussing Zubaydah was already in our hands or obtainable by other means.[33] From the outside, it is almost impossible to know whether these techniques were or were not successful. However, what we do know is that the use of these techniques also got us misinformation. Our information that Iraq was developing weapons of mass destruction, for instance, was one product of torture.[34]

We also know what torture has not led to. It has not led to the capture of Osama bin Laden or Mullah Omar in Afghanistan. It has not led to the capture of Ayman al Zawahiri. It has not ended the war on terror, the war in Iraq, or the war in Afghanistan.

Fear is not the most productive of emotions, and certainly not the most productive emotion for a state to embody or employ to implement policy. The use of torture is a prime example of the harms that come about from acting on fear. The consequences of torture are unpredictable. It is difficult, if not impossible, to tell when an individual is telling the truth. It undermines our moral standing in the world and acts as a rallying point for our enemies. It undermines our connection with the very communities that are most likely to provide the most valuable information for preventing future attacks. It emphasizes brute force over effective, proven intelligence techniques, undermining support for these techniques and therefore undermining our ability to deploy effective counter-terrorism techniques.

But most of all, torture is wrong. It is undeniably, morally, irrefutably wrong. It requires valuing ourselves so much more than others that we do not care that we may be punishing an innocent person, in which case we may be inflicting pain for no reason. Both of these are exemplified in the case of Maher Arar. Ignoring these facts requires an extreme level of selfishness. Even were it possible to know for certain that an individual had valuable information, torture is wrong. It is wrong to knowingly inflict that kind of pain. We know it is wrong, and by accepting it we injure ourselves not only in the moral standing of the world, but in our own eyes. To be torturers harms us as individuals, as a country, and as exemplars to the rest of the world.

Response to Karen J. Greenberg by Ronald P. Mahurin

In my brief response to Professor Greenberg's paper, I would like to begin precisely where she began her remarks...that is, with a confession. Or perhaps more accurately, a simple acknowledgment of what many of us may have asked ourselves from time to time, or especially today, on this seventh anniversary of the terrorist attacks of 9/11.

If Professor Greenberg's confession is one of doubt, of a fear of exaggeration, that somehow in the midst of her research she "may have gotten it wrong," I have two related questions that I would add to her own appropriate sense of doubt.

The first question is "How could we have gotten this wrong?" And when I say "we," I mean all of us—not simply the administration, or policymakers, or military leaders—but all those who are citizens of the nation, and who in some ultimate sense share in the responsibility to "get this right." Without simply going to the inevitable hand-wringing and finger-pointing that serves virtually no purpose in addressing the deeper issues revealed through the acts of torture that have now been substantiated beyond any credible doubt, we have the responsibility as citizens to ask why.

If Professor Greenberg's question is "How did we get here—to a place where the United States government though both a legal rendering and then through intentional acts gave sanction to the use of torture, as defined both in the Geneva Conventions and our own US Army Field Manual?" an implicit parallel question is "Why have we come to this place?" And I must confess that as I read the paper and have considered the official accounts of the use of torture at Abu Ghraib and elsewhere, the "why" haunts me just as much as the "how" haunts Professor Greenberg.

A June 2008 report on world public opinion and torture, a joint project of the Program for International Policy Attitudes at the University of Maryland and WorldPublicOpinion.org, summarized the results of an international survey of nineteen nations concerning public attitudes surrounding the use of torture. The poll of 19,063 respondents was conducted in nineteen nations, including most of the largest countries–China, India, the United States, Indonesia, Nigeria, and Russia—as well as Mexico, Britain, France, Poland, Spain, Azerbaijan, Ukraine, Egypt, the Palestinian territories, Iran, Turkey, Thailand, and South Korea. The nations included represent 60 percent of the world population. The survey was fielded between January and May 2008. Margins of error range from +/–2 to 4 percent. All of the countries polled are signatories to the Universal Declaration of Human Rights and parties to the Geneva Conventions forbidding torture and other forms of abuse. All but three have also ratified the 1987 UN Convention against Torture. India has signed but not ratified the convention, while Iran has not signed it.[35]

The survey presented respondents with an argument in favor of allowing the torture of potential terrorists who threaten civilians: "Terrorists pose such an extreme threat that governments should now be allowed to use some degree of torture if it may gain information that would save innocent lives." In fourteen nations, a majority or plurality rejected this argument in favor of the unequivocal view: "Clear rules against torture should be maintained because any use of torture is immoral and will weaken international human rights standards against torture."

In looking at the data for the United States, while Americans oppose the use of torture on the whole, the majority endorsing an unequivocal rule against torture is more modest than in other countries and has declined since 2006. A modest majority (53 percent) feels that torture should unequivocally not be allowed, while 44 percent favor an exception for terrorists. Thirteen percent say torture should be allowed in general.

Support for making exceptions for torture in the case of terrorists has grown among Americans since 2006 (44 percent, up from 36 percent), while the majority opposing the use of torture in all cases has fallen slightly (53 percent, down from 58 percent). These data are consistent with studies from the Pew Center for Research, which have tracked public opinion regarding the use of torture since 2004.

More than four in ten Americans (43 percent) say that the use of torture can be justified to gain key information sometimes (31 percent) or often (12 percent), according to a 2007 Pew Research survey. However, a 54 percent majority says torture is never (29 percent) or rarely (25 percent) justified. The number of Americans saying the use of torture against suspected terrorists is at least sometimes justified has been fairly stable since 2004.[36]

When Professor Greenberg asks how we got to Abu Ghraib, there will inevitably be multiple reasons, interpretations, justifications, and explanations given. And I'm afraid there seems to be no clear evidence that in a post-9/11 context, our national will and moral sentiments are any less inclined to end this debate. These data certainly do not tell the whole story. But in a nation that holds out to the world the ideals of freedom, liberty, and democracy, what are we sacrificing when nearly half the nation believes the use of torture is always or sometimes justified when pursuing the protection of the state and the security of its people?

In my remaining moments, I would like to speak out of my own experience in working for the past twenty-five years with Christian colleges and universities, both as a faculty member and most recently, prior to my current appointment at Houghton College, as a vice president at the Council for Christian Colleges & Universities—a national association of over 100 faith-based institutions. While these are colleges drawn from various church traditions, many, though not all, would identify themselves within the evangelical tradition of American Christianity.

It was in my capacity as both a political scientist with interest in human rights and someone who had broad knowledge and experience of the particular ethos and landscape of Christian higher education that David Gushee invited me to serve on the committee that helped draft the Evangelical Declaration against Torture. As part of that drafting committee, I sought the input of various colleagues and associates from across Christian higher education, including several Christian college presidents. And I'm very pleased that several of them are signatories of the statement.

During the drafting process, I gained a much deeper appreciation for the complexity and difficulty of getting evangelicals to agree on anything!

Those of you who are from this tradition will immediately understand what I mean by this. And there are many from other traditions who with great sympathy are nodding their heads in agreement. The rather non-hierarchical nature of the evangelical tradition means that declarative statements, even on what appear to be very basic matters or issues, make difficult any possibility of "speaking with one voice."

My observations about the broader evangelical community in this country, and in particular the educational institutions that represent many of the denominations that would be broadly associated with a group like the National Association of Evangelicals, is that unfortunately, our thoughts and affections have been at best misdirected and at worst, completely misunderstood, forgotten, or misrepresented.

As some of us on the steering committee have witnessed firsthand, the backlash over our Declaration against Torture statement has been rather strong, with many appearing to defend the indefensible by buying into the tortured logic of "How do we define torture?" or "In times of emergency, certain acts (we won't call them torture) are required in order to protect the lives of innocent people." Others, by virtue of their silence, have intentionally or unintentionally joined the chorus of the "disaffected" or confused in this country—the nearly 45 percent of the general public who somehow believe the use of torture can, at least on occasion, be justified.

Professor Greenberg's initial disbelief is that the actions of more than a few "bad apples" from our military and intelligence groups could be sanctioned by our national government and, more particularly, the executive branch of our government. I join her in that initial disbelief. To Professor Greenberg's disbelief and doubt, I add my own voice of dismay and concern.

While I am grateful for those leaders in my community who have stepped forward and demonstrated the courage and conviction regarding this basic statement against the use of torture, many voices have remained silent. I know some of the reasons for this silence, and I would be the first to acknowledge that for some in the evangelical community, while their personal convictions would absolutely and categorically reject the use of torture under any circumstances, they are bound by their church or denominational laws or governance systems to avoid signing such public statements.

For many others, however, the bar is quite low. If the events of Abu Ghraib have somehow failed to stir the moral consciences of these leaders in such a way as to at least ask why—why did our government, my government, not only permit but actually endorse the use of such violence and despicable acts in the name of "national security" in the aftermath of 9/11?— then I fear that we evangelicals have much more work to do in our own minds and consciences than I would have wanted to believe.

So, with Professor Greenberg, I return to my own confession or question—what will it take to get the broadest spectrum of evangelical leaders to affirm their opposition, on clear moral and biblical grounds, to the use of torture? Let us put aside any notion that there is no "moral high ground" on this question. Does anyone really doubt what happened in Abu Ghraib was anything less than torture? What further evidence do we need? What strained moral arguments are we prepared to make to suggest that it was something else—not really torture?

In the final section of her paper, Professor Greenberg postulates two reasons that led to the policy that has been in place from Guantánamo. The first is fear, and the second is a huge hole in our own national security apparatus and intelligence services. As we have learned more about both Guantánamo and the subsequent renditions policies and practices of our government, these two explanations have been offered from both inside and outside our government. These facts are no longer in dispute.

Yet in the end, as much as we are haunted by the images of torture, of human degradation and humiliation, we ought to be haunted by much more. We ought to be haunted by our own questions—about how as a nation we could seemingly tolerate such acts of violence, and what it says about our own national character. We should never equivocate. Professor Greenberg is right when she simply names the fact that "torture is wrong—it is undeniably, morally, irrefutably wrong." And if our nation is not haunted by the thought that we would have to think twice about how to answer the question "Is torture ever justified?" then we bear as much responsibility for the acts of violence perpetrated at Guantánamo and other dark places around the world as do those individuals who carried out those acts under the direct command of our government.

2

★

How the US Military Responded to the Drift toward Torture

Donald J. Guter

11 September 2001 was a beautiful, clear day in Washington, DC. The usual summer humidity had taken a break. I was still serving on active duty as the 37th Judge Advocate General of the Navy, and I was hosting an early morning meeting of our most senior leadership in my Pentagon office. Suddenly, my assistant, Nancy Miller, entered the room, apologized for interrupting the meeting, and told us that CNN was reporting that two planes had just struck the World Trade Center. This would be startling news under any circumstances, but thinking I must have misheard her report, I responded with the question "Two planes?" She confirmed her statement. I said, "Nancy, that is no accident." The words had just cleared my lips when a muffled thud sounded and the building shook. The mental connection with the events in New York was instantaneous. I stood up and said, "Gentlemen, we've been hit. Make sure we account for everyone, lock the safes, get your keys and phones, and evacuate the office."

What had happened was immediately clear; its implications were not. US interests had been the target of terrorist attacks in the past. World Trade Center I, the Marine Barracks in Beirut, and the USS Cole, to name just a few, come to mind. But these attacks, as brutal as they were, paled in scope and audacity compared to the attacks of 9/11, and the emotions they unleashed would alter both the mode and the intensity of the response. The brutality of this latest attack would be matched by new policies for discovering and responding to threats. The war on terror officially had begun.

First efforts focused on recovery and care for our own victims and their families, but on a parallel track, plans were pulled together quickly for a military strike on Afghanistan and its training grounds that had spawned this monstrous attack. The plans included the capture, detention, and interrogation not only of those who were directly responsible for the planning and execution of 9/11, but on those who would do harm to the United States, our allies, and our interests in the future. Anything and everything would be done to prevent a follow-on attack. Thus, the scene was set and the environment was supportive, but the signs that pointed to torture were not yet recognized.

My first notion that our interrogation posture might not be completely benign came early in 2002 during a meeting at the Pentagon that was chaired by then secretary of the Army Thomas White.[37] Secretary White said we would need a charter that would, first, formalize the working group and its interface with the Office of the Secretary of Defense and, second, make it clear that within the context of the investigation, the intelligence piece would control the interrogation plan. It would be necessary to build a firewall between the intelligence and criminal investigations so that the prosecution plan would not be harmed. That said, the overriding consideration and concern was that the administration not suffer the embarrassment of a follow-on attack to the 9/11 attacks while failing to obtain actionable intelligence from those being held at Guantánamo Bay, said to be senior Taliban and al-Qaeda and non-Afghan Taliban fighters. Although specific interrogation methods were not discussed at this meeting (or at any others that I attended), there was noticeable discomfort in the room when one of the attendees mentioned that we might not be getting actionable intelligence from the detainees because they might not have anything meaningful to reveal. At this time, we were still under the impression that it would be the policy of the United States to treat detainees humanely and within the spirit, if not the letter, of the Geneva Conventions.

How did we get to the point that torture was accepted—not just by a few "bad apples" in the military, as has been claimed by the administration, but by those highest up in the chain of command? How could anyone who was even remotely familiar with the Convention against Torture, who had studied international law, approve the use of such harsh interrogation methods under any circumstances? The 1984 Convention against Torture and Other Cruel, Inhuman or Degrading Treatment or Punishment defines torture as "any act by which severe pain or suffering, whether physical or mental, is intentionally inflicted on a person for such purposes as obtaining from him or a third person information or a confession…"[38] When the torture convention was ratified by the US Senate in 1994, it was a primary concern that there be a distinction between coercive but lawful interrogation and outright torture (the convention itself makes no such distinction). The Senate ratified the convention on the understanding that torture should be reserved for "severe physical or mental pain or suffering" resulting in "prolonged mental harm."[39] It is important to note that much of what has been called "torture" in the media was not torture, but what could be categorized as coercion or physical and mental abuse. However, the Third Geneva Convention (covering prisoners of war and ratified by the US Congress) states the following on the subject of coercion: "No physical or mental torture, nor any other form of coercion, may be inflicted on prisoners of war to secure from them information of any kind whatever. Prisoners of war who refuse to answer may not be threatened, insulted, or exposed to unpleasant or disadvantageous treatment of any kind."[40] The Fourth Geneva Convention also explicitly states that "no physical or moral coercion shall be exercised against protected persons, in particular to obtain information from them or from third parties."[41] In February 2002, President Bush had determined in an executive order that members of al Qaeda, the Taliban, and associated forces were not entitled to the protections granted by the Geneva Conventions,[42] not even those of Common Article 3, prohibiting both torture and "outrages upon personal dignity, in particular humiliating and degrading treatment."[43] This despite the fact that it has been almost universally acknowledged that "[e]very person in enemy hands must have some status under international law… *There is no* intermediate status; nobody in enemy hands can be outside the law."[44] However, Bush's order goes on to say that the values of our nation call for humane treatment of detainees and that, "[a]s a matter of policy, the US armed forces shall continue to treat detainees humanely, and to the extent appropriate and consistent with military necessity, in a manner consistent with the principles of Geneva."[45] This is in stark contrast to the definition of torture given in an August 2002 memo, which has come to be known as the "Bybee memo," in which torture was defined as treatment "equivalent in intensity to the pain accompanying serious physical injury, such as organ failure, impairment of bodily function, or even death."[46] It is this memo that many senior officers are convinced was a proximate cause of the Abu Ghraib torture scandal.[47]

The interrogation policy that developed following 9/11 has been labeled a "policy of cruelty" by Alberto J. Mora, former General Counsel of the US Navy, a policy that has "violated our founding values, our constitutional system and the fabric of our laws, our over-arching foreign policy interests, and our national security."[48] How did the definition for torture come to be stretched so far that the threshold greatly surpassed that of any international standards? How could we expect the world to treat our own soldiers, sailors, airmen, and marines humanely, when we ourselves were not giving others that right? The government's torture policy was a shameful downfall for a country that was known in World War II for having "really set the standard for the treatment of prisoners."[49]

On 11 October 2002, the military commander at Guantánamo, Major General Michael E. Dunlavey, sent a memorandum to the head of the US Southern Command, General James T. Hill, requesting the approval of certain interrogation techniques. Dunlavey had apparently come under significant pressure from higher levels at the White House to get more information out of interrogations.[50] In his memo, Major General Dunlavey states that though he is fully aware of the techniques currently employed in the war against terror, these methods "have become less effective over time."[51] He goes on to state his belief that, "the methods and techniques delineated in the accompanying J-2 memorandum will enhance our efforts to extract additional information."[52] The proposed interrogation techniques are set out in the accompanying memorandum, prepared by Lieutenant Colonel James Phifer and addressed to Major General Dunlavey.[53] The memorandum begins by identifying the following as the problem: "[the] current guidelines for interrogation procedures at GTMO limit the ability of interrogators to counter advanced resistance." Phifer goes on to divide the proposed interrogation techniques into three categories, Category I being the mildest and Category III the harshest techniques. Category I techniques include yelling and deception. Category II includes the use of stress-positions (such as standing) for a maximum of four hours, use of the isolation facility for up to thirty days, removal of clothing, and deprivation of light and auditory stimuli. Finally, Category III includes the use of scenarios designed to convince the detainee that death or severely painful consequences are imminent for the detainee and/or the detainee's family, exposure to cold weather and water (with appropriate medical monitoring), use of a wet towel and dripping water to induce the misperception of suffocation (also known as waterboarding, a term that has sadly entered the public consciousness during the media coverage on its legality), and use of mild non-injurious physical contact such as grabbing, poking in the chest with the finger, and light pushing. Phifer states that Category III techniques should be used only upon approval by the commanding general. In a memorandum on the development of interrogation rules of engagement, Alberto Mora writes that "even if the techniques as applied did not reach the level of torture, they almost certainly would constitute 'cruel, inhuman, or degrading treatment,' another class of unlawful treatment."

Lieutenant Colonel Diane Beaver, the staff judge advocate at Guantánamo, however, provides a legal review of the techniques in which she states her agreement that "the proposed strategies do not violate applicable federal law."[54] She attaches a more detailed legal analysis in which she examines the techniques in light of US law standards, including the Eighth Amendment to the Constitution (prohibiting "cruel and unusual punishment"), the federal torture statute, and the Uniform Code of Military Justice.[55] Beaver concludes that an international law analysis is not required, "...because the Geneva Conventions do not apply to these detainees."[56] Beaver has said that she based her analysis on the previous presidential decision to ignore the Geneva Conventions, later stating, "It was not my job to second-guess the president."[57] Beaver concludes that the techniques are legal "so long as the force used could plausibly have been thought necessary in a particular situation to achieve a legitimate government objective, and it was applied in a good faith effort and not maliciously or sadistically for the very purpose of causing harm."[58] She does express concern that the proposals to grab, poke in the chest, push lightly, and place a wet towel or hood over the detainee's head may violate Article 128 of the Uniform Code of Military Justice (Assault). She concludes that it would "be advisable to have permission or immunity in advance from the convening authority, for military members utilizing these methods."[59] After concluding with her recommendation that these techniques be approved, she goes on to state, "Since the law requires examination of all facts under a totality of circumstances test, I further recommend that all proposed interrogations involving category II and III methods must undergo a legal, medical, behavioral science, and intelligence review prior to their commencement."[60]

Beaver's legal review of the proposed torture techniques was described as "awful" by one renowned international lawyer.[61] Alberto J. Mora describes the memo as "a wholly inadequate analysis of the law and a poor treatment of this difficult and highly sensitive issue."[62] However, Beaver has stated that she was given just four days by General Dunlavey to write the memo, and that she had limited legal resources in Guantánamo.[63] Furthermore, though she requested help from other, more experienced lawyers, she received no feedback from them; she goes on to say that she "cannot help but conclude that others chose not to write on this issue to avoid being linked to it."[64] She also maintains that she believed senior lawyers in Washington would carefully review her memo and override it if necessary.[65] Clearly, under any normal circumstances, this legal analysis should not have been the last word on the legality of these interrogation methods. As presumed by Lt. Col. Beaver, her memo should have undergone careful scrutiny by other, more senior, lawyers. So how did it happen that this memo became the basis for approval of these interrogation techniques?

US Southern Command Cmdr. Gen. James Hill forwarded the Dunlavey request along with Lt. Col. Beaver's memo to Richard Myers, chairman of the Joint Chiefs of Staff, on 25 October 2002. The memo most definitely should have been subject to serious review at this level. In the past, Myers has claimed that he hadn't seen the memo or formally signed off on it before it traveled up to Donald Rumsfeld, most likely due to "intrigue" occurring between William (Jim) Haynes, Department of Defense General Counsel, and the Justice Department.[66] However, after hearings held by the Senate Armed Services Committee on 17 June 2008 on the origins of aggressive interrogation techniques, a more disturbing picture of Myers's role has come to light. Myers's legal counsel, Rear Adm. Jane Dalton, has testified that she was ordered to stop the review by Myers because of a request from Haynes, saying, "When I learned that Mr. Haynes did not want that broad-based legal and policy review to take place, then I stood down from the plans."[67] Despite numerous concerns that had been raised by a variety of military leaders as well as the Navy calling for further legal review, Myers and Dalton chose to do nothing. Dalton has testified that Myers himself was aware a number of people had voiced criticisms that the interrogation techniques might be against the law. In any case, on 27 November 2002, in blatant disregard for every concern voiced by the military, Jim Haynes sent a memo to Donald Rumsfeld recommending approval of all but three of the techniques requested for use at Guantánamo.[68] You will recall that these techniques include things such as stress positions, forced nudity, the use of dogs and sensory deprivation. The memo was approved by Donald Rumsfeld five days later, along with a handwritten comment stating, "However, I stand for 8–10 hours a day. Why is standing limited to 4 hours?" If this comment was intended to be funny, it goes far beyond inappropriate humor: the statement could be construed as an indirect approval for interrogators to go beyond what is stated in the memo, and could be used as evidence of such at a trial in the military commissions. In Alberto Mora's opinion, "The memos, and the practices they authorized, threatened the entire military commission process."[69] Mr. Mora first saw the memos on 19 December 2002; he immediately requested a meeting with Jim Haynes to discuss his view that some of the techniques could reach the level of torture. Mora would have to raise his objections to the approved techniques many more times before his concerns were heeded. It got to the point that on 15 January 2003, he informed Mr. Haynes that if the interrogation techniques did not stop, he would be officially signing out a memo declaring that the majority of the approved techniques were "violative of domestic and international legal norms in that they constituted, at a minimum, cruel and unusual treatment and, at worst, torture."[70] Rumsfeld suspended the authority to apply the techniques that same day.

It has since become clear that it was the administration's plan from early on to employ increasingly harsh and aggressive interrogation techniques. Concerns raised by the military were dismissed; those whose opinions did not coincide with those of the administration were categorically ignored. Nowhere has this become more apparent than in the handling of a working group that was established to develop interrogation techniques after Rumsfeld was forced to rescind his authorization of the harsh interrogation techniques. The working group included former Undersecretary of Defense for Policy Douglas Feith, officials from the Defense Intelligence Agency, representatives of the Joint Chiefs of Staff, and JAGs from all four branches of the military, and was headed by Mary Walker, Air Force General Counsel. However, from the outset the working group's legal analysis was crafted almost entirely by the Office of Legal Counsel at the Department of Justice. The OLC had issued a legal analysis by John Yoo, largely containing the views of the infamous Bybee memo (in fact, it incorporated parts of it verbatim). Those opposing the view of the OLC were simply disregarded in the drafting process; Alberto Mora stated that "contributions from the members of the Working Group, including [Department of the Navy Office of the General Counsel], began to be rejected if they did not conform to the OLC guidance."[71] In a series of memos written between 5 February and 13 March 2003, a number of JAGs voiced their concern that "[s]everal of the more extreme interrogation techniques, on their face, amount to violations of domestic criminal law and the UCMJ (e.g., assault). Applying the more extreme techniques during the interrogation of detainees places the interrogators and the chain of command at risk of criminal accusations domestically."[72] Furthermore,

> treating [Operation Enduring Freedom] detainees inconsistently with the [Geneva] Conventions arguably "lowers the bar" for the treatment of US POWs in future conflicts. Even where nations agree with the President's status determination, many would view the more extreme interrogation techniques as violative of other international law (other treaties or customary international law) and perhaps violative of their own domestic law. This puts the interrogators and the chain of command at risk of criminal accusations abroad, either in foreign domestic courts or in international fora, to include the ICC.[73]

Rear Adm. Michael Lohr wrote in his memo to Mary Walker, "Will the American people find we have missed the forest for the trees by condoning practices that, while technically legal, are inconsistent with our most fundamental values?"[74] Despite all these concerns, Donald Rumsfeld signed off on the final report on 2 April 2003. The JAGs had essentially been frozen out of the entire process. In fact, Alberto Mora has said that neither he nor anyone else in the Department of the Navy ever received a final copy of the working group's report; he assumed the report had never been finalized.

There is a marked difference between something that happens in spite of official policy and something that happens *because* of it.[75] The truth is that the administration had been looking into applying cruel interrogation techniques as early as 2002. In July that year, Donald Rumsfeld and Jim Haynes asked military psychologists about developing harsh methods of interrogation that could be used against Guantánamo detainees.[76] Richard Shiffrin, Haynes's former deputy on intelligence issues, sought information on what is known as SERE techniques. SERE stands for Survival, Evasion, Resistance, and Escape, and is a US military training designed to prepare US soldiers for abuse they might suffer if captured by a brutal regime. It was not designed to be used for US methods of interrogation. But the administration was interested in "reverse-engineering" the training into effective interrogation techniques, something that skilled, experienced interrogators have said "only a fool" would think he could do.[77] Upon the request by Richard Shiffrin, Lt. Col. Daniel Baumgartner Jr., Chief of Staff of the agency that oversees the SERE training, sent two memos to the Pentagon's general counsel's office describing SERE training techniques, including sensory deprivation, sleep deprivation, stress positions, waterboarding, slapping, sensory overload, and diet manipulation. In September 2002 interrogators from Guantánamo went to Fort Bragg, North Carolina, in order to attend training conducted by instructors from the SERE school. It was during this time that a meeting took place with a senior CIA lawyer, Jonathan Fredman, at Guantánamo, where the use of aggressive interrogation techniques was discussed. Lt. Col. Beaver has said that ideas did not come only from the SERE program, but from other sources as well: one such source was the hugely popular television show "24." Beaver recalls, "People had already seen the first series. It was hugely popular...Jack Bauer had many friends at Guantánamo...He gave people lots of ideas."[78] Minutes from the meeting show a frightening view of the legal limits of interrogation. Fredman tells the group, "It is basically subject to perception. If the detainee dies you're doing it wrong." Ironically, in 2007 the US military appealed to the producers of "24" to tone down the torture scenes because of the impact on troops and on America's reputation abroad. A brigadier general from the United States Military Academy at West Point traveled to California to meet with producers of the show and warn them about promoting illegal behavior in the series. The *Independent*, reporting on the incident, perhaps said it best when stating, "Forget about Abu Ghraib, forget about Guantánamo Bay, forget even that the White House has authorized interrogation techniques that some classify as torture, that damned Jack Bauer is giving us a bad name."[79] It is a sad day for our country when interrogation techniques that are deemed too brutal for television have been sanctioned by the administration.

Following Rumsfeld's December 2 authorization memo, senior staff at Guantánamo began drafting a standard operating procedure that specifically used SERE techniques in interrogations.[80] The FBI as well as the Department of Defense's Criminal Investigative Task Force raised concerns about the draft, saying that the use of aggressive techniques only "ends up fueling hostility and strengthening a detainee's will to resist."[81] However, again, objections and concerns voiced against such techniques were ignored. On 30 December 2002, two instructors from the Navy SERE school traveled to Guantánamo to teach interrogation personnel how to use techniques such as stress positions and slapping.[82]

Sadly, as we all know from the media coverage, abuse was not limited to Guantánamo: "When Secretary Rumsfeld approved the use of the abusive techniques against detainees, he unleashed a virus which ultimately infected interrogation operations conducted by the US military in Afghanistan and Iraq."[83] In fact, in September 2003, Major General Geoffrey Miller, who replaced Major General Michael E. Dunlavey as military commander at Guantánamo in November 2002, was sent to Iraq to assist with Abu Ghraib's start-up. He had instructions to implement Guantánamo techniques in the interrogation of Iraqi detainees. The *Washington Post* reported that "within weeks of his departure from Abu Ghraib, military working dogs were being used in interrogations, and naked detainees were humiliated and abused by military police soldiers working the night shift."[84] In an investigation by Major General Antonio M. Taguba into the Abu Ghraib scandal, Taguba concluded that "numerous incidents of sadistic, blatant, and wanton criminal abuses were inflicted on several detainees," calling the abuse "systemic and illegal."[85] Taguba maintained that Miller was partly responsible for the abuses.

Major General Miller was also in charge during the infamous interrogations of Mohammed al-Qahtani, the alleged "20th hijacker" in the 9/11 terrorist attacks. Qahtani, also known as Detainee 063, was subjected to increasingly abusive interrogation methods, known as the "First Special Interrogation Plan," that were authorized by Donald Rumsfeld. Qahtani's treatment was singled out in a letter from a senior FBI counter-terrorism official to the Pentagon complaining of abuses at Guantánamo. The letter reports that FBI agents were witnessing "highly aggressive interrogation techniques" and that Qahtani was "totally isolated (with the exception of occasional interrogations) in a cell that was always flooded with light" and "was evidencing behavior consistent with extreme psychological trauma."[86] Military investigators recommended that Miller be reprimanded for his failure to properly supervise Qahtani's interrogation. Disciplinary action against General Miller was, however, rejected by General Bantz Craddock, head of the US Southern Command, who stated that "the interrogation of [Qahtani] did not result in the violation of a US law or policy," and that the military achieved "solid intelligence gains" by using these techniques. The Army field manual always has made it exceedingly clear that everything an interrogator says and does must be within the limits of the Geneva Conventions. After the intense criticism following the treatment of detainees in the years following 9/11, the Army field manual was revised to explicitly ban beating prisoners, sexually humiliating them, threatening them with dogs, depriving them of food or water, performing mock executions, shocking them with electricity, causing other pain, as well as waterboarding. The Department of Defense simultaneously released a new directive on detention operations stating that all prisoners must—at a minimum—be treated in accordance with the standards of the Geneva Conventions.[87] These standards were most certainly not upheld during the interrogation of Mohammed al-Qahtani. Although it has become undeniably clear that this was not just the fault of a small group of rogue military officers, those higher up in the chain of command have not had to share in any of the blame. No one at a senior level has had to take responsibility for the horrors that have occurred.

Another notable fact stated in the Army field manual is, "Experience indicates that the use of prohibited techniques is not necessary to gain the cooperation of interrogation sources. Use of torture and other illegal methods is a poor technique that yields unreliable results, may damage subsequent collection efforts, and can induce the source to say what he thinks the [interrogator] wants to hear."[88] In fact, throughout history, the use of torture has proven to be ineffective. The desired response is almost never achieved through the use of torture, and at times simply produces a false response. It can also result in the death of a potential source of information. It is therefore surprising that so much has been made in the media of the "ticking time bomb" scenario. Some people have advocated the use of torture in a situation where a terrorist attack is imminent and torturing the perpetrator could save hundreds of lives. Alan Dershowitz has said that torture should then be authorized by the courts through the granting of "torture warrants." Besides the fact that this hypothetical scenario is very unlikely to happen, making exceptions for the use of torture in public debate most certainly does not adhere to the public values this country has always stood for. The ticking time bomb scenario is a dangerous one, because it justifies turning torture into an administrative process, and elevates its use into an acceptable standard. Torture should never become a part of public policy, even in the most extreme scenarios.

During questioning in the Senate Armed Services Committee Hearing by Senator McCaskill on the subject of the conditions at Guantánamo, Lt. Col. Beaver commented that she believed there was no violation of the law at Guantánamo and notes that "detainees were beaten to death at Bagram."[89] Senator Claire McCaskill replied, "It's a sad day in this hearing room when we say at least they weren't beaten to death."[90] This is one of the most disturbing aspects of a government policy that says it is permissible to torture—our moral standards are so lowered that what was once considered horrifying becomes commonplace. We cannot allow the normalization of torture in our culture. We should remain committed to unequivocal condemnation of torture. One cannot prevent cases of the use of torture by individuals who have chosen not to respect the law; those individuals should be dealt with accordingly in our justice system and made to take responsibility for their actions. We can, however, prevent torture from becoming an approved policy.

To that end, a number of retired judge advocates and general and flag officers from each service and within virtually every discipline have also taken up the fight against the government's policies. After noticing that various retired admirals and generals were speaking out individually on this issue, Human Rights First, a non-profit human rights advocacy group, brought the group together. As a united front, they have worked tirelessly to promote US adherence to international law.

In 2006, they wrote a letter opposing the nomination of Jim Haynes to a seat on the United States Court of Appeals for the Fourth Circuit.

They expressed profound concern about the role Mr. Haynes played in establishing interrogation policies. In November 2007, they wrote a letter to Patrick Leahy, Chairman of the United States Senate Judiciary Committee, condemning waterboarding and making it unequivocally clear that its practice is inhumane and illegal. The JAGs also met with a group of senators in August 2007 to express concern about a presidential order establishing rules for the treatment of CIA prisoners.[91] The executive order sets broad legal boundaries for the CIA's interrogations of suspected terrorists, in effect setting lower standards for the CIA. Though the order says that CIA interrogators may not use "willful and outrageous acts of personal abuse," giving as an example "sexual or sexually indecent acts," this is followed by the phrase, "for the purpose of humiliating or degrading the individual."[92] This phrase has caused the most concern, for it basically gives those undertaking abusive behavior an escape clause. So long as they can prove that their intent was not to specifically cause humiliation, they are not violating any laws. The JAGs warned the senators that this part of the order opens the door to violations of the section of the Geneva Conventions outlawing "cruel treatment and torture" and "outrages upon personal dignity, in particular humiliating and degrading treatment."[93] The group of ex-military officers also has been meeting with presidential candidates to discuss why they believe the United States cannot engage in torture. At a meeting sponsored by Human Rights First, which took place in December 2007, seven out of the then fifteen presidential candidates were present to discuss the role of the next Commander-in-Chief in ensuring that interrogation and prisoner treatment policies are consistent with American values and the Geneva Conventions.

Although, as this article demonstrates, the US military's response to the drift towards torture has not been monolithic, individuals such as Alberto Mora, Antonio Taguba, and the countless number of military officers who spoke out against the government's actions in the last years have all played a part in upholding our values during the war on terror. For their courage to speak out against these policies, they are true heroes.

Response to Donald J. Guter by Steven N. Xenakis

In her book, *The Dark Side,* Jane Mayer pays high tribute to the courage and moral fiber of our military lawyers.[94] Rear Admiral Don Guter, Rear Admiral John Hutson, The Honorable Alberto J. Mora, and many others spoke out early and stood up proudly in defense of the democratic traditions and laws that have kept our nation strong. RADM Guter and his colleagues deserve the highest praise for what they have done—and continue to do—to fortify our honor and pride here at home and abroad.

The attack on the World Trade Towers marked the beginning of the global war on terror. The rhetoric that has been drummed into our heads insists "the war on terror is a war like no other" and that "we must take all measures possible to stop the enemy." The plain fact is that every war is different, and nothing could be further from the truth. Nothing that has been claimed in the name of defending our country can justify cruel, inhuman, and degrading treatment of another man or woman. RADM Guter made the point eloquently—"...The government's torture policy was a shameful downfall for a country that was known in World War II for having 'really set the standard for the treatment of prisoners.'"[95]

Last June, Physicians for Human Rights (PHR) published its investigation on treatment and evidence of torture. Major General Taguba remarked in the preface to that report, "There is no longer any doubt that the current administration committed war crimes. The only question is whether those who ordered torture will be held to account."[96] Despite the growing public record, the incidents at Abu Ghraib and other sites have been blamed on a small group of rogue military personnel, have produced only a few court-martials of enlisted soldiers and one warrant officer, and have not touched one senior level official. The debate goes on, and strong voices continue to argue that we have done "nothing wrong"—which is why it is so important to affirm basic principles of human decency. With all due respect, we shouldn't need a lawyer to tell us what is right or permissible military conduct!

And yet, that is exactly what happened. As we have heard, the administration received legal advice justifying treatment of detainees that we—and most civilized countries— consider torture. The indefinite incarceration of the first 800 captives from Afghanistan in pursuit of dangerous terrorists barely drew a whimper of dissent. Our nation was absorbed by a climate of shock and fear—fear reinforced by the repetitive scenes of the World Trade Towers vaporizing over and over again. Most Americans didn't blink an eye when governmental authorities characterized the detainees as the "worst of the worst" and instructed interrogators to "take the gloves off" to dig deep for critical intelligence that would defend the nation against heinous acts. After all, the logic went, if roughing up a few prisoners could save innumerable American lives, the choice between torturing or not torturing seemed obvious.

Regrettably, physicians have been implicated both in the abusive interrogations linked to SERE (Survival, Evasion, Resistance, and Escape) training and in overlooking the harmful and dangerous treatment of detainees. Recently, I met an old colleague who served in Iraq at the time of the Abu Ghraib incidents. A colonel, still on active duty, who wishes to remain anonymous, remarked,

> Any of these (general officers) GOs who told you they were just "surprised" or "caught off guard" are the worst kind of officer the Army could ever have in its ranks. They actively worked to undermine people just trying to stay true to the law, the conventions, and the oath…I think we averted the worst but just barely—still many miles to go… Someday folks will realize that the medics sent to these places were actively manipulated to be proxy abusers. It was clear to me that these were sins of commission rather than omission.[97]

In 2005 the *Washington Post*'s Outlook section published my piece questioning the unhealthy silence from the military medical personnel. I explored the complicated issue of roles when the duty of military doctors—"first, do no harm"—comes in direct conflict with their duty as soldiers to obey orders. My arguments that the Hippocratic oath trumped military obedience came under heavy fire. With the help of PHR and others, I am delighted to report today that many of the governing policies and procedures have improved since then.

Since antiquity, the great nations have acknowledged that honor and civilized conduct must imbue the spirit of the warrior. It is no different for the global war on terror. Human Rights First has convened a group of retired admirals and generals—including RADM Guter and myself—who have forcefully spoken out to uphold these traditions. At one event, a presidential candidate asked a four-star participant about the circumstances of our gatherings—and our colleague answered:

> It may seem strange to have senior military officers collaborating with human rights groups—except when recognizing that the military shares important basic values regarding human rights—a common allegiance to the constitution and to the founding principles of our democracy. My fellow Americans—this is one topic when it truly is about the principle of the matter. Let me reiterate the four simple principles to which we subscribe:[98]

37

> 1. Torture is un-American. George Washington laid down the directive—American soldiers will treat the enemy humanely and conform to high moral and ethical principles on the battlefield.
>
> 2. Torture is Ineffective. Experienced interrogators acknowledge that information extracted by the use of torture is unreliable.
>
> 3. Torture is Unnecessary. Veteran FBI agents and military interrogators have spoken out publicly against the use of physical pressure in interrogation.
>
> 4. Torture is Damaging. "A person who is tortured is damaged, but so are the torturer, the nation, and the military."[99]

Sometimes, decent people get caught up in indecent acts. That is why it is so important to unite and affirm ethical principles and laws that stand the test of time and urgency, so that decent people can rely on the tested wisdom of what is right, especially when pressured by a compelling and prevailing contemporary notion that feels wrong to them.

This affirms our values as Americans and helps defend our service members in combat and citizens on our home soil.

Much has improved since the dark days of 2002, but our nation has been damaged. Where once the symbol of our great democracy was the Statue of Liberty, it has now become the image of that poor hooded man in detention with wires strung from his hands and feet. Our men and women on the front lines are endangered because of the increased risk of retaliatory measures. We are not safer because of these misguided policies and how we have acted as a country. It is time to right our wrongs, and we all have a collective duty to do so—to uphold our shared beliefs and convictions.

3

*

WHAT TORTURE DOES TO HUMAN BEINGS

Sister Dianna Ortiz

I wish to thank Professor Gushee and all who played a role in organizing this important summit on torture; and thank you for inviting me to share my reflections. I also wish to thank each of you for being here. Your presence reveals that like Jesus, you have refused to stand on the sidelines; instead you are saying no to torture—at least, I hope this is the case. I am both honored and humbled to be among you. It is my hope that my words will bring a small glimpse of the consequences of torture to the human spirit.

Over the years, I have found that images of one kind or another have served as useful vehicles to carry the words I have spoken before various audiences. Therefore, allow me to tell you that for some time, I was at a loss to explain a peculiar phenomenon. Strange as it may seem, from time to time I have received what appear to be gifts or "remembrances." They come by mail and are addressed to me where I live. There is no return address and no note—nothing to identify the sender, or senders—and no reason for the package. I choose to believe that the gifts are intended to remind me that there is an angel watching over me, accompanying me as I walk a path seeking to understand the experiences I have had, seeking to discover the why in the mountain of suffering that is visited daily upon the tortured.

Recently, I celebrated a birthday and with it came yet another gift—or, perhaps better, an "angelic reminder." At first, I found it vaguely irritating. When I opened the box, I found a rather odd shaped bottle with three pieces of parchment inside. On each was written a different word: Past, Present, Future. It seemed to me that my angel had sent me a fairly mundane message: forget the past, live in the present, hope for the future. I could have gotten that from a fortune cookie. And yet, those three words may serve another purpose—here today. They may serve as a framework, a superstructure for my words, words about myself and torture, and about you as well.

The past—that is, my experience of torture—keeps pace with every step I take. It is a dark, gray face that constantly peers over my shoulder. I have spent years struggling not to look back at what is following me, but to trust my footsteps to guide me onto a path where I can finally see beauty and goodness and embrace a lasting hope.

It is a difficult path to hold to if one also believes she should speak of the horrors of torture, as I do. You see, the past remains a constant threat, for speaking publicly about this horror often leads directly back to one's own experiences. By this I do not mean that one simply remembers them but rather that they are relived. At that moment, the present is indistinguishable from the past. This past has awakened again, both here and now. The smells of burning flesh and decomposing corpses, the mutilated bodies of children, the policeman's cratered face and button-like eyes devoid of feeling are returning. I have no wish whatsoever to return to that prison in Guatemala, nor do I wish to harken back to how I felt as I cried to a silent and deaf God. Yet, it all does come back.

Let me start my journey by taking you back for a moment to a time before my torture. Imagine, for a moment, the radiant face of God. We are nearly blinded by the glorious colors—shining from heaven's door. How magnificent it all is. But now, try to imagine a dark shadow falling across that face of God—eclipsing it, obliterating every sign of it. Hope is gone. Belief is gone. The God you once knew, you once trusted, is dead. Where are the colors now? What colors emanate from a dead God? "I will be with you always." That was the promise. Where is that promise now? What kind of a place is it where God dies—where trust in self and others dies as well?

Walk with me on the path that leads to that place. As we do, remember that there are thousands of others there at this very moment, some whose torture is being financed with our very own tax dollars. In

November 1987, I traveled to the highlands of Guatemala to live there, quite possibly, for the rest of my life. My ministry was teaching children to read and write in their native language—nothing extraordinary—nothing that should raise concern and outrage among those in power. At least you would think not. To me, being a teacher of Mayan children was a dream come true. I loved the Mayan culture. I loved the highlands. Even my bouts with head lice did not discourage me. In Guatemala, I had found myself—my purpose in life. I was at one with God and I was the happiest I had ever been. Nathaniel Hawthorne writes, "Happiness is like a butterfly which, when pursued, is always beyond our grasp, but, if you will sit down quietly, may alight upon you." That's how it was for me. I had found genuine peace in the highlands of Guatemala.

And then the butterfly was crushed and God died. First I received the death threats, then came the abduction by the Guatemalan security forces. I was taken to a torture cell—a place I came to know as Hell. In that clandestine prison, I was interrogated. My torturers played what they called a "game." If I answered a question in a way they liked, I would be allowed to smoke (although I didn't smoke). If I answered in a way they didn't like, I would be burned with a cigarette. These were the rules. For every answer I gave, they burned me. When I returned to the United States, a doctor found 111 second-degree burns on my back alone. That's how I know they asked me at least 111 questions. I was beaten, and I was tortured psychologically as well. I was lowered into an open pit filled with human bodies—bodies of women, men, and children—some alive, some dead. There were bodies that had been decapitated, caked with blood—and rats feasted on their flesh. I was also forced to witness and participate in the torture of another human being. Far worse than the physical torture was hearing the screams of the others being tortured. Even today, when I hear a scream or see the sight of blood, I think of those left behind in that prison.

It is not easy for me to admit that I was also gang raped. I sometimes blame myself. If only I had fought a little harder… I tried to be strategic, the way women are supposed to be in these situations. I really tried—but in the end, my torturers were much too strong for me. "Heads, I go first…tails, you go"—those were the words of the policeman, the most sadistic of the torturers. He was the first to rape me. I begged him to stop. But his actions roughened. I was his to do with as he wanted and he made sure I knew that. I still remember on the cement floor the last of who I was—a deep red stain.

Years have gone by, and still I carry the words he spoke when he had finished with me. In a tone of absolute triumph he said, "Your God is dead." I will never forget those words. Still, the policeman had left out one important fact: With God, I too had died—and dying with me was my trust in the human family. If this were not enough, my government was also in that clandestine prison—incarnated in the American I came to know as Alejandro, the one who was known to my torturers as their *jefe*, their boss—the one who could walk freely into one of Guatemala's notorious prisons and give orders: who to torture, how and when to torture. Before the Bush administration popularized this crime against humanity, the US government had long been involved in torture—but had done so in the shadows. I know this to be true from my own experience.

And now to the present: While the physical act of torture may be assigned to the past, its psychological effects permeate the present and blight the promise of the future. So often this is torture's intention. Torture is an attempt to obliterate a person's personality, to turn him into a quivering mass of fear, cowering in some corner of the world afraid to look for the dawn. Torture does not end with the release from some clandestine prison. It is not something we, the tortured, "get over." It is something we live with the rest of our days. It is forever strapped to our backs. It constitutes a permanent invasion of our minds and our souls. Someone in uniform, a scream, the smell of a cigarette, the sound of someone whistling, the sight of a dog, the sound of keys rattling, cutting a piece of meat with a knife—any of these may continually threaten a return to the past that walks so closely behind us. Imagine for a moment what it is like to be stalked by these images day in and day out. No one fully recovers from torture. The damage done by torture can never be undone.

In the midst of all this, we often search, not so much for why we were tortured, as for why we did not die in that awful place, as did so many of our sisters and brothers. Perhaps it is only out of desperation for an answer, for meaning, but many of us have come to believe, dared to believe that God, Allah, Buddha, or some other face of the Eternal, must have had some reason to keep us alive. What is the alternative—that we should see our present lives as but a continuation of the torture we experienced or that we live simply as a result of a random throw of some celestial dice?

Days, months, or years after our torture, the reverberations from our pasts echo in the paths we are now to walk. There standing before us are three doors—one of which we must walk through. Please understand, we judge no one door superior to the others. They are equal in value. The first leads to a life trying to hide, to denying the truth of what we witnessed and experienced. The second door leads to the easiest path, the most tempting one—closing one's eyes forever. The third is the most difficult—to accept, to face what happened squarely and then to use that terrible experience for some kind of good in the world. This is the least pleasant, the most hazardous path we might walk.

Of course, the choice of one door over another is not necessarily final. Over time, survivors may choose one path and then later follow another as they seek to find their way. So it was with me. In the clandestine prison where I witnessed the eclipse of God, I made a promise to those whose screams I heard: "If I survive, I will never forget you. I will tell the world what I have seen and heard." I returned to the United States shackled to that promise. Foolishly, I believed my government would welcome truth and demand that Americans—those, like Alejandro, who were involved in torture—those who knew of its practice and approved of it, would be held accountable. Instead, both the Guatemalan and US governments launched a smear campaign against me. What must I have been thinking? Instead of what I had expected, it became clear that I had to be silenced, discredited. First, it was said that I had not been tortured at all—that I was part of some political plot to deny the Guatemalan military funds from the US Congress. But there were all those burns on my back and elsewhere and so the governments' lies grew even worse.

I couldn't understand what was happening. What had I done wrong? I felt so alone. Was I like some tree stripped, grieving the ghosts of her departed leaves? I was grieving the life I had once lived—a life I could no longer even remember. And I was grieving the person I was becoming as a result of the torture. People tried to "fix me." But I was beyond repair. Many became frustrated and claimed I was feeling sorry for myself, that I was craving attention. Their advice: "Get over it…move on."

It was at that time that I made one friend—a razor blade. I carried it with me everywhere I went. It was my safety valve, if you will. At any moment, I could do what my torturers had failed to do. If I could do nothing else in this world, I could at least control the terms of my own destiny. And so one day years ago, I turned to my friend for comfort. My only escape was to close my eyes forever. I swallowed a handful of valium pills and slit my wrist. As I watched the blood stream, it was then that I realized I had opened the wrong door. I was not ready to die. I did want to live—to hope again.

If there was a reason that I survived other than blind chance, then this may have been it. Ten years ago, men and women from various parts of our world joined with me in walking through the third door. Together we brought into being an organization for torture survivors, known as the Torture Abolition and Survivors Support Coalition International (TASSC). With limited funds and the generosity of good people, TASSC has offered and continues to offer support and a range of services to our fellow survivors and their families here in the United States and abroad. At the same time, we have become one of the most uncompromising opponents of torture wherever it occurs. For this, we have been more often criticized than complimented.

These last several years have been dark times for torture survivors. Try to imagine what we felt as we witnessed the Bush administration embrace torture in broad daylight. In our despair, we expected outrage, massive demonstrations; instead, there was massive silence and apparent indifference. We spoke out but our words fell on deaf ears. We tried to mobilize and work with other NGOs—many chose to distance themselves from us, preferring to walk a more moderate path of compromise.

For TASSC, we do not see how moderation and opposition to torture fit into the same sentence.

Today torture stands triumphant over the wounded body of human rights. Torture's collective champion, the Bush administration, stands unchallenged by a weak, vacillating, fearful congressional majority. Are those words too harsh? They are not harsh enough. Congress has acquiesced to the systematic violation of human rights, preferring the role of impotent observer to active defender.

The future, what then lies ahead? We do. And by "we," I do not mean torture survivors alone. I mean all of us. We must begin to confront the massive obscenity that has become de facto US policy and those who have engineered this affront to human decency. Begin? Did I say begin? Yes, I did. But then comes the response: "We have already expressed our opposition to torture." Yes, I know, but it has not been enough; and so, we must begin to do enough. It is not enough simply to speak to power. Power is not listening. Power has dismissed truth. We must act—out of our seats and into the streets if necessary. Let this conference become one giant meeting on strategy and tactics. We do not need to reaffirm that torture is evil. We need to do something about that evil.

Let me offer my own first step toward defeating this sin that threatens our nation. Whether it be McCain or Obama, the government must restore the rule of law, and that restoration depends on the prosecution of any of our leaders who violated that law. Let the investigation of such suspects commence the day this nation has a new attorney general. Let us now begin the effort to ensure that the new administration will do precisely that.

Until my last breath, I will suffer the effects of torture; until that moment, quite possibly, the struggle between hope and despair will rage in me. There, that is enough about me. What about you? What about us? For those of you who, as I, are followers of the tortured Jesus, what does it mean to "do enough" about torture? What will you do? What *is* enough? Let the answers to that question fill the halls of this conference and return home with you.

What Torture Does to Human Beings

Douglas A. Johnson

When the first credible news emerged in late 2002 that the United States was using torture, we at the Center for Victims of Torture (CVT) were both appalled and surprised, because the United States had been a leader in the global effort to end torture; Republicans and Democrats alike held this as a bedrock American value. At CVT and throughout the torture treatment movement, we felt isolated and alone when so few voices spoke out to draw us back on course as a nation of deep values and self-respect. Worse still were invitations to debate talk show hosts and everyday Americans asserting that torture is moral when used to gain information to save lives, as in the fictional "ticking time bomb" scenario. We know the pain and the lifetime of suffering torture nails to its victims; why could others not see it? We know how easy it is to gain a confession, even from the innocent; how could anyone equate torture with truth telling? We know the pornographic, dirty, and shameful nature of the methods used to break people around the world; how could anyone paint this filth with a heroic, moral brush?

Our clients, who are principally refugees and asylum seekers, became deeply fearful. The nation to which they had come, fleeing the torture chamber for a harbor of safety and respect, now presented itself as a danger to those who were different. They came from countries in turmoil—countries full of violence and deeply divided, where through paranoia and hatred, those of a different ethnic group or set of thoughts and beliefs were terrorized. The reaction of our clients to their new fear was so profound that it had clinical implications, and our already difficult work of healing became more difficult. Speaking out and seeking allies became a clinical necessity; we needed to reassure our clients that our country was a nation of moral values and the rule of law, and that we would defend those people in our care to the best of our ability. But we despaired with them.

Emerging Voices

Two voices emerged in the United States that filled us with hope—stemming in part, I am ashamed to say, from their being unexpected. First, the Evangelical Declaration Against Torture[100] surprised us with both its moral clarity and outrage at the undeniable violation of the dignity of the human spirit, as well as its many prominent signatories, including the National Association of Evangelicals. The Declaration stated what torture survivors and we knew in our hearts, that applying consequentialist ethics to torture and cruelty is fundamentally wrong.

The other voice came from the military, especially retired general and flag officers, over forty of whom affiliated themselves with Human Rights First. We began to hear the sentiment from within the military that they had been asked to act dishonorably and employ methods they knew didn't work to obtain valuable intelligence and, in fact, endangered our troops and our nation. They were so alarmed at the cost to our nation's security brought about by decisions based on fear—not good practice—that many began to speak out. Our military leaders reminded us that our security comes not from our willingness to be cruel but from the values that sustain America and earn the world's regard. Those of us in torture treatment are grateful to them, as their voices provided us with certainty and strength, and heartened our clients with a vision of an America they can still believe in.

It is not at all a coincidence that both of these voices use a similar ethical touchstone, the Golden Rule. The US Army field manual *Human Intelligence Collector Operations* advises interrogators who are not sure they are acting ethically to ask this question before acting: "*If the proposed approach technique were used by the enemy against one of your fellow soldiers, would you believe the soldier had been abused? If you answer…yes, the contemplated action should not be conducted.*"[101] The *Declaration of*

Principles for a Presidential Executive Order on Prisoner Treatment, Torture & Cruelty was so successful at gaining a wide variety of adherents—conservatives and liberals, Republicans and Democrats, religious and security experts—because the very first principle is the Golden Rule.[102]

The Work of the Center for Victims of Torture

The mission of the Center for Victims of Torture is to heal the wounds of torture on individuals, families, and communities and to stop torture worldwide. Founded in Minnesota in 1985 by then Governor Rudy Perpich, CVT is the first organized program of care and rehabilitation for torture survivors in the United States and one of the very first in the world. Our core work and learning have emerged from the care of thousands of torture victims from nearly seventy countries, living in this country and abroad, over the past twenty-three years. We have reinforced our learning through our research and training of other health care professionals, both in specialized torture rehabilitation centers and among mainstream providers. We are currently providing technical assistance and small grants to thirty-three torture rehabilitation programs in the United States and another nineteen in countries across the world.

Abroad, in locations where human rights atrocities have been used to shape cultures through fear and the sheer number of victims hangs like a heavy millstone weighing down their future, CVT has organized major interventions to heal survivors of torture. We have trained hundreds of local people to become mental health clinicians and employed them to operate healing programs in Sierra Leone, Liberia, and the Democratic Republic of the Congo; in September 2008, we began operations in Jordan to aid Iraqi survivors. In the United States, we operate with a staff of about sixty-three full-time professionals, an equal number of part-time employees, and about 300 volunteers; in our programs abroad, we employ about 200 staff, mostly nationals from the nations where we operate, along with a small number of expatriates.

I report these details to underscore that torture is not a theoretical discussion for us. We know what torture is, and we know its impact.

There are approximately 500,000 survivors of torture who have fled to this nation's shores to seek safety and freedom from torture; about

30,000 now live in Minnesota. We currently have the capacity to provide intensive care to only 1 percent of those living in our state. Nationally and internationally, resources are even more scarce.

Torture's Impact

I have been asked to address "what torture does to a human being." I will look at this question from several points of view, but must emphasize that some of what we know is based on research and direct experience, while other parts of our learning are directed by hypotheses that point to new areas for further work and research. To have a full understanding of the impact of torture, we need to think on three levels—the individual, the family, and the community—and in the two dimensions of both the victim and the perpetrator. That is a difficult task, especially because torture treatment is a relatively new form of care and research is conducted by a fairly "resource-poor" set of collaborators. But, fortunately, there are now about 200 torture treatment centers in the world, and we are learning more each day.

We know quite a lot about the impact of torture and cruelty on victims through extensive care over more than two decades and a growing body of research. We have more limited research and clinical work that helps us understand the impact on families and their immediate network of loved ones and dependents. We have very limited empirical research on the effects of torture and cruelty on communities; much more is available on human rights atrocities in general and on war traumas. However, there is plenty of anecdotal evidence that is leading to the development of new approaches for helping communities heal—those larger collectives of individuals affected by the trauma of victims. As he tried to understand his experience, an African bishop told me his torture was intended as a message: "If they will do this to me, what will they do to my flock?" Certainly the fear engendered by the presence of past or present torturers does permeate the community.

We need more research about the impact on the torturer of being the abuser, but understanding is now emerging from a number of fields. We have some insight into the difficulties abusers bring into the lives of their own families, but our knowledge is much less complete. The impact on the community as abusers act out learned behavior or mental health issues has hardly been touched as a research or clinical subject.

On Individuals

Whatever we do learn about the impact of torture must first be placed in the context of what we know about the impact of intense traumas, and especially human-induced traumas, of which torture is the most extreme example. Some of this research has looked at the effects of unpredictable and uncontrollable traumas in animals. Findings have pointed to profound biological and behavioral changes induced by the trauma itself. New techniques in brain scanning have confirmed and expanded our understanding and have revealed more subtle measures of chemical and hormonal imbalances associated with trauma. Through these and other techniques, we now understand that the male human brain is not fully developed until the age of twenty-three or twenty-four, especially that part of the brain associated with judgment and moral reasoning. There are those studying how traumas can postpone or derail the developmental process for years. This disruption would explain, in part, why our clinicians find that men and women exposed to torture at an early age are so much more difficult to assist in healing than those tortured in their mature years. Having a mature sense of self and what you believe in helps a victim gain perspective and understanding and helps define a path to healing.

"The essence of trauma is that it overwhelms the victim's psychological and biological coping mechanisms. This occurs when internal and external resources are inadequate to cope with the external threat."[103] Two leading researchers in the field, Dr. Bessel van der Kolk and Dr. Jose Saporta, identify four fundamental aspects of traumatic events (incomprehensibility, disrupted attachment, traumatic bonding, and inescapability), "which account for the overwhelming nature of trauma and the overwhelming impact of the torture experience."

—*The trauma is so beyond the boundaries of normal life that victims don't have the language or the concepts to understand it; it is incomprehensible.* CVT's clients ask "How can this evil happen in the world?" Such difficult questions underscore that the normal patterns of thinking we use to get through daily life can neither explain the event suffered nor provide safe guidance for coping with it. And among torture survivors, who ask, "why did this happen to me?", those inadequate patterns of daily thinking may lead to blaming oneself for what happened. The evil happened because of something he or she did or failed to do. The result is "speechless terror."

—*We all have a biological need for attachment or emotional bonding to others to feel safe and secure, a pattern that begins with an infant's attachment to his or her mother.* We know more about how disrupting that particular attachment can lead to difficulties for a child. That biological need is particularly acute in times of intense traumas, when a sense of comfort and safety would be helpful. But it is often in these times when our normal friendships and supportive relationships are not there or are themselves unable to cope with what is going on. This is especially difficult for those imprisoned and isolated from others, "perpetuating the inner chaos and terror."[104]

—*The need to find a source of hope is so powerful that strong bonds are made during the trauma.* Van der Kolk points out that this process of "traumatic bonding" occurs with hostages, abused children, and abused spouses, as well as with torture survivors. To strengthen this bond, victims often blame themselves for their torment, a pattern that has been identified as "soul murder."

—*"When there is nothing that the victim can do to terminate the massive threat to safety, his ability to cope is overwhelmed."*[105] An Argentine psychotherapist, herself a torture survivor, once told me that torture was so much more difficult than other forms of abuse because there was never "hope of rescue." Even cooperation, or confession, does not always end torture, as that is seldom its purpose. Rather, the unpredictable and inescapable nature of the trauma challenges the individual's sense of competency and self-worth.

Isolation and sensory deprivation are especially damaging because they strategically utilize these traumatic responses. The literature on the biological effects of trauma has become increasingly rich. And so, it is particularly disturbing when those knowledgeable in the theory of trauma use their medical and psychological training to foster the destructive impact of a traumatic interrogation. Testimony in the Senate Armed Services Committee reported in June 2008 that a military psychologist and psychiatrist recommended creating an atmosphere of "controlled chaos," which would "foster dependence and compliance," through the creation of "psychological stress" by means of using such techniques as "sleep deprivation, withholding food, isolation, loss of time." Observing the sixteen-year-old Mohammed Jawad upset during interrogation, talking to pictures on the wall and crying for his mother, a psychologist recommended "ratcheting up" the pressure with prolonged isolation, which evidently led to his attempt to commit suicide at the Guantánamo site. Here, the need for attachment is clearly perverted to destructive effect.[106]

Jacobo Timmerman edited a daily newspaper in Buenos Aires in the 1970s. During the height of the military repression, his was the only Spanish-language paper reporting the increasing phenomenon of disappearances of political activists and their family members. As a result of his truth telling, he too disappeared for thirty months.

His moving testimony of his experience of torture in a secret military prison is called *Prisoner without a Name, Cell without a Number*.[107] His account was controversial, especially within his Jewish community, because he asserted that the whole repressive apparatus was designed and implemented by Nazis. Many agreed with him, arguing that the system of disappearances themselves was modeled on the "night and fog" methods of Nazi Germany. Those methods were premised on the view that a disappearance would cause far more fear than an assassination in that it would suspend families and communities by "unknowing" the fates of loved ones. But the Argentine Jewish community did not want to deal with the military dictatorship as a Nazi state; it was too threatening to the safety of the community.

Timmerman described in detail his cell and his torture chamber, both of which were filled with Nazi symbols: graffiti, posters, flags. Timmerman experienced the terror of being a Jew in the hands of his worst nightmare. His critics proposed that he was taken by a few bad apples who did not represent the honor of the Argentine military. The controversy raged. And yet, there is an alternative explanation of his experience. His captors had thought out how to maximize the terror they sought to instill in Timmerman. What better way to demonstrate their total disregard for his humanity? What method could be more effective to emphasize his vulnerability and to destroy the hope of rescue by those who respected his political and community standing? What means could be more effective than to terrorize him with imminent, nameless, and unheralded death, another victim among a cast of millions?

One of CVT's early clients from Ethiopia, a Christian, was nailed to the table by his Marxist captors, an obvious symbol of the state's disregard for religious freedom. But to ensure he did not gain the solace and possible strength of martyrdom, they also nailed him by his testicles, invoking also the symbolism of castration and the loss of manhood. It was the speech of hatred, the disregard for his most cherished symbols and identity, the purposeful unmanning that haunted his nightmares, not the memories of the physical pain.

The popular imagination equates torture with physical brutality in its most extreme form. And it often is, as Timmerman's testimony makes clear. But torture is also psychological. The body can truly be used as a weapon against the mind and the soul, but there are plenty of tricks to be employed directly against the mind itself. There are seventy-four different forms of torture reported in the United Nations Human Rights Documentation System or HURIDOCS.[108] Each is a testament to human ingenuity for cruelty and pain. We expect that list to expand, not shrink, as we in the torture treatment movement continue to document the brutality repressive governments exercise against their targets.

55

Physical Effects

Each technique of physical assault engenders short-term and long-term consequences, sometimes quite unique. There are countless variations of ways to puncture, burn, break, stretch, hang, beat, asphyxiate, drown, or otherwise abuse a human being. Some techniques leave physical scars or signs; others, such as rape or waterboarding, may leave no physical scar at all but leave long-term psychological suffering. Some forms of torture, such as being held for prolonged periods in very uncomfortable positions, have very subtle consequences that are sometimes difficult to diagnose in that they generally involve stretching and twisting of the spinal column. Depending on which vertebrae are most affected and nerves irritated, victims may experience symptoms that "simulate cardiac disease, gastrointestinal, genital or other conditions."[109] Because the survivor experiences the aftereffects as damage to specific organs, therapists may confuse diagnostic findings of normally functioning organs as indicative of primarily psychological symptoms and miss the actual nerve damage.

As our forensic capacities have increased, documentation of physical forms of torture has become more sophisticated, sometimes with unintended consequences. Our colleagues in Turkey, for example, developed a method of bone scintography[110] to prove the use of *falaka* or *falanga*, the beating of the soles of the feet with rods, once the most popular method of torture in the country. But where these new tests were available, police began to use methods more difficult to document, such as pressing victims between enormous blocks of ice. That may also explain the increasing sophistication of psychological forms of torture. Quite frankly, psychological forms of torture are the most damaging to the long-term health of the victim, as our clients' experiences demonstrate.

Emotional Impact

A torture survivor quoted by the Turkish physician and researcher Dr. Metin Basoħu said, "I didn't mind the pain so much. It was the cries next door I couldn't bear."[111] Purely psychological forms of torture, including being subjected to mock execution, sexual humiliation, or being forced to watch or listen to the rape of a loved one, may have exactly the same psychological consequences as physical torture. The captors of an Iraqi client played tapes of a woman screaming and told him that this was his wife being raped; that is what he could never erase from his mind. A number of CVT clients have said the worst thing they experienced was watching their child tortured (as a way of breaking the parent). They felt the pain of the child, but also their failure as a parent to protect the child. One study of CVT clients found that 25 percent had been tortured below the age of twenty-one, with children usually tortured as a weapon against their parents.

Another client from Ethiopia speaks about being taken out at night in a pickup truck with other prisoners; the truck stops repeatedly and one person is taken out and executed, his body left by the roadside. When he is the only remaining prisoner, the truck drives back to the prison, where he is placed in his cell, and his guards tell him to have a good night's rest. This sense of helplessness is the source of his nightmares, not the physical pain.

A key element of torture scenarios is the creation of dilemmas that have no satisfactory resolution. A client from Latin America was tortured in two different ways and then forced to say which she "preferred." She felt profound guilt and shame, somehow complicit and therefore deserving of torture.

When we hear stories of Americans carefully manipulating prisoners into painful stress positions, we are often told this is humane treatment since the victim can decide when he will be released by simply giving up information. As the position becomes more and more agonizing over time, the prisoner wonders, "Can I hold out for another minute, another five minutes, an hour?" And of course, if he has no information to give, the "trial by ordeal" will only be more prolonged. The illusion that the victim has any control over the traumatic situation helps instill shame and guilt about participating in one's own torture.

The likelihood of profound and long-lasting psychological effects from torture is independent of the intensity, nature, or duration of the abuse, although those effects may be partly related to poorly understood psychological attributes of the victim. The torturer may attack the body of the victim, but the ultimate target is the mind both during and after imprisonment. In fact, a study by Dr. Metin Başoğlu and his team com - paring the psychological impact of physical forms of torture with psychological methods found that "ill treatment during captivity, such as psychological manipulations, humiliating treatment, and forced stress positions, does not seem to be substantially different from physical torture in terms of the severity of mental suffering they cause, the underlying mechanism of traumatic stress, and their long-term psychological outcome. Thus, these procedures do amount to torture, thereby lending support to their prohibition by international law."[112]

There is a remarkably common pattern of profound emotional reactions and psychological symptoms that transcends cultural and national differences. The effects can include but are not limited to re-experiencing the trauma, avoidance and emotional numbing, hyperarousal, depression, damaged self-concept and foreshortened future, dissociation/ depersonalization, atypical behaviors such as impulse-control problems and high-risk behavior, somatic complaints, sexual dysfunction, psychosis, substance abuse, and neuropsychological impairment such as the loss of short-term or long-term memory, perceptual difficulties, loss of ability to sustain attention or concentration, and the loss of ability to learn.[113]

The main psychiatric disorders associated with torture are post-traumatic stress disorder (PTSD) and major depression.[114] While it is important to recognize that not everyone who has been tortured develops a diagnosable mental disorder, it is equally important to recognize that for many survivors, the symptoms and aftereffects of torture endure for a lifetime. We know, for example, that survivors of the Holocaust and the concentration camps during World War II have much higher rates of clinical depression and suicide even fifty years after the conclusion of that conflict. This suffering is not something that time simply heals.

What does this mean in human terms? A client was driving an ice cream truck in Minneapolis when he was rear-ended by a car traveling at slow speed. It happens; you get out, exchange insurance information, and go back to work. But he came out swinging, enraged and violent. He was a gentle man, and this was unexpected. He told me later that in his country of origin, his car was suddenly surrounded and pinned in by secret police cars; they arrested him and began a regime of brutal torture. He said that day in the ice cream truck, he suddenly thought he was back home again; he came out of his truck fighting for his life. This is what we mean when we talk about re-experiencing traumatic events. He had been a wealthy businessman in his country; now he was having difficulty driving an ice cream truck.

Another African client came to the clinic complaining of nightmares. They were so consistent and fearful that he routinely went to sleep in a chair so that, before falling into a dream state, he would fall from the chair and wake up. For at least six months, he had had little sleep and was exhausted, depressed, and suicidal.

On Families

We also know torture can profoundly damage intimate relationships between spouses, parents, children, and other family members, as well as between the victims and their communities. This level of trauma affects future generations, again as evidenced by the studies showing higher rates of suicide and depression among the children and grandchildren of Holocaust survivors. These findings have been repeated among survivors of other cruel and inhumane treatment.

On Communities

Through examination of and detailed work with survivors, we at CVT have reached conclusions about torture's nature and purpose that we believe to be relevant for the discussion that must take place in our nation about the tolerance or intolerance of torture and any practices of it. Torture in the modern world is not primarily a tool for gaining information, but rather a political weapon that invokes fear to shape societies.

Consider this: The death of Jesus is often so sanitized and ritualized that we fail to understand Jesus died under torture. What is the point of whipping a man bloody before his planned execution? Of impaling his face with a crown of thorns? Of nailing him to a cross or tying him up so that the weight of his body will gradually tear his limbs from his sockets in excruciating pain that will last for days until thirst and hunger ultimately kill him? Of displaying this cruelty—the humiliation and suffering of the crucified—on the public roads, on the hillsides for all—man, woman, and child—to see? As the bishop said, "If they will do this to me, what will they do to my flock?"

A great majority of CVT's Minnesota clients were targeted for torture because they were leaders in their communities. Their destruction through ritualized humiliation and shame was intended to eliminate their leadership from the community and to use their network of influence to induce fear and silence throughout the community. A high official in the Turkish human rights ministry once told me that in a nation of sixty million people, only one million were involved in any kind of civil society organization, including, he said, the administration of local mosques. "Do you know why so few people are active?" he asked me. "It is fear. Over generations, Turks have learned to be fearful of public life; we have retired to our families and our businesses." Fearful communities—traumatized communities—are more easily controlled by a few who can manipulate public power for their own private gain.

Though we may think of torture as bodily pain and suffering, we must remember that the body is merely a weapon to be used against the mind. It is breaking the soul that is torture's real purpose. And while we think of torture as a cruelty inflicted on the individual, it is a powerful political weapon used to shape cultures and societies through fear. Americans want to believe that if torture and cruelty are used, it is only to gain information to save lives; we do not see the broader purpose. We must remember that the rest of the world interprets our actions through their own experiences.

The Torturer

There is another important human being in the torture relationship: the perpetrator. We know far more about the processes of forming and training torturers than we do about the long-term impact on the individual who engages in torture. The processes are remarkably similar around the world. They involve:

—*Normalization of violence, often by being subjected to it oneself in a general training program, perhaps in the guise of resistance training to torture or abuse if captured;*
—*Controlled and constant indoctrination into the just mission of the perpetrators and the dehumanization of the victim.* As no one wants to see himself or herself acting for evil, it is important to believe one is contributing to a great good against those of great evil;
—*Participation in low levels of physical abuse, in the guise of "softening up" the target, including escalation to more and more violent beatings; perpetrators become numb and detached from their actions;*

—A winnowing out of those who appear to be upset or doubtful of what they are doing and offering of rewards and incentives to those who show themselves more likely to use violence in controlled but escalating ways. The Milgram experiments, where subjects are told by a researcher to inflict others with increasingly powerful electrical shocks, demonstrate how unfortunately easy it is for those in authority to push ordinary people to inflict pain on others, even when the authority is merely a researcher wearing a white coat.[115]

The successful creation of an abusive interrogation team requires managing the cognitive dissonance that arises in its participants' minds and personalities: that of being an abuser of others while also retaining a semblance of normal human relationships, such as being a father or husband or daughter or friend. This dissonance is actually somewhat difficult to maintain, and requires strong leadership adept at using group dynamics to reinforce the role and the willingness to continue in that role.

This pattern is well documented and appears repeatedly across all regions of the world and all ideological regimes, from the Marxists of Cambodia, China, and Ethiopia in the 1980s to the right-wing authoritarians of Greece, Argentina, and Chile. Given what we do know about the important role leadership and groups play in maintaining the productivity of torturers, we know remarkably little about what happens to those who are suddenly released from that psychological support and return to civilian life. If there are any studies of the costs to the soul and life of a torturer, I am not aware of them. But we have a number of important indicators of the personal and social consequences for torturers.

We have been approached by perpetrators seeking care at the Center for Victims of Torture, as have other treatment facilities. As far as I know, all of the programs within the United States have policies of not providing care to perpetrators of torture; this assures clients who are survivors of torture of their complete safety and confidentiality. Nevertheless, it may often take one or more interviews with potential clients to uncover their roles as perpetrators. And they often come with similar complaints: nightmares and sleeplessness, depression, thoughts of suicide. A number may have also been victims—through the violence in their training program whereby they felt forced to become perpetrators, or in retaliation from a new regime.

There is a case study of a perpetrator in Argentina who came to a team of psychiatrists looking for help to stop nightmares. They concluded they could not help him recover because he was unable to express remorse for his deeds. At the time, the Argentine military tightly held to the view that everything they had done in the "dirty war" was a justified act of patriotism, and anyone from the military who broke with that view was treated as a traitor to the country. For a significant time in the newly democratic nation, the military was able to maintain the strongly divisive "us versus them" language that worked against soul searching but could not protect from nightmares.

Over the years, a number of former American soldiers have told me of their participation or observation of atrocities during the Vietnam War or of the training they received in the use of torture and cruelty during interrogations. They have spoken to me of the personal costs to them, the fear, nightmares, and shame that have often taken years of psychotherapy to overcome. They have spoken of the difficulties of maintaining intimate relationships. These case studies and anecdotal evidence, bolstered by studies of abusive fathers and police, indicate deep wounds for perpetrators as well. In September 2008, I heard General Robert Nash talk to delegates at the Republican National Convention. As a commanding officer, he said he felt a deep obligation to the young men and women serving, and to their families, that they each return home a better person. He asked, with deep emotion, why we would ask any American man or woman, in or out of uniform, to engage in these activities, because he or she will not then return a better person.

Our Responsibilities to Heal

I hope this discussion helps you better understand the impact torture has on victims and victimizers, on families, on communities, and on nations. The impact is considerable, painful, and enduring. I have not helped you answer whether you should care if those consequences are visited upon terrorists and others who believe their religions justify killing innocents and civilians. This is what I know:

I know that I meet people everyday who gave a confession as part of the process of breaking them. I know that the victims' governments justified their actions by asserting the victims' guilt. And yet I know they all longed for death, and all tell me they would have said anything to get the pain to stop.

I know that at least one of those three who died on the cross so long ago was, in fact, innocent of all charges. But given the importance of torture in Roman law, I am convinced that all three were tortured to gain a confession and that at least two of them did so. I do not know whether they spoke the truth or just hoped to stop the pain.

I know that I am called to be concerned with all three. Hebrews 13:3 tells us "Remember those who are in prison, as though you yourselves were in prison with them; those who are tortured, as though you yourselves were being tortured." It does not tell us to concern ourselves only with the innocent. We can never really know who is and who is not innocent, but that doesn't matter. Torture is a crime against the human spirit and any who have suffered are deserving of our concern and care. I do not have the luxury of hating those who would harm our nation and our people, but must bear witness and offer healing to all. As the world watches us to see what we do, none of us has that luxury.

* * *

Response to Sister Dianna Ortiz and Douglas A. Johnson by Denise Massey

I want to share my emotional responses to learning about torture, in the hope that my responses will help you with your own. I will share with you the challenges and struggles I feel, the gifts I find in taking a second look at my feelings, and the actions I see as possible responses to these messages and gifts.

I am angry and outraged about the ways human beings hurt, destroy, and damage each other. I am also very sad. At times, thus far, I have felt hopeless and helpless. Another important issue for me and I am sure for many of you, is that this discussion has connections with painful experiences in my past. While my experiences are significantly milder than those of torture survivors, I too have experienced alienation, abandonment, helplessness, hopelessness, pain, isolation, and disillusionment with humankind and with the divine.

I confess that I want to avoid the topic, because these stories touch and amplify my own story. However, I know that meaning, hope, and healing are found in the connections between our stories. I also know that pain is a gift intended to show us something that needs to be healed. Physical pain gives us important information about how to take care of our bodies.

Being a pastoral caregiver, I have learned that avoiding painful realities only makes them worse. For example, I know a diabetic man who has lost all feeling in his feet. Because he couldn't feel his pain, he got a bad infection that was left untreated. He ended up having a toe amputated. His experience reminded me that our pain really does call our attention to issues that need healing.

Let us find hope and courage from the knowledge that listening to our pain leads us to the actions that bring about healing. I applaud the courage and hope you have already expressed in choosing to read this information about torture. I invite you to draw upon all of your spiritual and emotional resources to join me in moving through pain toward healing.

Let's begin with our painful feelings of anger and outrage. I believe anger, like many feelings, is a signal that something is wrong and needs our attention. Anger provides energy to make changes, the energy to protect the things that are important to us.

Dr. Andrew Lester, a pastoral counselor who has studied anger extensively, teaches us that anger is a sign that something deeply important to us is being threatened. He suggests we ask ourselves, "What is being threatened?"[116] For many of us today, some of our strongest and most deeply held spiritual beliefs are seriously threatened by the facts about torture we are learning. For example, many spiritual traditions teach us the following truths: we all are one (what happens to one of us affects the rest of us); how we treat each other matters (the Golden Rule); human beings have great potential and can do much good in the world; and we are to love other people, the divine, and ourselves. These and other spiritual principles are important to many of us.

We are angry because these precious principles are disregarded and violated. Torture is a great offense to our spirituality, our morality, and our humanity. One of the gifts of anger is that it reminds us of our values, the things that are precious to us. Another gift is that it gives us the energy to make changes, to confront injustice, and to restore our deepest spiritual convictions. We can allow our religious faith to confront the realities about torture that diminish our national soul.

I have worked as a chaplain in a variety of settings, including a mental hospital, a VA hospital, an addictions treatment unit, and a psychiatric unit. I saw a number of individuals with post-traumatic stress disorder, and some survivors of torture. I've seen the havoc torture causes emotionally, physically, mentally, and spiritually. The concepts Douglas Johnson discussed really do happen to real human beings. And it is quite disturbing to see what torture does to people.

Perhaps most distressing to me were the injuries and distortions to the potential of so many wonderful people. The losses to the world are incalculable. I saw so much damaged and wasted human potential. I feel both angry and sad about these losses.

We've already discussed anger, now let's look for the gifts within our sadness and despair. There is much real sadness regarding the effects of torture on human beings. Sadness gives us the important message that something is dreadfully wrong and needs our attention. Sadness calls for us to do two things: to release something and to restore something. We must ask ourselves, "What must be released?" and "What must be restored?"[117]

When I examine my sadness about torture, I realize the need to release several things. I must release my denial telling me these things can't really happen. I must release the desire to ignore the painful realities of our world. I must release the helplessness and hopelessness that tempt me to avoid action toward change and healing.

The next question about our sadness to reflect upon is "What must be restored?" I see several answers. You may have others. As I release my denial and ignoring of painful facts, I must restore my willingness to see and respond to the truth. As I release my feelings of helplessness and hopelessness, I must restore my belief that what I do matters. I also restore my belief that I can participate in changes brought about by powers greater than myself, such as organizations, communities, and the divine mystery.

I was thrilled in my research to discover the number of organizations working to bring an end to torture and healing to torture survivors. I encourage each of you to find a community or organization that you join to help bring an end to torture.

We need our spiritual resources to help us end torture. Our faith traditions have important contributions to make for the healing of our national soul. I hope we can learn from each other and grow stronger as a result. I believe our interfaith work brings healing for our national soul.

In community with the divine and with other people, we can learn from our emotional responses to what torture does to human beings. Remember, our emotions are meant to tell us something is wrong and to provide energy for actions that can bring about healing. Let me share with you some of the actions you and I might choose to take as a result of this conference. I invite you to consider this list and to consider additional possibilities.

I will stay attuned to the holy one in my life and work, and will seek to bring about healing and restoration. I will learn more about our nation's policies and ways to influence them. I will listen to the stories of torture survivors. I will read the literature about these issues. I will learn from people who are knowledgeable about ending torture and healing its effects. I will contribute in some way to the healing of torture survivors. I will choose one organization to join and one concrete action to support the call for "no torture, no exceptions."

This is a list of possibilities. You may think of others. You must discern what is right for you. I encourage you to choose one small, manageable, and concrete step to move in the direction of healing. I encourage you to pay attention to what you feel energized to do and to choose an action in that arena. Remember that you are not alone; you can have the support of spiritual communities and of the divine.

May we each experience the grace to play our part in the healing and restoration of our national soul through a commitment to "no torture, no exceptions."

4

★

What the Torture Debate Reveals
about American Christianity

David P. Gushee

The Righteous Gentiles Paradigm

My own understanding of how individuals and societies, including people of faith, respond to the encroachment of government wrongdoing has been shaped profoundly by the first major intellectual project of my career. In my doctoral dissertation I studied the ways in which Europe's Christians responded to the Holocaust.[118] I wanted to know how the resources of Christian faith functioned (or failed to function) when Europe's Christians (beginning in Germany) discovered that their Jewish neighbors were being persecuted, deported, and annihilated by Nazi Germany. I was especially interested in learning about those who rescued Jews—those persons the Jewish community, drawing on its own tradition, decided to honor as the "Righteous Gentiles of the Holocaust."

Obstacles to Resistance

Among the many things I have learned from that study is that when governments misuse their massive power in order to harm people and violate their basic human rights, they have numerous built-in advantages over those forces of resistance that might come to be arrayed against them or on behalf of their victims.

They have an informational advantage, as only the government (actually, a small number of persons within the government) actually knows in detail what its policies are and how and where those policies are being implemented. Even in a society with a free press and a political opposition, there will always be a time lag between the development and implementation of (secret) government policies and the public discovery of those policies. Thus, any resistance will always be playing catch-up and operating on the basis of less than complete information—often information purposefully distorted by the government.

Governments also have an authority advantage, in that the presupposition of most ordinary citizens, at least in a democracy, is that the government has both the right and the obligation to undertake the policies it deems necessary to protect national security or advance the common good, and that citizens should trust government with that power. This authority advantage is exacerbated among Christians who are raised with an understanding of the Bible (cf. Romans 13) that teaches them to submit unquestioningly to government authority.

Governments have an intimidation advantage, in that if they choose, they can impose considerable costs on any individuals or groups within the society who might decide to resist their policies. In Nazi Germany and Nazi-occupied Europe, such intimidation was a major factor inhibiting resistance. Most people are not terribly brave.

Finally, resisters have a resistance-process disadvantage. The process of moving into resistance—or into any active rendering of help to someone in need, even help that is minimally costly to the helper—is actually more cumbersome and elaborate than most of us imagine: The resistance/helping process begins with noticing something is wrong or someone needs help. This requires not only access to information, but also a basic attentiveness to realities outside the self, in particular, attentiveness to the injustices and miseries suffered by others, so that if information is available it will actually be noticed. This can be blocked by perpetrators who purposefully hide the wrong and the wronged, and by the self-centeredness or particular distractions and stresses faced by the potential helper.

Beyond noticing, the potential helper/resister must be able to discern the significance of what is noticed. At one level this is a moral judgment rooted in the observer's worldview, character, and moral values, but many factors feed into that judgment. This perception of significance can be blocked by all kinds of factors, including, for example, perceptions of the worthiness of the persons needing help.

Once having discerned the significance of an event, observers or potential helpers must still somehow shake off the inertia created by their engagement with other people, problems, projects, interests, or concerns. They were headed in one direction and circumstances now suggest they must do something different. This directional shift rarely happens quickly.

One critical factor affecting whether that inertia is shaken is a sense of personal responsibility to act. I can notice a car accident and discern that it is a significant one without then accepting that I have a personal responsibility to do something in response to it. There is a gap between the sense that "someone should do something here" to "I must do something here." This is why first-responders are trained to say, "You, in the blue shirt, call 911," instead of "Someone call 911." Especially where there is no context for relationship between the victims and potential helpers, this sense of personal responsibility can be quite attenuated.

Once sensing a personal responsibility to act or help, still further steps are required. The ones sensing that responsibility must believe they have the capacity to act in a constructive way. This sense of efficacy, which many lack in the most basic aspects of everyday life, must then be coupled with the capacity to develop a plan of action. There is yet one more step from developing such a plan of action to actually executing it. Advanced resisters soon learned during the Holocaust that against such massive state-sponsored evil, they needed not only such an implemented personal plan of resistance, but also the resources available through networks of resistance. These then needed to be discovered, or developed. It is easy to see that many ordinary human beings lack the needed efficacy, strategic sense, follow-through, and networking skills.

Finally, resistance must be sustained over whatever length of time is required to aid the victims and end the wrong being done to them. In the case of Christians resisting Nazis in occupied Europe, this took as long as six years. Many began rescuing Jews but could not sustain the effort due to the fear of discovery by the Nazis, the costs of rescue, or both. Those of us who have extended ourselves in less demanding ways to friends or family members will understand the limits of human energy and courage even in causes we believe in and with people we love deeply.

For all of these reasons, it was sadly predictable that civilian resistance and rescue of Jews were able to save only a relatively small number of Jews, perhaps 250,000 out of 7,000,000. The great majority of European Christians proved to be bystanders, neither helping the Nazis nor helping the Jews. A relatively small number of perpetrators killed a large number of victims against the backdrop of a massive number of bystanders, with resistance offered by a small number of rescuers—perhaps one-half of 1 percent of the Christian population.

These structural factors inhibiting resistance most often prove far more powerful than the resources provided by religious faith. Those of us who are idealistic about the impact of our weekly preaching and teaching in church or synagogue should be quickly sobered up by these hard facts. We will never give up our belief in the significance of what we do. But we dare not forget what we are up against. A doctrine of sin—especially structural sin—helps considerably.[119]

Torture, Resistance, and Evangelical Christians

I am not saying Nazi genocide and American torture are morally equivalent. But I do contend that the same basic pattern has characterized the response of American Christians to the use of torture and cruelty by our government in the "war on terror." I will speak primarily of my own home community, white evangelicals, and allow other presenters to speak more specifically about their communities. Probably a similar analysis could be undertaken of the sluggish religious or evangelical response to a number of issues in a number of other nations.

First there is the time lag. There was a gap of more than two years between the development of secret new government interrogation policies and the coincidental discovery of the abuses at Abu Ghraib in 2004. Once again, government had a head start over those who would check its behavior, and has retained an informational advantage as the Bush administration has sought to keep its paper trail as hidden as possible, despite being pursued doggedly by relentless advocates for justice such as Karen Greenberg.

After Abu Ghraib's unveiling, evangelical Christian leaders remained almost universally silent. Undoubtedly most accepted the government's contention that the abuses at Abu Ghraib were the acts of a few bad apples. They had no way of knowing then—and still show little sign of accepting now—that at least some of the acts of cruelty, torture, and degradation that took place at Abu Ghraib (and elsewhere) were explicitly authorized by officials within the Bush administration.

George Hunsinger deserves great credit for moving in 2005 to plan the Princeton Seminary torture conference (which took place in January 2006) and then for helping to birth the National Religious Campaign Against Torture (NRCAT) in 2006. Even here, though, the time lag factor is evident, as we see a gap of four years from the development of torture policies to the formation of a religious resistance organization.

The first evangelical effort to deal with torture as a moral problem, as far as I know, was launched by our flagship magazine, *Christianity Today*, in late 2005 when it asked me to write a cover story on the morality of torture. It is most interesting to know that requests from evangelicals serving in our military and intelligence services for moral guidance in dealing with their orders helped motivate CT to seek out this article. The article, which came out in February 2006, argued unequivocally that torture is "always wrong" and can be seen as launching the evangelical anti-torture movement. Evangelicals for Human Rights (EHR) was later midwifed by NRCAT and has managed to secure the support of at least key leaders in the center and to the left of the evangelical community, as evidenced by signatures on our documents in 2007 and earlier this year.[120]

Still, I must be realistic about the limits of our success. Following the paradigm established earlier, I believe evangelicals have proven susceptible not just to government's informational advantage but also its authority advantage. The latter is especially strong in our particular faith community for several reasons. One is that many white evangelicals have been schooled on a traditional reading of the biblical text Romans 13:1–7, which tends toward a high degree of respect for, trust in, and subordination under, government authority, especially in its exercise of the "sword," that is, state violence. This is related to a broader evangelical authoritarianism, especially in our most conservative quarters, that elevates the role of the man over his family, the (male) pastor over his church, the president over his nation, and our nation over the rest of the world. All of these authorities are viewed as having been put into place by God and as answerable primarily or only to God. The kinds of checks and balances provided by democratic constitutionalism, the wisdom of other nations, and international law are devalued.

Another factor specific to events of recent years is that the particular administration that has altered longstanding American policies on torture has been Republican, and has been led by the "evangelical" president, George W. Bush, a favorite of white evangelicals even now. In my view, this default acquiescence to government, to state violence, to the Republican (or any) party, and to a favored political leader is a grave theological error that leads Christians to violate our baptismal commitment to Jesus Christ alone as lord of our lives.

In terms of the dynamics of the resistance process, white evangelicals proved especially unable to notice the transition to policies of torture and especially the moral significance of that transition. For conservative white evangelicals, a generation of treating Christian public witness as focused entirely on the "life and family" issues such as abortion and homosexuality systematically hid other moral issues from view. It took a major fight within evangelicalism for the evangelical center-left to gain much ground with the claim that a broad human dignity and common good agenda are more biblical than a narrow abortion and homosexuality agenda.[121] It is clear to me that my side is winning this argument within evangelicalism, but we weren't winning it from 1980 to 2004.

Overcoming this systematic evangelical self-blinding to issues beyond "family values" and pushing evangelicals to a broader moral vision are important projects for many of the evangelicals gathered here. Part of that broader vision, which Glen Stassen will discuss more thoroughly tomorrow, has been addressing evangelical weakness in developing a theology of justice and human rights. Despite a biblical record full of the demand for justice and the affirmation of human dignity, despite the commitment to justice and human rights of the Radical Reformers, despite the nineteenth century evangelical reform groups that fought for abolition, women's rights, and the rights of workers, despite the Catholic social teaching tradition with its careful theology and ethic of justice, despite the Christian liberation movements and the civil rights movement anchored in the black church, and despite the justice witness of many other faiths, late-twentieth-century white evangelicals have often acted as if justice and human rights are strange, alien, irreligious concepts imported from the Enlightenment. This has left us with weak antennae for sensing injustices in society—or for that matter, in our own churches. What an incredible tragedy that evangelicals lost touch with their own tradition and with the broader Christian tradition, and with such horrifying implications.

I noted above that a sense of the relative worthiness of the victims of injustice affects whether potential rescuers become actual ones. This is closely related to whether the potential helper has any context for knowing or caring about those whom government is mistreating. Christians were most likely to rescue Jews in Nazi Europe if they had Jewish friends whose fate mattered to them. This made Jews not strangers or aliens but friends and "neighbors," worthy and valuable human beings. It also helped if the version of the faith these Christians embraced included a high valuing of the Hebrew scriptures and belief in God's ongoing covenant with the Jewish people.

It is clear to me from the nature of conservative evangelical discourse about Islam and terrorism that many evangelicals after 9/11 perceived Islam as an intrinsically dangerous religion and Muslims as the enemy of both America and Christianity, as the international cultural Other. In the environment of post-9/11 fear, anger, and grief, it was hard to find many evangelicals who could generate much sympathy for suspected (Muslim) terrorists. All too few evangelicals had any pre-existing context of ongoing friendships with Muslims, and conversations between leaders at the national and international levels were rare. Dealing with the "otherness" of Christians and Muslims from each other is the extremely important goal of those Muslims and Christians who have gathered together in the "Common Word" dialogue process about which we will hear tomorrow. Clearly, much work must be done for evangelicals to come to see the Muslims indefinitely detained at Guantánamo and elsewhere as their neighbors.

Once a group of evangelicals decided to resist torture, we found communities of fellow resisters both within the Christian family and far beyond. It has been profound to get to know people whose sensitivity to government abuses of power and whose commitment to justice and human dignity are often much more acute than in my own family of faith. Whether they know it or believe it, I believe these bulldogs for justice are doing the work of God.

At the same time it has been tempting to fall into despair over the resistance to resistance still visible among some evangelicals. At every stage, our efforts have been attacked by our co-religionists. We have been charged with everything from being soft on terrorism to being closet leftists to offering shoddy definitions of torture to being naïve for not realizing this is a new kind of war against a new kind of enemy requiring new kinds of policies. We have been met by a wall of rejection or, at best, silence from the most visible voices in the Christian Right, none of whom have agreed to support anything we have attempted in or through EHR. And we have found a significant number of sympathetic evangelicals (bystanders, one might say) who have been hesitant to add their names to our documents for fear of negative professional consequences in their politically and theologically conservative contexts.

In short, both at the leadership and the grassroots level, evangelicals were slow to notice torture or to sustain attention to torture. We were confused and divided in our moral judgments of torture once we were finally forced to notice. Many who did notice, and felt uncomfortable with torture, felt little or no personal responsibility to do anything about it. It did not have an appreciable effect on how evangelicals voted in 2004 and was not treated as a "moral values" issue. When a group of evangelicals mobilized against torture in 2006, we made considerable headway but also gained intense resistance from within our own community, with opponents who simply could not believe criticism of a Bush administration policy could be morally rather than politically motivated. Once again our instinctive political conservatism and authoritarianism and our narrow understanding of "moral values" betrayed us.

But it seems to me that the acquiescence and silence of many leading evangelicals to torture have helped finally to discredit these evangelical leaders. If our faith's leaders can't figure out that waterboarding and freezing people to death is immoral—people who have been disarmed, deprived of protection from international law and the US Constitution, defenseless against their abusers, made in the image of God, loved by Jesus Christ, and sacred in God's sight—we need some new leaders. I think the shifts happening in the evangelical community right now bear witness that new leadership is in fact emerging.

What did the torture debate reveal about American evangelical Christianity? It revealed that government has incredible power and must be watched vigilantly and resisted forcefully when it strays, and that evangelicals are not very good at that. It revealed that evangelicals had gaps and weaknesses in our public theology and in our public leaders that proved fateful in limiting our resistance to the government evil of state torture. But it also showed that we had resources in our theology and in other leaders that can help us do better. The most important of these resources is the recognition that the gracious savior whose forgiveness we claim is also the sovereign lord who demands our entire lives, our setting aside of all ideologies, loyalties, and fears that hinder our faithfulness to his will, and our embodied love for the enemy, the alien, and the abandoned of the earth.

★   ★   ★

RESPONSE 1 TO DAVID P. GUSHEE BY BRIAN WALT

In his soul-searching and inspiring reflection on the response of the Evangelical community to the torture crisis, David Gushee raises two critical questions: (1) Can the moral imperative of our faith traditions to seek justice and dignity for all human beings overcome the formidable social and political factors that inhibit resistance to injustice in general, and to the practice of torture by our government specifically? (2) How have our respective communities responded to the torture crisis? What is our "track record"? In my response I want to focus on these two questions from the vantage point of Judaism and the Jewish community.

David Gushee's outrage as a Christian at the indifference of so many Christians to the murder of the Jews is so inspiring. His effort to understand what motivated "Hasidei Umot Ha'Olam," "the Righteous Gentiles," the minority of Christians who actually did save Jews, is essential to our efforts to improve the response of our own religious communities to current and future injustice.

As a Jew, born seven years after the Holocaust, growing up in South Africa under apartheid, the question of why people—and especially religious people and institutions—often stand idly by the blood of our neighbors was a central moral question we wrestled with every day. What did religious faith mean to those who attended church services during the time of the Holocaust yet were silent about the extermination of the Jews? Growing up in South Africa under apartheid, I had to confront the sobering reality that the response of many in my own community to the injustice of apartheid was not that different from the response of the Christian community during the Holocaust. It is true and a source of pride that Jews were disproportionately represented among the most courageous resisters to apartheid. Yet notwithstanding a few inspiring exceptions, it was precisely those Jews who were seemingly most disconnected from our community and its religious traditions who were most active against apartheid. Most of our rabbis, religious institutions, and the members of those religious institutions were either silent or did far too little to end apartheid. As a young person I was particularly grateful to those rabbis and Christian clergy who did challenge apartheid.

David Gushee reports that the response of the Evangelical community to torture is mixed. While we all are inspired by those people and institutions in our traditions who courageously uphold the rights of all, most of our faiths have been far too silent in the face of injustice.

One of the great blessings of Evangelicals for Human Rights, Rabbis for Human Rights, the National Religious Campaign Against Torture, and this conference is that it offers us an opportunity to reclaim the integrity of our faiths by giving voice to the prophetic vision calling us to resist injustice, even when it is scary, even when it may be unpopular, even when, or especially when, it involves a group that is seen as the other.

Now I want to address the second question regarding our individual faith traditions' response to the torture crisis. How has the Jewish community responded?

As in the Christian community, there was a lag of about four years in the response of the Jewish community to the torture crisis. Rabbi Arthur Waskow was the first to raise the issue of US-sponsored torture in the Jewish community. Shortly thereafter, Rabbis for Human Rights-North America launched our North American Human Rights program. We chose to make torture the first issue of our new program precisely because there was so much silence on this issue in our community.

Our participation in the Princeton conference and in the National Religious Campaign Against Torture strengthened our work. We started by enlisting rabbis to sign a rabbinic statement against torture. We created a rabbinic educational resource on Jewish values and torture, and we joined with other Jewish organizations such as the Religious Action Center of Reform Judaism and the Jewish Council on Public Affairs in working on this issue in our community.

Torture is now on the agenda of our community and we have successfully created a large network of Jewish leaders and communities passionately involved in the struggle to end torture. However, we do face a few challenges: While there is general agreement in much of the Jewish community that torture is wrong, many in our community are unsure about an unconditional opposition to torture, citing the hypothetical scenario of the "ticking bomb." This is of particular concern to many Jews in relation to Israel. Also, despite the fact that the Israeli Supreme Court has banned the use of torture in interrogation, and Rabbis for Human Rights has held up this decision as a model for the United States, many Jews fear that the focus on US-sponsored torture may raise the issue of the illegal use of torture in Israel. This concern constrains the opposition of some in our community. Finally, we have not been very successful in gaining the support of the Orthodox Jewish community.

In the first chapter of Exodus, we are told of the two midwives who refused Pharaoh's order to kill the Hebrew children. They refused to obey this order because of their "fear/awe of God." The Hebrew text, *hameyaldot ha-ivriot,* can be translated either as the "Hebrew midwives" or the "midwives to the Hebrews." This textual ambiguity gives us the insight that all peoples have this *yirat Hashem,* this fear of God that we need to sustain in all our traditions. A fear of God is what makes it impossible for us as people of faith to do acts of injustice to others, or to be silent in the face of acts of injustice. The killing of the firstborn was an act that shocked the conscience. Torture too is such an act.

May we all have the clarity of the midwives, and may we all be guided by our shared awe of God that will make it impossible for us to be silent or complicit in any act of injustice. May God bless our efforts.

★ ★ ★

Response 2 to David P. Gushee by M. Cathleen Kaveny

My task is to give some brief perspective on the response to torture within the Roman Catholic community, particularly in the United States. The Roman Catholic community of faith, of course, is both highly international in terms of its membership and highly centralized in terms of its leadership. While each bishop is an authoritative teacher within his own diocese, and local conferences of bishops have some authority to deal with matters in ways that address the unique social, cultural, and national circumstances of their people, the ultimate teaching authority rests with the Pope in Rome, especially when he acts together with his brother bishops throughout the world.

For our purposes, this means there is authoritative teaching on the matter of torture. The catechism of the Catholic church situates the discussion of torture under its discussion of the second great commandment: You shall love your neighbor as yourself. It is a part of a subsection outlining the requirements encompassed by the fifth commandment of the Decalogue: You shall not kill. The Catholic tradition does not view negative moral commands as isolated and arbitrary; the prohibitions outlined in this section of the catechism are meant to support the positive insight that human life is sacred, because from its beginning it involves the creative action of God, and it remains forever in a special relationship with the creator, who is its sole end.[122]

The exact prohibition in the catechism reads, "Torture which uses physical or moral violence to extract confessions, punish the guilty, frighten opponents, or satisfy hatred is contrary to respect for the person and for human dignity."[123] In *Gaudium et Spes*, the Second Vatican Council's Pastoral Constitution on the Church in the Modern World, torture is referred to as an "infamy."[124] In his encyclical *Veritatis Splendor*, Pope John Paul II prophetically called torture an "intrinsic evil."[125] The United States Catholic bishops have also issued an extremely helpful study guide entitled "Torture is a Moral Issue,"[126] which frames the question in terms of a reflection upon the meaning of Jesus' injunction to love not merely our neighbors, but also our enemies.[127]

So Catholic teaching is clear that torture is impermissible. When it works as it ought, the teaching authority of the universal Church acts as a counterweight when Catholics are tempted to associate our faith narrowly with the interests of our own nation, region, or political party. At the same time, however, it needs to be said that in the United States, Catholic voices protesting torture are more muted than they might be, and the response of the faithful is lukewarm to this teaching. Why? I see three reasons: first, the way in which the culture wars have played out in this country; second, the tensions within the Catholic community over development of doctrine; and third, the primacy of abortion as a moral and political issue for many influential American Catholics.

The Convergence of Two Culture Wars. In 1995, Pope John Paul II introduced the dichotomy between the "culture of life" and the "culture of death" to describe the clash between traditional Christian values on social issues such as abortion, euthanasia, and the family, and liberal individualist values. In 1996, Samuel Huntington published a book entitled *The Clash of Civilizations and the Remaking of World Order*, which stressed the fundamentally different value systems and interests of the Islamic world and the West.[128] My suspicion is that these two very distinct theses merged in some minds after 11 September 2001. Catholic Christians, particularly traditionalist Catholic Christians in Europe, saw themselves as beleaguered on all fronts.[129] On the one hand, the faith was being eroded by the pervasive materialist and secularist atmosphere of the West. On the other hand, the increasing population and vibrant faith of Muslims in Europe threatened to eclipse an old and tired Christianity. After September 11, some traditional-minded Catholics in the United States also saw themselves in two converging culture wars, one against a hedonistic mindset that would destroy us from within, and the other against Muslim terrorists who would destroy us from outside. More than one commentator pointed out that it was precisely America's loss of traditional values and a God-fearing morality that incurred the wrath of Muslim fundamentalists in the first place.[130]

The actions of a few terrorists, a tiny minority in the Muslim community, crystallized a broader fear that Christianity, and Catholicism in particular, was facing mortal challenges to its future. After September 11, the Republicans presented themselves as defenders of the United States as a Christian nation, as a city on a hill on both fronts. They promised to restore traditional Christian values and would protect America against those who would attack her. Many American Catholics found this a powerful combination. Consequently, they were reluctant to criticize the actions of the Bush administration, or to view with skepticism their explanation of the abuses at Abu Ghraib as the work of a few enlisted men who turned out to be bad apples.[131]

The Problem of Development of Doctrine. On a theoretical level, the question of the church's teaching on torture raises the issue of change and continuity in its teaching in general, and ultimately, the degree of its reliability as a teacher of the natural moral law. It is no secret that the church not only failed to protest the use of torture by Christian governments, it also engaged in such practices itself as part of the Inquisition. In fact, the catechism explicitly acknowledges the church's dark past, albeit in small print. In times past, cruel practices were commonly used by legitimate governments to maintain law and order, often without protest from the pastors of the church, who themselves adopted in their own tribunal the prescriptions of Roman law concerning torture.[132]

The question of change and continuity, and potential further change in church teaching on the moral law, is a controversial topic within our faith community. Some more progressive thinkers, such as John Noonan, outline change that has occurred in the church's teaching and practice on issues such as slavery, religious liberty, the law of marriage, and the death penalty; their arguments suggest that the church could also change its teaching on matters such as contraception.[133] In response, more traditionalist thinkers, such as Cardinal Avery Dulles, play down the changes; they stress continuity in order to provide a bulwark against further change and to strengthen the church's teaching authority here and now.[134] In my view, the significant development in the church's stance toward torture is a particularly difficult case for the traditionalists to smooth over; it is hard to find continuity between practicing torture and prohibiting it categorically. They are understandably reluctant to discuss it.

The Primacy of Abortion. Even a casual observer of the political scene in the United States would notice the overriding attention given to abortion by Roman Catholic bishops, as well as by committed groups of Catholic faithful. In their longstanding battle to overturn *Roe vs. Wade*,[135] pro-life activists, in my view, have adopted some strategies that have made it harder to see what is wrong with torture. Catholic teaching prohibits intentional killing of the innocent under all circumstances. Understandably, pro-life activists emphasize the utter vulnerability and innocence of the child to be aborted. The unborn baby is tiny, beautiful, helpless; its status is often summed up in the insistence that it is innocent, which seems to encompass all these descriptions.

But as a technical term in moral theology, innocent doesn't mean free from sin, or little, and least of all, beautiful. Innocent does not mean free from all sin. The natural law prohibitions against harming others do not and cannot depend on the state of the potential victim's soul. Who among us would be safe? Even the unborn, according to traditional Catholic and Christian teaching, are marked by original sin, which is the plight of the entire human family.

For purposes of immunity from attack, an innocent person is simply a person who is not currently in the act of unjust aggression. We see this in the doctrine of just war. An innocent civilian is not somehow less innocent because she prays for her country in a war against our country. A twenty-year-old rousted up in the middle of the night and tossed into the bowels of a secret prison is not little or cute, but he is equally innocent for purposes of the moral prohibition against harming the innocent.

Catholics will need, I think, to draw more links, more connections, between abortion and torture if we are to persuade the hierarchy and our fellow believers about the moral importance of torture. One aspect of this task is straightforwardly academic and theoretical: reflecting on the meaning of the word "innocent" for purposes of immunity from violent attack.

There is also a second aspect of the task, which focuses on the development of distinctively Catholic sensibilities in ways that support the moral prohibition against torture. Catholic imagination is quintessentially iconic; Catholics tend to think in pictures. For example, the prohibition on abortion is supported by countless images of a Christmas Mary holding the baby Jesus in her arms. That image, I think, needs to be supplemented by one of Mary on Good Friday. Many Catholic churches incorporate the Stations of the Cross, a series of plaques or statutes that mark key moments in Jesus' progressive suffering on Good Friday. In the fourth station, Mary encounters her badly beaten son, the man who her baby became, carrying his cross on the way to his death. Common depictions of the thirteenth station depict Mary fainting in the arms of St. John the Evangelist as the horribly battered body of Jesus is removed from the cross. Every man subjected to extraordinary rendition is some mother's son.

The image of torture is, in fact, central to Catholic imagination. The word "crucifixion" comes from the Latin word *cruciare*, which means to torture or to torment. Catholic churches generally give pride of place not simply to crosses, but to crucifixes, which display the body of Christ on the cross. Moreover, in many cases, they depict the suffering and dying Christ, not the risen and triumphant Christ.

I think the first task facing American Catholics with respect to torture is to pay attention to the crucifixes we see before us every Sunday, reflecting upon them in conjunction with Jesus' admonition from Matthew 25: "Whatsoever you do to the least of my brothers, that you do unto me."

★ ★ ★

Response 3 to David P. Gushee by Mohammed Elsanousi

I want to characterize this conference and all the efforts to combat torture by the following saying of the prophet Muhammad (peace be upon him), who said: "A person should help his brother, whether he is an oppressor or is being oppressed. If he is the oppressor, he should prevent him from continuing his oppression, for that is helping him. If he is being oppressed, he should be helped by stopping the oppression against him." That is exactly what this conference and the sponsoring organizations are doing today, so my deep appreciation goes to Professor Gushee and his terrific team for organizing this conference and to all sponsoring organizations.

In his paper Professor Gushee expressed his dissatisfaction about the Evangelicals' efforts to speak out against torture despite a biblical record full of the demand for justice and the affirmation of human dignity. The situation with the American Muslim community is not much different.

Dr. Gushee mentioned an interesting point in his paper about evangelicals who are sympathetic about the issue of torture, but are hesitant to add their names to his documents for fear of negative professional consequences in their politically and theologically conservative contexts. Imagine, if this fear exists within the evangelical community, it's even stronger in the Muslim community because of the sensitivity of this issue and because the majority of people who are victims of torture are followers of the Islamic tradition. I remember when I took a delegation of American Muslim community leaders to participate in the founding conference of the National Religious Campaign Against Torture in January 2006, they were reluctant to speak out against torture because of the fear of being associated with terrorists. Therefore, in these few moments that I have I would like to talk abut the Islamic affirmation of human dignity.

Islam is a tradition that highly values the dignity of the human being and considers that dignity to be the essence of humanity. In the event that dignity is affected by torture, oppression, or any other means, that humanity becomes questionable. According to the religion of Islam, God created human beings and honored them by making them his vicegerents on earth and responsible for taking care of the rest of the creation in the universe. The concept of vicegerency is repeatedly mentioned in the Holy Qur'an to emphasize the responsibility of the human being on this earth. The human being is commanded by God to do justice to his creation. The Holy Qur'an 17:70 states: "We have honored the sons of Adam; provided them with transport on land and sea; given them for sustenance things good and pure; and conferred on them special favors, above a great part of our creation." In this particular verse, God speaks about how much a human being is honored and valued in comparison to his other creatures. He was honored by being created to be the best of God's creation, including the angels. Even the angels protested the fact that they were not given the same honor as the human being. In fact, the rebellious angel became Satan! Therefore, the human being needs to contemplate deeply on this honor, and it should be carried out into his real life with responsibility.

This kind of honor comes with a tremendous responsibility and duties toward all other creatures, especially fellow human beings. What that means is that God would like to see this honor demonstrated to his entire creation. What that entails is treating others with dignity and as humanely as possible in all kinds of circumstances. This is a real test for those who violate the dignity of human beings by torturing and humiliating them in a way that clearly contradicts the basic understanding of this honor.

We have seen so many people abuse and violate this attribute, which was bestowed by God himself, and as a consequence they are violating God's command. I believe this happens when God-consciousness is weakened and people forget they might be in a similar situation someday. Islam considers all humans as one family created from one source. If these torturers would realize they are torturing their own brothers and sisters, they would never think of doing such a terrible act.

Islam perceives the rights of the human being from the viewpoint of this honor as well as a vicegerent on this earth. These two concepts clearly describe how the human being should be treated in all circumstances, including at a time of war. Islam strongly encourages its followers to practice the utmost compassion and mercy at the time when the individual, group, or state has the power and the upper hand. In this kind of situation, Islam expects from the people falling in that category to be just and to practice their power with justice and compassion.

Fourteen hundred years ago, the prophet of Islam instructed his companions to be just and deal with their enemy with mercy and compassion. He forbids them from torturing any individual. And in fact, he orders them to ensure that those who are in their custody are well fed and given proper care. The greatest example on this prophetic teaching is represented here:

The prophet (peace and blessings be upon him) passed by a prisoner who was in chains, and he called out, "O Muhammad, O Muhammad!" He came to him and said, "What is the matter?" He said, "I am hungry, feed me. I am thirsty, give me water." The prophet (peace and blessings be upon him) commanded that his needs should be met. And no doubt medical treatment is what the sick person needs.

In another Qur'anic verse (6:165) God says, "It is He Who hath made you (His) agents, inheritors of the earth: He hath raised you in ranks, some above others: that He may try you in the gifts He hath given you: for thy Lord is quick in punishment: yet He is indeed Oft-forgiving, Most Merciful." In this verse, God again emphasized the concept of the human being as an agent of God on this earth and assigned with higher responsibilities than the other creations, so that those who are more privileged with power and wealth should be humble and considerate to others because God is testing them with these bounties.

This honor of responsibility, which is bestowed on human beings, requires great vigilance toward all of God's creatures, including fellow human beings. To make someone as an agent to act on your behalf means there is a huge level of trust, confidence, and honor, and this trust should clearly be reflected in the honoree's behavior. It also indicates that the agent should execute his/her responsibility with utmost justice and transparency. This responsibility also entails giving greater attention toward those who are weak and cannot exercise their right, especially

89

when the agent has the power to exploit this weakness and the vulnerable state of the powerless.

Torture is opposed by Islam because it not only negatively impacts the dignity of the human being; it also contradicts the notion of establishing justice on earth, which is the most crucial value next to the belief in God. Islam emphasizes justice even when one is overwhelmed with hate and malice. God commanded the believers not to let their anger and abhorrence of a people deviate from justice, and asks us to fear God and apply justice whether the person is a friend or an enemy, because justice is next to piety.

As far as prisoners are concerned, Islam always treated prisoners with dignity and respect, categorically opposing the torture of captives and prisoners. It is regarded as a violation of justice and human dignity and abuse of the concept of vicegerency, which I have mentioned in the previous Qur'anic verses.

The prophet of Islam, who is described in the Qur'an as the "mercy to the Universe" (Rahmat al-Alameen) actually showed more mercy in his dealings with criminals who came to him voluntarily admitting their crimes. He asked them to repent and seek forgiveness from God. The prophet also emphasized the rule of presumption of innocence and affirmed this through his sayings and practice. Fourteen hundred years ago, the prophet said, "Prevent punishment in case of doubt." What it tells us is that evidence obtained through torture or any way against the will of the human has a doubtful status. Therefore, punishment should not be given on the basis of such doubtful evidence. We should also learn from this prophetic tradition that forcing prisoners or the accused to make confessions is legally unacceptable and morally wrong.

Islamic law is very clear on the issue of conviction. It should be based on confidence that the accused is guilty of wrongdoing, leaving no doubt or probability. Therefore, if there is any doubt, the case should be settled in favor of the accused person. This particular principle is based on the saying of the prophet Muhammad: "Prevent punishment in case of doubt. Release the accused if possible, for it is better that the ruler be wrong in forgiving than wrong in punishing" (Al-Saleh). This very Hadith is telling us that if the judge was not satisfied by the evidence presented before him or her and has reasonable doubt, then that judge should decide the accused is not guilty.

There is no room in the American creed of human dignity for torture. There is no room—we condemn torture. Islam condemns torture. Fourteen hundred years ago, the prophet of Islam said, "The people that have the greatest chastisement on the Day of Judgment and in Hell are the people who tortured people—that is the teaching of our Prophet (peace be upon him). We cannot accept torture."

In conclusion, I would like to emphasize that Islam brought an unprecedented wealth of human and spiritual values to the people with whom it came into contact. Primary among these values was the knowledge and certainty that God Almighty bestows the gift of dignity upon every human being. It is an unqualified and unconditional gift, freely offered to the pious and sinful alike, irrespective of gender, religion, race, social status, age, power, etc. It is offered without restriction, in times of peace or times of war.

91

5

★

GUANTÁNAMO: AN ASSESSMENT AND REFLECTION FROM THOSE WHO HAVE BEEN THERE

John A. Chandler[136]

In the recent movie *The Dark Knight*, a crucial suspect with knowledge of mafia and other criminal operations flees the country.[137] District Attorney Harvey Dent wants the man back, but China will not extradite a Chinese national. Batman volunteers: "If I get him here, can you get him to talk?" Dent agrees and asks, "How will you get him back?" but the caped crusader has already disappeared.

As it turns out, Batman performs an extraordinary rendition, using an early CIA test program called "Skyhook"[138] in order to kidnap the Chinese national from an office building in Hong Kong and then bring him back to the United States by private plane for interrogation. The new Batman movie is a case of art imitating life: since 9/11, the United States has been complicit in the kidnapping, interrogation, and torture of over a hundred human beings. The CIA has either "rendered" these men for torture to countries like Jordan and Egypt or kept the men in secret CIA prisons known as "black sites" for CIA interrogation. The process by which suspects are kidnapped and sent to foreign gulags for torture and interrogation is known as "extraordinary rendition."

On 6 February 2002, our client Shergawi Ali al-Haj, a Yemeni citizen, was arrested in Karachi, Pakistan, a thousand miles from any battlefield in Afghanistan. He was arrested by the CIA and Pakistani intelligence officers.[139] At four A.M., Shergawi and others were herded into a Pakistani intelligence facility. Over the course of twenty-one days, Shergawi was interrogated by CIA officers, but not tortured. Late one night, however, the Americans came back for him. Saharawi was stripped down, fitted with a diaper, blindfolded, covered, and shackled. His escort said, "May Allah save you from the Americans." He was put on a plane to Amman, Jordan, where Shergawi spent the next two years. For nine months he alternatively was questioned and tortured. "Flange," or foot whipping was the Jordanian specialty. It is a favored punishment because, although extremely painful, it leaves few physical marks. Foot whipping is effective because of the cluster of nerve endings in the feet and the structure of the foot, with its numerous small bones and tendons. The wounds inflicted are particularly painful and take a long time to heal. For nine months, Shergawi responded to questions submitted by the CIA and had his bare feet beaten when his answers were unsatisfactory.

A Brief History of Extraordinary Rendition

Extraordinary rendition has its roots in the depths of the Cold War. Stephen Grey describes the experience of a 1965 Uruguayan "proxy" that tortured and questioned a man for the CIA.[140] CIA proxies were not directly employed by the agency and created plausible deniability.[141] Grey notes, however, that along with deniability came a "loss of control."[142] The CIA might issue guidelines or obtain assurances about the interrogation techniques the proxy planned to use, but ultimately the CIA "knew full well that the Uruguayan police questioned their suspects by torture."[143] Thus, the CIA, while keeping its hands technically clean, became morally culpable when they "outsourced" their torture.[144]

Over the years, the CIA rendition program grew in scope. The "Air America" program, in which the CIA carried out air missions in Southeast Asia, doing "what the military either couldn't or wouldn't do,"[145] became a notoriously well-known symbol of CIA covert action.[146] As the Vietnam War ended and America moved into the 1970s, the program was largely abandoned, eventually becoming decommissioned after a Senate investigation in 1976.[147]

Modern-day renditions usually concerned returning nationals to their countries of origin for trial[148] or bringing nationals to the United States for trial.[149] During the Clinton administration, for instance, a number of Egyptian nationals were kidnapped from countries such as

Albania and Croatia, and returned to Egypt.[150] As Secretary of State Condoleezza Rice put it, "For decades, the United States and other countries have used 'renditions' to transport terrorist suspects from the country where they were captured to their home country or to other countries where they can be questioned, held, or brought to justice."[151]

Extraordinary Rendition Post-9/11: The Gloves Come Off

After 9/11, America's practice changed radically. The two strains, CIA torture by proxy and use of secret flights for covert purposes, merged to become the morally and legally objectionable extraordinary rendition program. Instead of rendering suspects back to their own countries for trial or punishment, the United States, through the CIA, began to kidnap suspected terrorists and render them to third countries for torture and interrogation. Like the proxies of the Cold War days, the CIA took a puppet-master approach to torture, keeping its own hands technically clean while guiding the detainment, transport, interrogation, and torture of numerous suspected terrorists.

Stephen Grey extensively researched and documented the CIA's extraordinary renditions, tracking the flight records and reports of torture through informants and victims.[152] Early in 2001, Grey spoke with Congressman Porter Goss, a former CIA agent who would later become director of the CIA from 2004 until 2006. On 14 December 2001, Grey asked Goss about the possibility of kidnapping Osama bin Laden. Goss responded, "It's called a 'rendition.' Do you know that?" clarifying, "Well, there is a polite way to take people out of action and bring them to some type of justice. It's generally referred to as a rendition."[153] About a year later, Cofer Black, then in charge of CIA counter-terrorism, addressed the House and Senate Intelligence Committees. Referring to CIA "operational flexibility," Black said, "This is a highly classified area. All I want to say is that there was a 'before' 9/11 and 'after' 9/11. After 9/11 the gloves come off," adding later that "[w]e must go on the offense and stay there."[154]

As a result of growing alarm and public investigation, the CIA's program was exposed. On 6 September 2006, President Bush admitted that a "small number" of suspected terrorists were being "held and questioned outside the United States, in a separate program operated by the Central Intelligence Agency," though many would soon be transferred to Guantánamo.[155] Of course, the president and the CIA remain quiet about the extent and details of the program for alleged national security reasons;[156] no one really knows how many persons are being held abroad, in either secret CIA prisons or in foreign countries at the behest of the CIA.

The Legality of Extraordinary Rendition

In response to 9/11, President Bush and Congress greatly expanded the intelligence, investigative, and enforcement powers of various US agencies.[157] As part of this expansion, President Bush authorized the use of interrogation methods by the CIA, likely including extraordinary rendition.[158] A 2005 *New York Times* article claimed that in the days after 9/11, President Bush gave the CIA power to transfer suspects abroad for interrogation, acting on a case-by-case basis with approval from the White House.[159] In January 2005, then White House counsel Alberto Gonzales had said in written testimony that "the policy of the United States is not to transfer individuals to countries where we believe they likely will be tortured," yet the *Times* article quoted half a dozen unnamed current and former government officials as believing that "in practice, the administration's approach may have involved turning a blind eye to torture."[160] Additionally, Porter Goss, in 2005 testimony, assured Congress that the CIA has "a responsibility of trying to ensure that [suspects] are properly treated, and we try and do the best we can to guarantee that," though "once they're out of our control, there's only so much we can do."[161]

For many years, the CIA refused to admit any such authorization or documents existed, even when prompted by a lawsuit by the ACLU.[162] On 10 November 2006, the CIA finally admitted in a letter to the ACLU that the documents existed, though refusing to disclose their contents.[163] The CIA's admission describes two documents, a legal memorandum from the Office of Legal Counsel at the DOJ to the General Counsel of the CIA, and a memorandum from President Bush to the Director of the CIA.[164]

Extraordinary rendition is illegal under both US and international law. The primary law that governs extraordinary rendition is the 1987 Convention Against Torture (CAT), a treaty signed by the United States in 1988 and ratified in 1994.[165] CAT requires a country to take steps to prevent torture in any territory under its jurisdiction and prevents the use of any "exceptional circumstances," such as "a state of war or a threat of war, internal political instability or any other public emergency," to justify torture.[166] More important for extraordinary rendition, however, is article 3: "No State party shall expel, return ('refouler') or extradite a person to another State where there are substantial grounds for believing that he would be in danger of being subjected to torture."[167] In secretly transporting men to Egypt, Syria, and Jordan for questioning—countries that have a record of torturing detainees well documented by both the United States State Department and many international agencies[168]—the United States has acted illegally.[169]

The Bush administration, however, has in a series of infamous memos argued that many methods of interrogation considered to be torture are legal, as well as the practice of extraordinary rendition.[170] For the defenders of extraordinary rendition, the key part of CAT is the term "substantial grounds."[171] As the *New Yorker* put it, "the Administration appears to be relying on a very fine reading of an imprecise clause" in CAT.[172] Martin Lederman, a former Office of Legal Counsel attorney, argues that CAT "only applies when you know a suspect is more likely than not to be tortured," a position echoed by John Bellinger, the chief legal counsel to the Department of State, in a 2006 report and testimony to the Council of Europe and the United Nations Committee Against Torture.[173] Bellinger's comments before the Council of Europe are particularly instructive:

> For those who say we're not following our international obligations in certain cases, I have to say that sometimes it comes down to a disagreement on what the obligation is. With regard to Article 3 of CAT, this is a technical issue.... For more than a decade, the position of the US Government, and our courts, has been that all of those terms refer to returns

from, or transfers out from the United States. So we think that Article 3 of the CAT is legally binding upon us with respect to transfers of anyone from the United States; but we don't think it is legally binding outside the United States.

Similarly the Senate of the United States and our courts for more than ten years have taken a position that the words "substantial grounds" means "more likely than not."[174]

These arguments over "substantial grounds" are supplemented in other ways. John Yoo's infamous 2003 memo spends a number of pages arguing that certain methods of interrogation do not meet CAT's definition of torture.[175] As well, he argues that the United States can use certain legal defenses, such as the traditional notions of self-defense and necessity, to justify the interrogation techniques being used.[176] Finally, the Bush administration has repeatedly claimed that it makes sure "we have assurances that people won't be tortured if—or before we render them to a country."[177] However, such assurances are not monitored by the United States and are known by our government to be empty promises.

The Reality of Rendition

Shergawi spent two years in the intelligence prison in Jordan. He was brutally tortured for his first nine months. In addition to flange, he was beaten and shocked with electricity many times. He was constantly threatened with beatings, other forms of torture, and rape.

Several times during his torture in Jordan, Shergawi witnessed men who looked like Americans present during interrogation sessions. These men never actually conducted interrogations, but the Jordanians told him the Americans wished to know information and that the questions were coming from them. Shergawi was shown thousands of pictures of detainees and suspects and asked to name them or give information about them. Though he recognized none of them, Shergawi made up answers and finally began randomly to identify some as al Qaeda operatives in order to please his questioners. After two years the CIA came to get him.

On 7 January 2004, Shergawi was removed from the Jordanian prison. At 11:00 in the evening, he was taken by car to an airport. There, he was stripped, full-body-cavity searched, dressed in a diaper, shorts, and shirt, and then fitted with plastic handcuffs. After being held in a room and photographed, he was thrown into a luggage cart on top of another man and transported to a plane, where he was thrown in and tied down. Two Americans in the back of the CIA chartered plane kept watch over him. From there, Shergawi was taken to Kabul, Afghanistan. Flight records of the CIA's rendition plane, a private Gulfstream jet, tail number N313P, based in North Carolina, confirm the flight.[178]

In Afghanistan, Shergawi was subjected to some of the techniques the Department of Justice and the Bush administration had determined did not meet the standard of torture: sleep deprivation through loud music, freezing cold with inadequate clothing, sensory deprivation due to light manipulation, withholding of food depending on interrogation performance, and psychological abuse and shaming. Shergawi was interrogated every day by CIA officers, but generally regarded CIA treatment at its Kabul site as preferable to the Jordanian prison. After one to two months in Kabul, Shergawi was transferred to Bagram Air Base in Eastern Afghanistan, again being shackled, with eyes taped shut, and generally treated like luggage. After another six months of interrogations at Bagram, Shergawi was finally transferred to Guantánamo Bay on 19 September 2004 and has been there ever since.

Life at Guantánamo is better than in Jordan and Afghanistan, but still debilitating. Shergawi is given very few amenities and constantly is denied food and medical attention. Though he no longer suffers physical beatings, he says his captors beat him "in [his] food, medicine, and religion." In addition, he is often threatened with return to the Jordanian prison where he suffered the harshest torture of his captivity.

Conclusion

After 9/11, the United States was determined to get tough on terror. It instituted programs, both domestic and international, to stop terrorists and their plans. One of these programs was an amalgam of earlier CIA practices that became known as extraordinary rendition. CIA officers began to recruit other countries to torture and interrogate suspects for them. As Stephen Grey makes clear, the CIA took steps to insulate the agency. Grey writes, "The idea was that legally speaking the…prisoners would never be in US custody. America, on this occasion, would just be a travel agency."[179]

In doing so, our country has acted immorally and illegally. We have surrendered the values generations of Americans have fought to protect.

★

Guantánamo: An Assessment and Reflection from Those Who Have Been There

Mark Denbeaux

I am the son of a Protestant minister, a theologian. I was raised on the social gospel of Walter Rauschenbusch. My father was a chaplain with General Patton. He was responsible for supervising the liberation of two concentration camps. He became very involved in the civil rights movement in a variety of ways, and one of his concerns always was that the Christian church was simply not active in the way it should be. And my father would be fascinated and very optimistic about this gathering. He would be proud that you have asked me to be here, so I am really quite touched by this.

What I want to talk about is the fact that we have collected data and we do know the truth about who is in Guantánamo. And the reason we know it is because we took government records and we assumed that every single fact the government said was true. So we are not arguing with the government; we are reporting what the government itself says is the basis for the detention of these people. Many years ago, the father of the current mayor of Chicago, Mayor Daley, was reported to have said, "Never write a letter and never throw one away." Well, our government has been writing letters and I think to a large degree they did not believe they would be read. And if you systematically go through them, you can find out the truth not only about who is there, but also about the government having the wrong people, along with the fact that they have known it and they did not care. And you can tell that step by step—and I would like to go through that today.

One of my father's great heroes was Immanuel Kant and his proposition that you never use people as means, only as ends. It is pretty clear that those people in Guantánamo have been held as means and not as ends. So I am going to start with a few things. The first part we ought to recognize is that the government was forced, as a result of the Rasul case, to go through the process of explaining its basis for detention. They published them and we reviewed them. And there are some important things to understand about the government's basis for detention. If you look at the profile, approximately 5 percent of the people in Guantánamo were captured by US forces. That means the evidence against the other 95 percent is dependent upon non-US officials and the weight we choose to give to Pakistani and Afghani tribal warlords, tribal chieftains, and others. And as you may know, a central part of that was the use of bounties.

But there was more to that, and here is where I am going to talk about what I consider to be evidence that they knew they were wrong. You have all heard that those we are holding are the worst of the worst. Well, if they are the worst of the worst, then we can give up airport security, because the fact of the matter is they have collected a bunch of people down there whom we do not even claim were fighters. Eight percent of them are alleged to be fighters. As a matter of fact, 60 percent of them are there only because they are alleged by our government to be associated in some way with either the Taliban or al Qaeda. One of my students was going through the evidence and came to me and said, "I do not get it. Where is Mr. Big?" And he pulled out a paper and said, "Here is somebody, and this is his entire paper." He was conscripted by the Taliban to be an assistant cook. His hostile act was when he surrendered to the Northern alliance in Afghanistan. My student was enraged. He said, "I do not get it. We have the assistant cook, so where is the cook?" He said, "We are holding the sous chefs of Afghanistan." The fact is, when you go through, you realize those are the government's documents.

So when Rumsfeld and the government have said these are the worst of the worst, they are talking about people who have been conscripted to be assistant cooks for the Taliban.

Another part of this is that 55 percent of those detained in Gitmo are never once alleged to have committed a hostile act. It is very simple. They put out a chart. There are two ways to be an enemy combatant. One is you are affiliated, associated, a member of, or fought for the Taliban; the other is that you can be an enemy combatant if you have engaged in hostile acts against US and coalition forces. In the case of 55 percent of those detained, the allegation of hostile acts is missing. There is not a syllable, not a letter. They do not allege that they have committed hostile acts. My students refer to them as the 55 percent who are enemy civilians. And I might add to this that when we look at the enemy civilians, the assistant cook who was conscripted, the government said he surrendered to the Northern alliance. They consider this his hostile act. So of the 45 percent who are alleged to have committed hostile acts, one is the assistant cook who surrendered. That was a distressing feeling as we went through this profile. But our position was to give the government the benefit of the doubt; things have changed a little bit. Because if the premise is that we genuinely believe these people were in fact who our government claims they are, you have to say to yourself, how could that happen? Why are they in Guantánamo?

This is where the ends and means problem comes in. Gitmo is the equivalent of a "perp walk." Nobody was captured there. They were all moved there. And they were moved there in a highly visible way, so the public would know how well we are doing in the way on terror. And they had cameras and pictures, but you have seen all that. This was obviously done as a public relations gesture.

If you wanted to look at the evidence that our government did not believe their own claims about their detainees, you could look at their policy of release. Now bear in mind that no court has ever released a detainee. That is part of the embarrassment of our profession and our legal system. But the fact is, the government has been releasing lots of them. Now let me ask you this: if you believed your own evidence, and if you had identified numbers of people to be al Qaeda fighters, and if you had identified people who were in fact associated with the Taliban, and it was the basis for holding people, who do you think you would release first? I submit that if our government had believed its evidence, they would have released people who never committed hostile acts and were perhaps just associated with the Taliban. And I would assume they would hold people whom they claimed to be fighters for al Qaeda and have committed hostile acts.

We are now able to determine that this is not what happened. And I think this is the most chilling part of it. The government never announces who they release, or where, or when. We discovered a way to figure out when people were released—by looking at the published weight figures for detainees. Due to hunger strikes, the government did publish such weight charts. It was not hard to figure out that the last month a detainee was weighed was the last month he was there. So if you looked at the months when they stopped, you could find out who had been released. We did a profile of those who had been released, and if you are an al Qaeda fighter, you will be released at exactly the same rate as if you merely had been associated with the Taliban. If you have in fact committed hostile acts, you will be released at exactly the same rate as if you have not. There is absolutely no correlation. If our government believed its own evidence, they would not be releasing the people they alleged to be the worst of the worst. But they are.

There is one correlation and that is nationality. If you are from Pakistan, Afghanistan, or Saudi Arabia, you will be released in large numbers without regard to any of the evidence. No matter how severe the allegations, you will be released. But if you are from Yemen or Algeria, you will still be there no matter how slight the evidence. And we have the equivalent of the assistant cooks who are from Yemen who are still there. So it obviously deals with politics. It has absolutely nothing to do with the credibility of the evidence.

One last point: I think when people lie, there is an inference that can be drawn that they have a reason to lie. There is a Latin phrase meaning "false in one, false in all." Our government has claimed they are the worst of the worst, but that is obviously false. One way to determine this is to consider what is known about their behavior while detained. The government has revealed there are 759 people who were held in Guantánamo. During the period of time when they released them, the detainees were alleged to have committed 460 acts over a thirty-month period of manipulative or self-injurious behavior. In 2003 and 2004 there was an average of one such act every day and a half. Detainees committed 499 disciplinary violations over those thirty months, an average of one incident every two days. And it is important to understand that as bad as they are, more than 70 percent of the disciplinary violations are for trivial offenses. And even the most serious are offensive but not dangerous. Spitting is the primary assault that is reported by the government. And the disciplinary reports reveal that the most serious injury sustained by guards as a result of misconduct are a handful of cuts and scratches.

These are "the worst of the worst," who have to be chained to the floor not because they are dangerous, not because they really have to be incarcerated this way, but because they are a part of the charade of using them as props for another purpose. If you assume no recidivists (which is unlikely), that means two-thirds of the detainees in thirty months committed one disciplinary act. The rest never did anything. Nearly half of the reported violations are spitting. Almost half of all the disciplinary violations occurred during a ninety-two-day hunger strike that followed allegations of Koran abuse. And for 736 of the 952 days covered, or 77 percent of the time, the government has no evidence of any disciplinary violations. The point is, they know their evidence was a sham to begin with and they did not expect people to look at it. They knew when they released people that no one would be able to figure out who since they did not publish the numbers. We now know they have arrested and held people for bogus reasons that were inadequate and they knew were not valid. Now we know from the way they released them that it has to be true. And we know that every time they try to characterize them as dangerous or evil or bad, it is actually a manipulative device; they are certainly not being treated as ends, but merely as means.

GUANTÁNAMO: AN ASSESSMENT AND REFLECTION FROM THOSE WHO HAVE BEEN THERE

Gita Gutierrez

I am a human rights attorney, and I want to talk to you today about what "human" means in this phrase. I could certainly talk about rights. I work at the Center for Constitutional Rights. I have been involved in this litigation for many, many years. I am also an attorney, and I am a ferocious advocate for the men I work for at Gitmo and their families. I have met with over forty men at Gitmo since I started going to the base. I also represent a man who grew up in Baltimore and was put in CIA secret detention and shipped to Gitmo in September 2006. And I cannot talk about what happened to him because it has all been classified. His experience, and he himself, have been deemed top secret, and if I were to give witness to his experience, I could be prosecuted and put in a federal prison. As an attorney, working with my colleagues at the center, we have pursued prosecutors in other countries to bring war crime prosecutions against officials in this country under principles of universal jurisdiction because of the atrocities they have committed.

But what I want to talk to you about today on 11 September 2008 is what "human" means for human rights attorneys. I invite you to set aside your expertise whether you are a theologian, a lawyer, an academic, a political scientist, a dean, a policymaker, or a doctor. I ask you to set that aside and to join me and sit at the human circle and learn each other's names. Questions about faith and torture and our nation's soul are issues I have struggled with since September 2004 when I first went to Gitmo and sat across the table from two British citizens—one a young man exactly ten years younger than myself—who had been tortured and placed in isolation, one for a year and half and one for nearly two years, when I sat across the table from them. And that was a frightening experience. I was not afraid of the clients I was going to meet. I was afraid and nervous about the environment I was going into. It seems silly now to look back on it because now there are so many lawyers going to Gitmo. But that was shortly after Abu Ghraib, when the photos came out and I was asked to sign rules allowing attorneys access to go down, that said I could submit to searches of my person and property. It did cross my mind—whether they would try to strip search me when I got down there, which was not something I felt like I could tolerate.

It was a very tense week of intense meetings with my clients and very tense relations with the lawyers at the base and the military police. I had a lawyer from the general counsel office at the Department of Defense who was more or less my babysitter, who followed me around everywhere except for my meetings with my clients. But we got through the week. And since that time I have gone down to the base often, and some years I spend a quarter of my time sitting in rooms with men there.

What I want to talk to you about today is Mohamed al-Qahtani. He has one of the most well-documented torture interrogation regimes at Gitmo, evidenced by government documents and not just his own self-reporting. He is a young man from Saudi Arabia who was subject to the first special interrogation plan. The details of the plan itself are still classified, but an interrogation log from that time was leaked and goes through what happened to him in detail in fifteen- or thirty-minute increments.

I have often been asked how the Center for Constitutional Rights became involved in his representation. Everyone is someone's child. Mohamed's elderly father traveled to Bahrain to meet with human rights attorneys from the center and from an organization called Reprieve. Very early in 2002 and 2003, lawyers from the US went to these countries and worked with local human rights organizations to get the word out among the community that American lawyers were coming, and if you were a father or an uncle or a brother who had a relative disappear, the American lawyers could take an authorization from you to try and help your relative. And Mohamed's elderly sick father filled out an authorization to get help for his son because everyone is someone's child.

We recruited a firm to represent him, and they had not filed his case yet in 2005 when *Time* magazine released a story about the interrogation log and allegations against him that he was one of the twenty alleged hijackers. The firm had not approved this pro bono project and they dropped him like a hot potato. I try to be forgiving but I cannot forgive that act because I have always believed lawyers are here to serve. These lawyers abandoned an individual when he most needed someone to step forward into the public dialogue and defend him.

So the center looked at the issues surrounding the torture and decided to represent him. We filed for him ourselves because of the documentation of his torture and because of the issues around his case. We believe firmly that no one should be tortured and recognized this was not a case of rogue individuals in Gitmo being creative with his interrogation. It was a very calculated plan that was developed and approved within the highest levels of the administration.

I usually preface any talk about Mohamed and his experience with a charge to the audience, because Mohamed is sitting in prison today. He is there tonight and will be there tomorrow, and I have a concern about our culture's voyeurism with respect to violence and torture. I do not want to contribute to that, so I will usually tell the audience I am going to give them a list of five things at the end of the talk and ask everyone to take action based on what they are going to witness. And I actually will pause for a full minute and ask anyone who is not ready to take that step to leave. Most people think it is a rhetorical move, but I will actually stop long enough for them to get uncomfortable enough to realize that I am, without any judgment or hostility, giving them an opportunity to leave. Because I think it is important to take this information and do something with it. We are way past words.

So when Mohamed first arrived in Gitmo in early 2002, he was treated to the same kind of interrogation all of the men experienced: stress positions, exposure to the elements, manhandling, being beaten, watching people beaten by the extreme reaction force that would come in if a detainee would not leave his cell or be compliant. But around August 2002 Mohamed's fingerprints matched fingerprints that were on file with the FBI. They became concerned he was one of the individuals trying to come into the country before September 11, and at that point his interrogations shifted. He was placed in severe isolation and threatened with military working dogs. At the end of this three-month period, an FBI agent named T. J. Harrington observed Mohamed in his cell in isolation and wrote an observation that this was potential detainee abuse and that Mohamed exhibited signs of psychosis from the trauma he was experiencing. He sent it up through his chain of supervision.

From that point Mohamed went into almost sixty days that are covered in the interrogation log. The log is available on the Internet. It reads as a very dry, rather clinical observation of what happened to him. During that time he was subjected to twenty-hour-a-day interrogations and was permitted to sleep only from seven until eleven A.M. So for any of you who can remember being students and pulling an all-nighter, or for those of you who still experience that and are familiar with the sort of delirium you feel the next day, Mohamed went through that for almost sixty days. He was shackled and restrained, and at various times he would go on hunger strikes and was given very painful IVs. The medics and the doctor were fairly intimately involved in his interrogation, which has raised a number of concerns within different agencies. He was poked often for IVs and they had a very difficult time finding veins. He was overhydrated and then shackled down and left without being permitted to use the bathroom. He would urinate on himself and then could not pray. He was stripped. He experienced forced nudity in front of both men and women. He was basically sexually assaulted when MPs would hold him down and a female interrogator would straddle him and touch him. This again was all in the context of being utterly deprived of sleep and often not eating or drinking.

To give you some perspective on how violating this was to his person and to his soul, when I visit Mohamed I do not wear a veil, but I do cover. I wear fully black clothing, long-sleeve shirts, and a long black skirt, and he still has never looked me in the face. It is almost impossible for me to conceive him being held down, with a woman laying on top of him that way or straddling him and touching him in that way, and what that must have done to him. He was hospitalized during this time. His heartbeat dropped so low that there was a concern he would actually die or lapse into some kind of severe medical condition. He was rushed to the hospital at Gitmo, an EKG was given, and a cardiologist was flown in from Puerto Rico to review his results. That was the only night during the interrogation log period when he slept more than four hours in the morning. And he was interrogated on the way back to his interrogation.

This is all from the interrogation log. Mohamed has certainly gone into other details and descriptions of what it was like, but that is in the government records. His treatment has been the subject of multiple detainee abuse investigations by different agencies. The authorization for his treatment has been the subject of numerous congressional inquiries. An entire book has been written about the authorization for his treatment. There is no dispute about what happened to him. There have been a few people today who touched upon where these kinds of interrogation tactics came from and about how, when these methods—sleep deprivation, for example—were used against Americans by North Koreans, we called it torture.

When we originally started looking at these methods, they were part of survival school training for military personnel. When these aggressive enhanced-interrogation methods were being started at Guantánamo, people from Gitmo went to the SERE school to observe. CIA personnel came to Gitmo to advise how to use these methods, and many of them are reminiscent of things the CIA had laid out in the Kubark manual. General Jeffrey Miller, who was the commander at Gitmo during some of this time after Mohamed was interrogated, then went to Abu Ghraib and provided advice there. So these methods traveled, and I think they were deliberately shared there.

I first met Mohammed in December 2005, after he had been through all of this. He has been in a maximum-security facility in Gitmo called camp 5, based off of similar maximum security facilities in the United States. He had been there for over two years when I first met him. And I cannot really convey to you what Mohamed has felt and endured, and I won't objectify him that way. I hope someday he is able to tell his story himself. But I can tell you what I experienced as a person meeting with him. The first day he refused to come out of his cell and I fought with the military lawyers about that—whether I could go into the cell block and meet with him. And we just fought, yelling at each other all day in front of camp 5.

That night I went back to the room I was staying in. It was not the first time I had been to Gitmo. I had been there often enough before then. I reached out to my own faith community and asked for their prayers. They prayed for me and for Mohamed that he would be able to see through his fears and resistance and come and meet with me.

The next day he was actually tricked into coming. He did not know he was coming to meet with me. We met in a tiny, tiny holding cell. And he was curled up, turned into the corner, would not turn around and look. I went in with an interpreter who kept having to ask him to pull his hands away from his face so that he would speak. His affect was of someone who had been damaged and injured. He had incredible difficulty following the lines of logic and having a conversation. He would talk here and there. We had the same conversation almost every day for five days in a row.

Over the course of the next two years, I met him fairly often every month or every other month, often for a week at a time. I sought the assistance of the Bellevue Center for Survivors of Torture on how to work with someone who not only was a victim of torture, but was still being held in the place where he was tortured. At times we met in the same type of room where he was tortured. So this was not like working with an asylum seeker, who is now safe and back in the United States, but instead going into the place where he was still held. They helped me understand his affect, his presence, the challenges of trust, his loss of his sense of humanity, his paranoia that was not entirely irrational, his feeling that he was surrounded by people who were out to get him. In many ways we had the same meeting over and over for years. It would have the same rhythms, the same questions, the same trust issues.

I just want to close with a few reflections on what the experience has been like meeting with him. One is that I realized the system in Gitmo is designed for lawyers to fail at our work with someone who has been a victim of torture. We have not failed the Constitution and we have not failed our country. The victory in the Supreme Court this year was historic. But as clients, as men who we are going to work for, who we are trying to assess, the system is set up for us to fail. This does not mean we *will* fail, but it is set up that way. And as lawyers we have to recognize that our profession plays a very small but crucial role. Without a court order, I would not be able to stand before you today and talk about Mohamed's experience. But too much time has passed. He ended up there in 2002. Too much time has passed for the legal cases to restore the loss of years or to offer justice for the loss of those years.

I think back on *Brown vs. Board of Education*. It took ten years before that case was implemented, and that was ten years of individuals who went through segregated school systems. To me that is the limit of the law. Looking at our national soul is perhaps what has been most troubling to me; it has been hard to have to question my faith in my country. These comments may be provocative, but in my tradition and in my belief and way of walking in the world, I am not here to comfort the afflicted but to afflict the comforted.

In witnessing my client's experience, I have seen the violence and dehumanization that allows torture to occur. I think there is some inconsistency in our notion that Gitmo is an exception or that it is shocking or different. It is true that the backwards step in Gitmo is alarming. We have moved backwards. But we have with Gitmo looked at the underbelly of our country. We have two threads in our historical narrative. One is of democracy, of respect for rights, of a shining upholder of human rights in the world. But we have another thread in our history, of dehumanization based on race, ethnicity, or nationality. We see this in what was done to Native Americans and to native-born black Americans, or when we hear words like "chink" and "gook" used to dehumanize the other. "Towelheads," "terrorists," and most recently, "Islamofascists" —I have been on panels where people have used that word. We have a capacity in this nation to see other human beings as less than human, and that is part of our history too.

It is also part of our present day. There are prisoners in state and federal prisons in this country right now who have had similar experiences of strip searching, hunger strikes, the restraint chair. The facilities the men in Gitmo are held in, the isolation, are based on practices in the United States. I think it is a very slippery slope from torturing someone we call a convicted criminal to potentially feeling comfortable torturing someone we only suspect of terrorism.

So I leave you with an invitation. The resisters are waiting for you; we have been waiting for you. Our nation is in the midst of a long, dark night of the soul. I invite you to step into this darkness, open your eyes widely, witness this darkness with unflinching strength of spirit, reach out and grab a hand to pull our country through this night. In this darkness you may touch the hand of a Muslim in Gitmo, you may touch my hand, you may touch the hand of a torturer. You will touch the hand of God.

★

GUANTÁNAMO: AN ASSESSMENT AND REFLECTION FROM THOSE WHO HAVE BEEN THERE

Thomas Wilner

I believe passionately in this country and in the ideals of this country. And it is why I first got involved in this issue. People have asked me before why I am so passionate about these things. I was thinking about it. In part it is my background and to some extent my religious background. My great-grandfather was the rabbi of Vilna in what was then Russia. He was apparently a very important and learned guy. In the 1870s he read the Gettysburg Address and the Declaration of Independence, and he said, "If there is a country like this, I want my children to live there." My grandfather came to this country in 1883, when he was thirteen. He was a passionate patriot.

My father and uncle used to tell the story that when they first went to Gettysburg, my grandfather took the podium and recited the Gettysburg Address and the Preamble to the Declaration of Independence to them perfectly. My father tells me he said it with a slight Russian accent. He had tears in his eyes and it was as if he was saying a prayer. And I realized that as I grew up, my religion in a sense was belief in the principles of the country, a place that gave the little

Jewish kid the opportunity to be free and live under the rule of law and have a civilized existence.

I also will tell you about my own experience. I have been an international lawyer all my life, representing companies and countries around the world. And everywhere I have gone around the world, I have felt an intense pride in being an American. And I have seen that returned. You know people complain about people in other countries not liking Americans; I have found that that is wrong. They may feel we are sort of cowboy-ish, that we sometimes make mistakes, but everywhere I have gone around the world Americans were looked at as the good guys. We make mistakes but we are still the good guys—not self-interested. We screwed up in Vietnam but it was well motivated.

That has changed and it disturbs me greatly. People say it is our moral authority in the world; it has changed in the last few years. I was approached in 2002 by a group of Kuwaitis looking for their children, who we found out had been sold for bounties and ended up in Gitmo. We brought a case asking for one thing—simple due process, for the right to a fair hearing. That is all the Gitmo cases have ever been about. It has been a long time and I have considered it a struggle for the soul of our nation.

I have some overall reflections of what I have seen in the last six years. The first is just looking at torture. It is just extraordinary to me that we can even be debating this issue in the United States. When I grew up, torture was something the bad guys did. You get comic books as a kid and that is what the bad guys did to Americans. That is what the Nazis did. It was never what we would do. It was what the bad guys did to John McCain, and yet there is no doubt now that America is torturing. When they told me the way they have been treated by Americans, my stomach turned. Clearly we have tortured people, I do not care about the legalisms we use or the words we use. Moreover, we have done it without any real debate in this country. And we have done it without an empirical study to see if this is effective or good. We did it and there still has not been a debate.

We have allowed this to go on. Everyone in this country has allowed this to go on, me too. Another thing that gets lost in this is that we have held people without any hearings. And for my guys down at Gitmo, that is more important than physical torture. I will tell you a story about this that actually appeared in the *New York Times*. When I was down there, a guy asked me, "Do you mind me asking what religion are you?" I said no, and that I am Jewish. He said, "You know what the interrogators told me? How can you use your lawyer when you know he is a Jew?" Another guy told me that as well. I reported that to the *New York Times*, which ran a tiny little piece about it.

Nobody seemed to care. The next time I went down, he said, "You told them about that, didn't you?" I said yes. He told me, "The interrogator came in and threatened me, and I looked at her and said, 'What are you going to do? I have had the heck beat out of me, I have been shot, and I have been strung up. Beat me all you want, just give me a fair hearing.'" We now have facts proving that most of them were held there without evidence and were innocent. The CIA did a report in 2002. They were not getting information out of these people so they went down and checked it out. They concluded that most of the people were innocent. They sent it up to the White House, and Addington and Gonzalez in the White House said to bury it, that we have made the decision on these people and do not care if they are innocent. That is true and it is extraordinary. That, to me, is evil.

Another thing I think we have to consider that I have seen is the relativity of truth. What happens when we torture the innocent with no hearings and the government just denies it? We can look at the reports and the facts and see there is no evidence against these people, but the government just says, no, they are all bad guys. We know we torture but the government says, "We would not torture; we are Americans." It is a terribly dangerous thing, because you cannot even have a debate about it. Nobody gets to the truth. I am asked about the role of the press in this. The press reports what people say; usually they do not go behind it and say what the truth is. Then when they do report it, we do not do anything about it; nobody cares. It goes on. Maybe there is no political opposition.

And what has happened to religious groups? How can they tolerate this? How can they go in their congregations and bury it? This is intolerable.

Another thing that has disturbed me in all this is the feeling of a "tough guy" attitude. I remember seeing the movie *True Grit* years ago, and there is a scene where John Wayne is going to shoot and kill people in a cabin and someone says, "How can you do this?" and he says, "Tell them we mean business." That is the sort of attitude. Tough guys do not worry about laws or principles. In this administration, if you raise considerations about the law or principles or ideals, you are considered a wimp.

That is an extraordinary thing to me, and it goes against what I was taught. I was taught that someone who gives up their principles in the face of opposition is not strong but weak. The strong person is the person who sticks to their principles when it is tough to do so. That is what this administration should be doing. This is a struggle for the soul of our nation, and I think it is important to always ask what we stand for as a nation. I always thought this nation had a dark side, but in my mind we were always working against that and making progress. And I believe that we are different than other nations because we are not bound together by a common race or a common religion. What makes us Americans are our principles of liberty, justice, and the rule of law. President Eisenhower said we are proud to be Americans, because in America anybody can stand up without worrying he might be thrown into jail to rot without a hearing, because we have habeas corpus and we believe in it. These principles of habeas corpus, liberty, and the rule of law are really the soul of our nation. They are our greatest strength and we should realize it.

That is why President Clinton said the world has always been more impressed with the power of our example than the example of our power. And this is not a Republican or Democrat thing. President Reagan said the exact same thing in his great speech in 1992 to the Republican convention. He said our greatest strength derives not from our wealth or power but from our ideals of freedom and justice. This is a struggle for the soul of our nation, and it is a struggle we must continue to fight as long as it takes. I do not see this as a partisan issue, but I am disgusted that the people who did this are still in power. Whether you come from a liberal or a not so liberal area, we have an obligation to stand up for what this nation stands for and I think what a true religion would stand for. I cannot imagine a compassionate, loving, just God tolerating this. I do not care what other issues are on the table. This is the issue of most importance. This is the issue of our soul.

Part II

RECOVERING OUR MORAL BEARINGS: WHERE DO WE GO FROM HERE?

6

SERMONS AND REFLECTIONS

＊

Sacred Bodies: Inspirited Flesh

Cheryl Bridges Johns

The book of Genesis records for us the beginnings of humankind. Two things stand out in this ancient story. First, human beings are created in the image of God (1:26); and second, God formed us from the dust of the earth and breathed into us the breath of life (2:7). Since the dawn of creation, all humanity bears this dual distinction of the *imago dei* and the breath of God. Thus is foundation laid for the sacredness of life.

The *imago dei,* the imprint of God, is a great mystery. Its meaning is often obscured by human constructs of God. However, at its most basic level it means the life that is in God is in us. We are made for that life—its beauty, its fellowship, and its wonder. God gave to humanity not just the gift of life, as in all creation, but the gift of God's life—extending by grace a portion of the divine into human flesh.

This gift of life means humans are somehow enchanted beings—more than mere flesh and dust. Enchanted beings are inspirited. They are "gestalts of grace" in the sense that God has graced dust with God's very likeness. So, in a real sense, in every human being heaven and earth are joined in an enchanted microcosmos. This is beauty and this is mystery. We are, in the words of the psalmist, "fearfully and wonderfully made" (Psalms 139:14).

As enchanted beings, the special reality of being human creates the possibility of divine visitation: We are designed for the indwelling of God's spirit because God has created us with divine image. Life is thus gifted and it is sacred.

Furthermore, to live in an ecology of community reflects the divine life. This ecology is characterized by mutual respect, delight in the other, and appreciation of the gifts of others. To live in the divine life is to live without greed, self-centeredness, and a desire to control.

Humankind not only shares the divine image, it breathes the divine *ruach* or breath. So, by inference, human life springs from God and is sustained by God. Humans bear the mark not only of sacred image but sacred breath.

In my own tradition, Pentecostalism, we hold it sacred that God poured out his spirit on all flesh on the day of Pentecost. The mighty wind of God filled human vessels—inspiriting them, filling them with divine life and power. Dust once again was infused with the divine *ruach*. God and humanity were intimate once again. In Pentecost, people become, in the words of Flannery O'Conner, "Temples of the Holy Ghost," habitation of the holy. They may be common people. However, it seems to delight God to visit the most common, profane flesh: the poor, the outcast, the alien. In some special way they are open to receive, to become enchanted, to live in a power not their own. In the ministry of Jesus it was such ones that welcomed Christ and received his gift of sharing in the divine life.

It is of ever-growing concern that our world is one of disenchantment. The earth is no longer sacred and we are no longer connected to it in an organic unity. The modern era has made us masters over the world. And we have played this role all too well. As masters we have subdued the earth, using its resources for our own perceived well-being. We no longer see the gestalts of grace found in nature. And in so doing, we have ravaged the earth for its resources. For profit, we have turned deaf ears to the groanings of creation.

Can it be too far of a jump in moral reasoning from ignoring the groans of creation to ignoring the groans of human flesh? Just how far apart are mountaintop removal and waterboarding? When everything is objectified and commodified, then everything is open to use, sell, buy, and yes, "if need be," abused for what is perceived as the greater good.

So it has come to be that human beings, just as the larger world in which we dwell, are disenchanted. They exist not for their inherent qualities of the divine; rather, they are utilitarian instruments in a larger economy. The real greater good, namely that the earth is the Lord's and all who dwell in it belong to God, is lost in pursuit of competing interests.

Gus Speth, dean of the School of Forestry and Environmental Science at Yale University, points out in his recent book *Bridge at the Edge of the World* that in most Western countries, while the GDP has risen significantly over the last decades, the Index of Sustainable Economic Welfare has indicated decline. Imagine, more products to consume, more money for consumption, and yet the general well-being of people is in decline. There is more pollution, less health care, more prisons to support, and wars on terror to fund.

At the same time, during the war on terror, there has been an increase in measures such as torture. But corresponding to this, people do not feel safer; they feel less safe.

What I am saying is that there is a connection here. We have more commodities to buy and sell and yet, there is less quality of life. We have more tactics against terrorism, such as torture, yet people do not feel safe. More is not always better; in fact, "more" can lead one to the abyss.

This connection reveals that we have lost sight of the primal garden, the giftedness of creation, and the sacredness of human flesh. Like a guilty Adam and Eve, we no longer seek to hear "the sound of the Lord God walking in the garden at the time of the evening breeze" (Genesis 3:8). Instead, like our ancestors we seek to hide ourselves from the creator so that our transgressions might not be discovered.

Deeds of violence done in the darkness may be hidden from public view, but before the one who made the day and the darkness, nothing is hidden. For God, the darkness is as the light, and before the eternal gaze, transgressions are discovered. From the ground human blood continues, as did Abel's, to cry out to the creator. Before the creator come not only the cries of tortured bodies, but the moans of inspired flesh, enchanted beings whose breath carries tones of the divine wind. God, who is not impassable and unmoving, participates in each moan and each cry. The spirit of God, with sighs too deep for words, carries human suffering into the divine presence. "I have observed the misery of my people...I have heard their cry" (Exodus 3:7).

So the divine creator becomes the judge who condemns Cain, who judges the harsh Egyptians, and who judges those who claim privileged relationship. While humans may turn their gaze from the suffering, God turns toward it, ever demanding justice. Prophets such as Isaiah are sent to remind those who claim privileged status that God indeed sees and hears: "The earth lies polluted under its inhabitants, for they have transgressed laws, violated statutes, broken the everlasting covenant. Therefore, a curse devours the earth, and its inhabitants suffer for their guilt" (Isaiah 24:5–6).

Speth warns that if destruction of the world's environment continues, there is the abyss ahead. Quoting Robert Jay Lifton, he continues, "If one does not look into the abyss, one is being wishful by simply not confronting the truth."

We are at this conference to stare into the abyss. We are here to reveal that which is hidden. Such work is not easy, for it forces us to see what we would rather never see. It forces us to hear the cries of those hidden away from normal, everyday life. Yet, for the sake of the sanctity of life, for the sake of inspirited flesh, we are compelled to move forward in calls for justice. All the while we know that we are being judged. The one who hears every cry, who sees every tear, who hears every moan is on watch.

So there is an urgency about our task—yet another task to build a bridge at the edge of the world, keeping us from hurtling into the abyss. It is not the first time our nation has faced the task of righting wrongs and restoring justice. We can build bridges. We can restore broken walls. We can acknowledge the dignity and sacredness of all flesh, even the dignity of "terrorist flesh." So, in light of our past, it is appropriate for us to recall the words of Martin Luther King, Jr. on 4 April 1967 at Riverside Church in New York City:

> We are now faced with the fact that tomorrow is today. We are confronted with the fierce urgency of now. In this unfolding conundrum of life and history there is such a thing as being too late. Procrastination is still the thief of time. Life often leaves us standing bare, naked and dejected with a lost

opportunity. The "tide in the affairs of men" does not remain at the flood; it ebbs. We may cry out desperately for time to pause in her passage, but time is deaf to every plea and rushes on. Over the bleached bones and jumbled residue of numerous civilizations are written the pathetic words: "too late."

★

IMAGINE THE SOJOURNER

Fleming Rutledge

The Lord your God…loves the sojourner, giving him food and clothing. Love the sojourner therefore; for you were sojourners in the land of Egypt. (Deuteronomy 10:17–19)

You may know of—or you may be a fan of—the wildly popular *Number One Ladies' Detective Agency* series, by Alexander McCall Smith. Its lady detective, Precious Ramotswe, is one of the most endearing characters ever to emerge from the printed page. She is called Mma Ramotswe, in the dignified, respectful way of her native country, Botswana, and she is so richly human, wise, and kind that you want to spend as much time with her as possible. There are nine books in the series so far and their appeal does not fade.

Here is a little snippet from the reflections of Mma Ramotswe. She has just witnessed a case of petty theft. She recalls her beloved father and how he taught her always to be "scrupulously honest":

> It was difficult for Mma Ramotswe to imagine how anybody could steal from another, or do any of the things which one

read about in the *Botswana Daily News* court reports. The only explanation was that people who did that sort of thing had no understanding of what others felt; they simply did not understand it. If you knew what it was like to be another person, then how could you possibly do something which would cause pain?

The problem, though, was that there seemed to be people in whom that imaginative part was just missing. It could be that they were just born that way—with something missing from their brains—or it could be that they became like that because they were never taught by their parents to sympathize with others. That was the most likely explanation, thought Mma Ramotswe. A whole generation of people, not only in Africa, but everywhere else, had not been taught to feel for others because the parents simply had not bothered to teach them.[180]

It was difficult for Mma Ramotswe to imagine, but she made the effort just the same. She worked hard at figuring out human behavior. It was important to her to know "what it was like to be another person," to understand "what others felt." But let's not fail to note that she made the effort to understand not only the victims of crimes but also the perpetrators. Either they had been born with something missing, or they had not been taught empathy the way she had been taught by her father.

Samantha Power is the author of *A Problem from Hell*, the Pulitzer-Prize-winning book about genocide and America's failures to respond to it.[181] Her project is to examine all of the genocides of the twentieth century, beginning with the Turkish massacre of the Armenians and continuing through to Rwanda and Kosovo in the 1990s. If she has one theme above all, it is failure of imagination.[182] Each genocide had its Cassandras, its figures who begged and pleaded with the world community to pay heed, only to be met with varying degrees of disbelief and incomprehension.[183] It was, she writes, a lack of imagination. Government officials, diplomats, United Nations personnel, the intelligence community, congressmen, senators, and presidents—they could not or would not imagine genocide. In the 2000s, Nicholas Kristof is a voice in the wilderness; for years he has been trying to help his readers imagine what is going on in Darfur.[184]

Sympathy and pity are not enough. Sympathy and pity come to the other person as if from a distance, from a safe height. Imagination, empathy, and understanding must come from within, from the same level as the other. One has to imagine "what it was like to be another person," even when the "other person" is a criminal.

More than forty times in the Torah, the Lord speaks of the "sojourner(s)." This is not a word we use very much in everyday conversation, but it is obviously very important in biblical thought.[185] The dictionary definition is "one who lives temporarily." God expects his people Israel to have special regard for the sojourner. The people of the covenant are asked, in effect, to imagine themselves into the place of the sojourner, to see things from the sojourner's perspective. They are not to do this because of universal rights or general moral principles; those are not really biblical concepts. Even the idea of our common humanity is not central here. The motivation for the care of the sojourner arises out of the memory of the community, the teaching handed down from one generation to the next. The people of God are to use their imagination to remember, to envision their condition before the lord delivered them at the Red Sea and forged them into a nation. Their care for the sojourner is to arise out of their own recollection of slavery and exile in a foreign land, their experience of being at the mercy of someone else. That is what they must not forget.

The classic passage is from Deuteronomy (10:17–11:1): "The Lord your God is God of gods and Lord of lords, the great, the mighty, and the terrible God, who is not partial and takes no bribe. He executes justice for the fatherless and the widow, and loves the sojourner, giving him food and clothing. Love the sojourner therefore; for you were sojourners in the land of Egypt...." God loves the sojourner. That is the primary fact. Therefore and for that reason, God's elect people love the sojourner, for we were once sojourners ourselves before the lord delivered us with his mighty hand and an outstretched arm. The care of the sojourner arises not from general principles, but from the power of the shared story. As Mma Ramotswe reflects, "A life without stories would be no life at all."[186]

There is a poverty of story in the churches today, even in the more conservative congregations. The Bible is just not known as it should be for our good. There is a lot of talk about "Abrahamic faith," but what we really need to know and remember is the prodigious reach of the promise made to Abraham: "By you, Abraham, *all the nations of the earth* will be blessed" (Genesis 12:3). That is the pledge made by God to "the father of us all" (Romans 4:16). The covenant made with Abraham is a central episode in the biblical story. It reveals God's purpose from before and from beyond all time, to bless "all the peoples of the earth"—not just the favored nation, but *all* the nations. The covenant God made with Abraham was comprehensive in a way that unaided human imagination could never have discovered. That is why God brought Abraham out of his tent at night to look at the immense canopy of stars. What a sight that must have been in the pure desert air, with no pollution to obscure the distant galaxies! And God said to Abraham, "So shall your descendants be" (Genesis 15:5). This was God's way of lifting the imagination of his people. We need Abrahamic vision so that, when we look at the stars, we wonder not only at the glory of the cosmos and the lord who made it, but also the promise of God to be gracious to humanly unimaginable numbers of people.

The story of Abraham, as it continues, gives us an archetypal picture of the Christian life. God had blessed Abraham in his old age with great riches, but even so, there was something precarious about his situation. Abraham does not live to see the covenant fulfilled. He is a sojourner in the land of promise. Listen to the way the New Testament picks up the theme: "By faith Abraham *sojourned* in *the land of promise, as in a foreign land,* living in tents with Isaac and Jacob, heirs with him of the same promise. For he looked forward to the city which has foundations, whose builder and maker is God" (Hebrews 11:9–10).

Because Abraham, the prototype of the sojourner, has pitched his tents in a foreign land, there is always a certain amount of insecurity involved. He must live by faith, with no permanent home on this earth as it is presently constituted. In the New Testament, the letter to the

Hebrews expands this theme far beyond Abraham, declaring in no uncertain terms that all Christians are foreigners, "strangers and exiles on the earth" (Hebrews 11:14–16).[187] The synoptic gospels give us a fully developed picture of the "foreign land" as territory occupied by an enemy whose legions are repeatedly attacked and defeated by Jesus in his exorcisms. This adversary is referred to three times in the Gospel of John as the "ruler of this world" (John 12:31, 14:30, 16:11).[188] "His doom is sure," as Martin Luther puts it in his famous hymn,[189] but in the meantime the principalities and powers continue to serve this ruler and are allowed to make war on God's creation. Thus the sojourner suffers not only from estrangement and dislocation, but also from the assaults of this dehumanizing enemy, referred to by Paul the apostle as the power of sin and death.

So the motif of the sojourner in scripture carries with it two parallel meanings depending on the circumstances. If the Christian community is being asked to recall its own story, the emphasis is on our present status as temporary residents who are not at home. Some of the important novelists have referred to this. Walker Percy, for instance, created a whole gallery of characters who cannot accommodate things as they are. They are not "adjusted." One of them says, "I cannot tolerate this age."[190] This is the sojourner theme.

But the other meaning of the sojourner has to do not with the status of the people of God as figurative "strangers and exiles on the earth," but with the literal stranger in our midst. To return to Deuteronomy, God has called for acts of imagination on our part.

The lord your God loves the sojourner, giving him food and clothing. Love the sojourner therefore, for you were sojourners in the land of Egypt. In that one clause, "for you were sojourners in the land of Egypt," the whole history of God's gracious mercy to Israel is summed up. The lord says to Moses: Remember that you were powerless in the hands of an enemy population. Remember that you would still be enslaved were it not for my mighty acts of deliverance; you would be forgotten skeletons in the wilderness without the food, water, guidance, and protection I, the lord, provided. Remember these things and you will understand why I have commanded you to care for the sojourner.

Here is an example of someone who did not remember who he was before God. When Donald Rumsfeld was still secretary of defense, he wrote these words (he later acknowledged them as his own) on a memo outlining US interrogation policies: "I stand for 8–10 hours a day. Why is standing limited to 4 hours?"[191]

What is this if not a staggering failure of imagination? The secretary of defense stands to command. Perhaps he prefers to work at a stand-up desk.[192] He has a staff to bring his lunch, to carry his messages, to bow to his demands. He works in air-conditioning in the summer and heated rooms in the winter. He likes what he is doing and he can throw his weight around any time he pleases. The captive at Guantánamo, or in a secret CIA prison where the Red Cross can never come, is surrounded by people who wish him harm. He does not choose to stand as Rumsfeld does; he is forced to stand. The room where he stands is too hot, or too cold. Perhaps there is ear-splitting rock music playing. Very possibly he has not been allowed to sleep. Even if this prisoner is the worst sort of terrorist, the unwillingness of the secretary of defense to perceive these differences is a good illustration of an abject failure of imagination. The difference between a terrorist who must be subdued and a helpless captive is a difference of power and powerlessness. Once a man (or woman) becomes powerless, then he is a sojourner. A sojourner is by definition at the mercy of someone else, some other group. It is this person who God loves; it is this person who is commended to us for particular care.

Nearly all men can withstand adversity, that other Abraham—President Lincoln—said; but if you want to test a man's character, give him power. As the most powerful nation—for the present—we Americans are being especially tested. We have become like those whom another novelist describes as men who exhibit "an easy confidence known only to those for whom it has become second nature to decide other people's fates."[193] Those other people, the sojourners in Guantánamo and in the clutches of the CIA, are out of sight and out of mind most of the time. The witnesses to the lord's story are the very few who have come forward to testify, who have done the work of imagining what it is like to be without human contact, without sleep, without sight of the sun.[194] A captive who is powerless is our ethical responsibility no

132

matter what he has done, because we also were powerless in the grip of sin and death until the one who was at a great height came down below, until he stepped out of his position and made himself of no consequence, until he gave up his power and placed himself at the mercy of torturers. In the manner of his death, Jesus Christ made himself the representative not only of all victims but also of all perpetrators. In this solidarity with us he became the quintessential sojourner with nowhere to lay his head and no one to come to his defense in a foreign land occupied by his enemies—that is to say, occupied by ourselves.

Christians, imagine therefore the sojourners, and hold them in your heart as fellow sufferers like yourself. We do this in imitation of our lord, who knowingly suffered torture and death at the hands of those who in his time represented the greatest empire and the best religion the world had ever known. And out of the love of Christ we will teach the children. Remember the story; remember who we are before the lord:

> Love the sojourner therefore; for you were sojourners in the land of Egypt. You shall fear the Lord your God; you shall serve him and cleave to him, and by his name you shall swear. He is your praise; he is your God, who has done for you these great and terrible things which your eyes have seen. Your fathers went down to Egypt seventy persons; and now the Lord your God has made you as the stars of heaven for multitude. You shall therefore love the Lord your God, and keep his charge, his statutes, his ordinances, and his commandments always. (Deuteronomy 10:19–22)

Let me close with these important words from J. K. Rowling:

> One of the greatest formative experiences of my life preceded Harry Potter, though it informed much of what I subsequently wrote in those books. This revelation came in the form of one of my earliest day jobs. Though I was sloping off to write stories during my lunch hours, I paid the rent in my early 20s by working in the research department at Amnesty International's headquarters in London.

There in my little office I read hastily scribbled letters smuggled out of totalitarian regimes by men and women who were risking imprisonment to inform the outside world of what was happening to them. I saw photographs of those who had disappeared without trace, sent to Amnesty by their desperate families and friends. I read the testimony of torture victims and saw pictures of their injuries. I opened hand-written, eye-witness accounts of summary trials and executions, of kidnappings and rapes.

Many of my co-workers were ex-political prisoners, people who had been displaced from their homes, or fled into exile, because they had the temerity to think independently of their government. Visitors to our office included those who had come to give information, or to try and find out what had happened to those they had been forced to leave behind.

I shall never forget the African torture victim, a young man no older than I was at the time, who had become mentally ill after all he had endured in his homeland. He trembled uncontrollably as he spoke into a video camera about the brutality inflicted upon him. He was a foot taller than I was, and seemed as fragile as a child. I was given the job of escorting him to the Underground Station afterwards, and this man whose life had been shattered by cruelty took my hand with exquisite courtesy, and wished me future happiness.

And as long as I live I shall remember walking along an empty corridor and suddenly hearing, from behind a closed door, a scream of pain and horror such as I have never heard since. The door opened, and the researcher poked out her head and told me to run and make a hot drink for the young man sitting with her. She had just given him the news that in retaliation for his own outspokenness against his country's regime, his mother had been seized and executed.

Every day of my working week in my early 20s I was reminded how incredibly fortunate I was, to live in a country with a democratically elected government, where legal representation and a public trial were the rights of everyone.

Every day, I saw more evidence about the evils humankind will inflict on their fellow humans, to gain or maintain power. I began to have nightmares, literal nightmares, about some of the things I saw, heard and read.

And yet I also learned more about human goodness at Amnesty International than I had ever known before.

Amnesty mobilizes thousands of people who have never been tortured or imprisoned for their beliefs to act on behalf of those who have. The power of human empathy, leading to collective action, saves lives, and frees prisoners. Ordinary people, whose personal well-being and security are assured, join together in huge numbers to save people they do not know, and will never meet. My small participation in that process was one of the most humbling and inspiring experiences of my life.[195]

Unlike any other creature on this planet, humans can learn and understand, without having experienced. They can think themselves into other people's minds, imagine themselves into other people's places.

Tortured Truth

Tyler Wigg-Stevenson

As one who has become deeply involved in the moral opposition to the practice of torture by the United States, I am increasingly convinced that our national debate on the issue must move beyond mere good and evil. There are many reasons to oppose torture, and for those of us who oppose it on religious grounds, the moral standard seems clear and unambiguous. And yet our moral standards sometimes seem to count for very little in policy discussions. We who have argued that the United States should be the gold standard for human rights have found to our dismay that gold can be twisted into virtually any shape its owner desires. And many of the commentators who are among the loudest to decry our nation's moral relativism are also, when confronted with the issue of torture, the quickest to bend to facile and often specious appeals to national security.

No one in America, of course, attempts to argue that torture for the sake of torture is justifiable, as the Romans did in Jesus' day, and as the worst contemporary dictators do in ours. Such a position is too easily rebuked. Instead, when we loudly condemn torture as immoral, we hear from torture's defenders variations on the following two themes: (1) that torture is wrong, but that American "enhanced interrogation practices" aren't torture, no matter how severe; or, (2) that torture is wrong, but necessary for the sake of national security, and this necessity morally outweighs the wrongness of the act itself.

When confronted with assertions like these, there is simply not much that our moral arguments can do. In both cases, torture's defenders have thoroughly defanged our moral attack by admitting that torture is immoral, while simultaneously justifying our practices of detainee treatment. Consider the first defense: "We don't torture." The government agrees with our moral condemnation but declares by fiat that what we do to detainees isn't the thing we condemn. And in the second defense, torture and national security are placed on a moral balance and security is simply found to be more worthy.

So, when we shout "torture is wrong," they are coolly able to reply, "We thoroughly agree, and by the way, be so kind as to pass us that waterboard." For moral values to be important to the resolution of a policy dispute, we must have a debate about what right and wrong means to the issue—as we do with abortion, same-sex marriage, stem cell research, assisted suicide, etc. With the issue of torture, our opponents have undone us with their agreement, their nonresistance.

Of course, we all know that agreement about the immorality of torture is not really agreement when it is justified in these two ways: that what we do isn't torture, or that it's morally necessary for security. When we hear these responses, we counter with questions that sharpen the point: How do you define torture? And, can torture truly be employed in the interest of national security? These questions are where the debate is really at. But consider them closely for a moment; such questions are *not* questions about morality, about right and wrong. No. These are questions about truth. And until the national conversation about torture shifts its center and begins to revolve around issues of truth and untruth, veracity and deceit, I fear we will be stuck in the same fruitless, frustrated agreement in which we presently find ourselves.

With this in mind, it's instructive to note that one of the New Testament's most profound conversations about the topic of truth is also a story of torture. I'm referring, of course, to John 18, Jesus' famous exchange with Pilate. Jesus answered [Pilate]: "You are right in saying I am a king. In fact, for this reason I was born, and for this I came into the world, to testify to the truth. Everyone on the side of truth listens to me."

"What is truth?" Pilate asked.

"What is truth?" Does Pilate ask it breezily—as if to dismiss as insignificant the strange testimony, the *raison d'etre*, of this odd Jew standing before him? Or does he ask it wearily, as would a world-weary politician who realizes appearances are everything in the game of empires?

In any case, it would seem that he asks his question rhetorically, not expecting an answer, given his immediate willingness to hand Jesus over to torture by flogging. Pilate is a politician who knows full well that truth will have little to do with what happens next, because the mob outside his gates wants the death of the one standing before him. It is the way of the fallen world that truth is often lynched by those willing and able simply to shout it down with cries of "Crucify, crucify!"

In a situation like this, truth is a luxury Pilate can't afford. And this tells us something of what Pilate thinks about truth. It exists, certainly— a thing is true or not. But when it comes to Pilate's politics, the truth of a thing is largely irrelevant to the outcome. To Pilate, the truth is incidental. If, as Henry Kissinger purportedly said, something "has the added benefit of being true," terrific. But if political expediency is not served by the truth, then truth will become a casualty of necessity. This is the case, that is, if you believe only in a little-t truth. But what if we're dealing with big-T Truth? What if Truth itself is a thing? What if Truth has a name, a face, a personality? What if Truth has a will? What if Truth refuses to be ignored or misportrayed?

Many will have heard the East Indian legend about the blind men who, gathering around an elephant, say that the elephant is like different things. The man by its leg says an elephant is like a tree, the man by its tusk says it is like a spear, the man by its tail, a rope, and so on. The moral of the story is supposed to be that truth is relative, and depends upon perception and location. This observation isn't entirely without merit. But what goes unspoken in this story is that the elephant in question must surely be dead. Because if the elephant is alive—if Truth is a living being—it matters far less what the blind men think about the elephant they are manhandling than it does what the elephant thinks of them.

It isn't clear whether Pilate even believes there is such a thing as big-T Truth. But if he even believes that the elephant exists, so to speak, he surely also believes that it is dead and harmless. Otherwise he would not—could not—have been so indifferent and world-weary about his own rhetorical question, "What is truth?" He could not have been so willing to place political expediency over the truth of the matter if he believed Truth was a thing unto itself, a living and likely angry elephant. And clearly he could not have been so cavalier about Truth if he had recognized that Truth in human flesh stood before him to be condemned or set free.

If big-T Truth does not exist, then we have no final responsibility for the lies we tell. If you can cover something up, you can get away with it. History may be written by the victors to reflect positively on them, and when all who remember the events have gone to the grave, there will be nothing left but the official lie, and the lie will become the truth we all believe, with no voice raised to cry it down. This is the case if truth is not itself a thing. But if Truth exists to itself—if Truth is a thing—then our lies do not go unnoticed. If Truth is itself a thing, then all deceit is an offense to it. And even if nobody else gainsays our deceit, big-T Truth sees and remembers.

More to the point: if Truth itself is a thing, and God is in fact Truth, then the lies we tell are not offenses to be given lightly. Because then the Truth we have offended is not some passive, heavenly ideal, some moral abstract. No, if God is Truth, then the Truth we offend is a Truth that comes looking for us. The Truth we offend is the one who created the world in truth and will judge it truly at the end of history. This is what it means to say that the triune God—Father, Son, and Holy Spirit—is Truth: God the son testifies in perfect truthfulness, by the power of the holy spirit, to God the father, who is Truth. In the Trinity, we see Truth truly known: Truth testifying truthfully to Truth, or Truth's true recognition of itself. That is, in Jesus' words and person we have a perfect representation—the Truth—of the God who, as creator, established the reality upon which all truth is based. This is why Jesus says that he is the "way and truth and life"; it is why Paul says of Christ that he is the image of the invisible God; it is why the author of Hebrews calls Jesus "the *exact representation* of God's very being." Jesus Christ, the man Pilate cavalierly dismissed, is the true picture of Truth itself. And the reason that such Truth should have caused Pilate to quake in fear is that it is not some passive object, a dusty implement that may equally be employed or not depending upon the situation. No, when we recognize that the triune God is Truth, we see that Truth is an active, willful, unstoppable force that confronts each of us at every moment.

The way Pilate imagines it, Truth is eminently ignorable: what mattered to him was not truth but practicality, results, getting things done, even by lies and deceit. But Truth as a man—Truth with a capital J, so to speak—will not be ignored, cannot be pacified or tranquilized, cannot be pushed aside without consequence. What Pilate didn't recognize was that Truth *always* pushes back. When Pilate stood before the Truth incarnate and rhetorically asked, "What is truth?" as he prepared to crucify the Truth, Pilate did not recognize that his situation was like that of a man who, standing in the path of a raging conflagration, idly remarks, "What is fire?"; or like that of a man who, falling from a great height, casually reflects, "What is gravity?"

Truth has a personality. Truth has power. In Jesus, Truth has a *name*. And it—no, *he*—will not forever tolerate being dishonored by deception. So Pilate sent the man who was himself the resurrection and the life, who was sinless before God, who was the reflection of God's glory, to die a sinner's humiliating death on the cross. But the death that is the true consequence of sin for the rest of us was for this man a lie. And the period that lie attempted to place at the end of that man's story was brushed aside by God as easily as that stone covering his tomb. In the resurrection, God says: This story can never be stopped, for this is a story of life and a world without end. And the true speech of God about Truth—*He lives!*—could not be overcome by Pilate's indifferent lie, no matter how loud the cries to crucify.

We find our rebuttal to the defenders of torture in our proclamation that Truth is a living and terrible and awesome God. In the face of this active Truth, torture's champions simply cannot stand. Consider first the argument that the United States categorically does not torture: that whatever we do is, by definition, not an act of torture, no matter how horrific it is. This defense employs such twisted logic that it can excuse waterboarding as "enhanced interrogation," rather than torture, even though we ourselves prosecuted a Japanese soldier for waterboarding an American civilian in World War II. The solidity of such a defense requires a Pilate-like conception of truth: that is, a dead and absent object, to be employed or ignored or manipulated according to political expediency. Only if truth is as Pilate believed it to be could we accept such a brazen assertion of truth's utter relativity, wherein torture is defined not by some external, objective judgment—which, admittedly, we must always interpret—but rather that we would define the moral category of torture by what America does or does not do.

Imagine a child arguing with his parent that he ought not to be spanked for stealing his sibling's toy, even though he roundly supported such punishment when it was his sibling doing the stealing. "Mother, when Jimmy took my action figure, that was stealing. But as everyone knows, *I* don't steal. When I took Jimmy's truck, it was enhanced vehicular borrowing." We who know how poorly such defenses would fare in our own homes can readily envision how much worse they will do in the celestial courts before God our heavenly father. To say that "we do not torture" when the evidence is so patently to the contrary, and thus to seek to define truth by our own actions instead of its divine standard, is effectively to call God dead and irrelevant. Now, if he were dead and irrelevant, this would be an inoffensive crime. But those of us who know that God is very much alive and relevant, know that a lie about Truth itself is a blasphemy of God's very name. And the name of the lord, the true verbal representation of God's very self, is not a matter he takes lightly—having dedicated his third commandment to that very topic.

Those in government, therefore, should tread carefully in their pronunciation about the truth of torture. There is far more at stake than how well their words will play with the chattering class of pundits. Policymakers who say they are believers—who hold that Truth has a face and a name and a memory and a *will*—should be cautious. Their cavalier remarks may gain them political points, but they make a mockery of one who will not indefinitely suffer it, who will repay, and whose judgment is terrible and timeless. It is one thing for people like you and me to call out our government's lies where we find them—but we ourselves have unclean lips. It is quite another to say that such lies are denounced by the one whose tongue is a two-edged sword "capable of dividing soul and spirit, joints and marrow," which is as able "to judge the thoughts and intentions of the heart" as it is to strike down all the nations of the earth. Of course, if our public servants believe, like Pilate, that truth is but one instrument in the toolbox of political spin, no more superior to deceit than a screwdriver might be said to be superior to a hammer, then by their own standards they have nothing to worry about.

But this defense of torture—the simple counter-assertion that we do not do it—is only one defense and it is by far the most readily rebuked as a simple act of untruth. The second defense—that the moral *gain* of national security outweighs the moral *cost* of committing torture—appears at face value to be honest, and almost brutally so. This defense rightly recognizes both the wrongness of torture and the goodness of security. Where does an active and seeking, big-T Truth enter into this picture?

The untruth of this defense occurs at a much more fundamental level, requiring that we believe two simultaneous lies. First, it asks us to believe that human beings are *less* than God created us to be, and second, it asks us to believe that the power and purpose of government is *greater* than God has ordained it to be. And this is a far more profound deception than the simple deceit of saying we do not torture when we surely do. To say that what we do is categorically not torture is like saying "black is white" or "up is down." But to defend torture by making human beings less and governments more is like saying, "black is not black" and "up is not up." For us to believe that torture can ever be justifiable, we must first pretend that an individual—the one who is tortured—is less than the image-bearer of God that the Genesis creation account tells us each person is. To be made in the image of God, as God created us, means that all of us are vessels of something greater than ourselves. We can and regularly do dishonor and obscure this image with our sinful behavior. But no matter how despicable our actions—and if someone is guilty of terrorism, then those actions are despicable indeed—we cannot stop bearing this image. We can no more cast God's image away from us than we can discard our brain, our heart, our lungs. What this image of God means for how we treat each other is that another human being can never be regarded simply as an object or a means to an end. This is the religious basis for modern human rights: that the human person bears the inalienable mark of God and must be accorded with a basic dignity that that image commands. And yet the practice of torture flatly requires that we deny God's image in the tortured person: torture treats its victims as if they do not bear the inherent dignity that God saw fit to give them. God is the lord of life: he created life, he loves it, and he intends it for good. So we can see how prohibited it must be for anyone intentionally to consume another human being's life in torment, even temporarily. We can see that to do so is to enact blasphemy: transforming the good gift of God into a manifestation of evil, inflicting pain on another's body as if God had not deigned to make that body—just as much as the body of the torturer—a mirror of his own image.

The fact of our being image-bearers of God does not, let's note, establish some unattainable ethical standard. There are ways to govern, imprison, war against, and even kill each other that do not fundamentally violate the created image of God in one another. This doesn't mean that such actions are never sinful; they certainly can be. But they do not necessarily require that the person become simply an object, a means to another end. There is no way to torture a body and mind, however, while simultaneously acknowledging the image of God in it. Torture is thus an enacted lie about God and the nature of his creation. Whereas he perceived what he had made and called it "very good," when we torture we look at what God has made and call it worthless, fit only for pain, an object for our own mortal purposes.

The second lie we must believe in order to buy the national security argument is that the purposes and power of human government are vastly more than God has ordained them to be. The paramount passage for understanding this truth is Romans 13:1–7. These verses show that God's purpose for governmental power is the flourishing of good, the punishment of wrong deeds, and the maintenance of basic order. Toward this end, Paul writes, the one in authority "does not bear the sword for nothing," and "everyone must submit himself to the governing authorities, for there is no authority except that which God has established."

Wrongheaded interpretations of this passage seeking to maximize governmental authority have been employed by history's worst regimes in order to give divine sanction to their oppression. But a true reading of this passage reveals that God has a relatively humble purpose for the exercise of violent force by governments: namely, to maintain a basic order where life can ultimately flourish. Interpreted most narrowly, "the sword" that is not wielded in vain refers to a police authority. Interpreted most broadly, it is the authority to inflict capital punishment and to conduct war. (We should note that God's granting the authority to war and kill does not also convey the corollary that he is pleased by such activities.) But this passage cannot be interpreted in a complete maximalist sense, in which the exercise of violence—no matter the type or degree—is absolutely justified simply by the governmental office of the person wielding the sword. God does not endorse tyranny. Governmental violence is justified only by the purpose for which God has vested the authority to inflict it. Any exercise of violence that violates that purpose, therefore, is to bend toward evil that which God has given for good. But, some might say, isn't torture therefore justifiable by the state's authority of the sword: a temporary use of force for the lasting good of the whole nation? Far from it. Torture is a perversion of governmental authority because it offends the principle upon which the authority is granted. Torture takes life that God has given and turns it into hell.

Consider the example of the ancient Israelites, who were given the historically unique authority and mandate to destroy completely their pagan enemies in the wars of the lord. This was for the purpose of creating Israel as a holy people, through which salvation and life would come to the entire world. Yet even in God's instructions that the Israelites not leave anything alive in the lands that they conquered—horrifying and even incomprehensible to contemporary ears—we also see the command not to cut down fruit trees to build siege engines. The reason? "Fruit trees are for the benefit of humankind" (Deuteronomy 20:19). Surely from a tactical level it would have been easier to make siege weapons from any kind of tree. Yet even in the midst of total war, God's purpose that life might continue out of death meant that these life-giving trees could not be used for the purpose of killing.

Destruction is sometimes necessary and permissible for the sake of maintaining life. But violating the very principle of life is never allowed, and this is precisely what we do when we torture, due to the violation of the *imago dei*. God does not allow us to inflict hell for our own purposes. For the state to torture is to cause the intentional desecration of the very human life it is ordained to protect. Just as an athlete who cheats in competition can never truly win, having violated the very terms of the sport, neither can a nation employ in the name of protecting human flourishing means like torture that violate the interest for which the authority to employ violence is given in the first place. Anything the government does should be for the welfare of its citizens, but a government does not have license to do anything in the name of its citizens' welfare.

Some practices, like torture, exceed the authority granted to governments by God. To endorse torture is to perpetuate the untruth that the nation is more than God has made it to be. Christians who believe in the eternal punishment of the unrighteous believe this to be merited by the offense done to God's holiness. But no interest of the state—not even security—is anywhere near commensurate with God's holiness. Romans 13:1 prohibits individual rebellion against the state, based on the principle that no individual's interests are significant enough to overturn the order that God has established for the benefit of all. But as it is between the individual and the state, so too is it between the state and God. Human government is simply not important enough to justify the violation of God's law.

Because of these two truths, the moral calculus of torture's defenders fails to add up. They make human life worth less and the government worth more than God would have either to be; thus confusing their negative and positive signs, they arrive at a sum that is the inverse of the truth. And because the Truth that is violated is the Truth whose image humans bear, as well as the Truth who put government in place for human well-being, this is not a minor miscalculation. Those of us who seek to live according to that Truth, as his disciples, cannot simply agree to disagree with those who would permit our government to torture. Nor can we allow ourselves to be intimidated by the godless pontificators who claim the name of the lord in one breath, and then with another denigrate the crown of his creation and idolize the nations that sit under his feet—and all in the name of patriotism. Security obtained at the cost of a lie against God and his creation is a fleeting security indeed. Not for nothing does Revelation set "all liars" at the climax of the list of those whose place is the lake of burning sulfur.

Simply put, we cannot allow our government to torture and thus sin against the God we serve. I hope our witness on this account will be clear and honest. I hope we will be firm and unyielding in our conviction that, as Paul writes, "we cannot do anything against the truth, but only for the truth." This conviction is a sure one: trust that Truth is not some still, defenseless object, but a man to whom all power in heaven and on earth has been given—and who, as Truth, will be vindicated in the end.

145

7

★

The Religious Roots of Human Rights

Glen H. Stassen

The committee asked me to address the religious roots of human rights, because they hope we will spread a deeper ethic that gives us solid ground on torture and on other important parts of our lives. We are not only Evangelicals Against Torture; we are Evangelicals for Human Rights. So my purpose is to try to be helpful for teaching and spreading human rights more broadly as the basis for a deeper ethic that stops torture and other injustices too. What this whole experience with the corruption of our nation's and many churches' morality says to us is that we deeply need better ethics.

Human rights are about caring. David Gushee wrote *Righteous Gentiles of the Holocaust* and "Why Torture is Always Wrong" not because he is a Jew, not because he has been tortured, not because he is pushing simply for his own rights, but because he cares—for Jews and other defenseless victims of evil, of injustice. And he cares about growing a next generation and a nation that cares. We all are here because we care.

The identifying feature of human rights is that when we focus on human rights, they call our attention to those whose rights are being violated. They call us to care for the victims. As Cathleen Kaveny said, in Catholic teaching it is based on "Love your neighbor as yourself"—and on human dignity. Furthermore, human rights embody that caring and justice in law and custom as well as in persons and churches. The defenseless need the protection of justice, law, and custom.

In all my experience of those who participated in the civil rights movement in North Carolina and Kentucky, and those who successfully brought about the Revolution of the Candles in the former East Germany, toppling the terrible dictator Erich Honecker and the Berlin Wall, and the struggle for human rights for retarded persons in Kentucky, and my study of Barth and Bonhoeffer affirming human rights and leading opposition to Hitler's horrible violations of human rights, I have never heard anyone talk selfishly about "my individual rights." They were concerned about injustice to the relatively defenseless. It was the defenders of the unjust status quo and unequal privileges who said that Christians should not push for human rights because human rights are selfish. Some of us still hear echoes of that ideology of privilege even from friends who do not realize how that ideology has influenced them unawares.

Human rights have grounding in Islam, Buddhism, and other religions in addition to Judaism and Christianity, as you may read in books by Swidler, Sachedina, and Evans.[196] I have worked extensively with Muslim and Jewish scholars to develop just peacemaking as the new paradigm for the ethics of peace and war. We are publishing books and a monograph together working for just peacemaking, including the practice of advocating human rights, based on all three of our faith traditions.[197] I am very pleased that Graham Walker will fill in a bit of what I do not have the space to develop here—attention to growing support for human rights in other faith traditions. But within my limits here, my important task is to show something about Christian grounding for human rights. And historically, there is special reason for Baptists to claim our heritage of human rights.

The Free-Church Baptist Origin. The historically first full concept of human rights was developed and articulated as early as the 1640s, during the free-church struggle for the right of religious liberty in Puritan England, by the Baptist Richard Overton. Overton was one of those very first Baptists who, with John Smyth, founder of the first Baptists, joined the Waterlander Mennonite church in Holland in 1615, where they had fled from religious persecution. Later Overton returned to England and general Baptist membership.[198] He advocated human rights first in his satire, *The Arraignment of Mr. Persecution*, in 1645. His arguments are based on an extensive knowledge of the New Testament. He also argues from natural law and from historical experience of religious persecution by a state church as himself a part of a persecuted minority, the Baptists and Mennonites. He argues that religious persecution causes wars, divisions, bloodshed, and hypocrisy. Most wars, and especially the Thirty Years' War that killed one-third of the people of Germany, were fought over which religion would dominate and exclude the other. Overton understood German as well as Latin, and it seems he may have experienced some of the Thirty Years' War firsthand, which greatly intensified his caring for the victims of the war. In his *Arraignment of Mr. Persecution*, eight of the ten accusers against religious persecution speak of the wars and bloodshed it causes. The right to religious liberty would be a dramatic peacemaking initiative: there would be no need to fight a war to get "our" faith to control the government.

Overton was also motivated by caring for justice for the poor, based on biblical teaching and then intensified when he got to know the poor who were jailed for their debts, as he was jailed for his faith. His writing is infused with objections against a tax system that was designed to benefit the wealthy and to put disproportionate burdens on the poor and the middle class. We can empathize. Overton's human rights grew out of his caring. When he was arrested and imprisoned for printing his books and articles calling for the right to religious liberty and justice for the poor, his brave wife continued printing yet more books and pamphlets. The government authorities came to arrest her. They sought to snatch her small baby out of her hands so they could take her to jail, but she held on with so much moral strength, conviction, and caring, that they gave up. The government had sent a whole group of police to arrest her, but they were so impressed with her witness that they too refused to arrest her. Finally they sent a group of hangmen, who by their profession of killing alleged criminals had become callous and uncaring enough to carry out the arrest. They picked her and her baby up bodily, brought them out in the street, tied them to the back of a horse-drawn wagon, and dragged them to jail through the streets. Overton published the story of her courageous and strong witness with dramatic details, so the people would know this dramatically uncaring injustice and be moved to care for the victims.[199]

Overton's comprehensive doctrine of human rights as belonging to all persons—including Protestants, Catholics, Jews, and Muslims—was born fully developed, comprehensive even by present-day standards. It included three major categories of rights: (1) *religious liberty and civil liberty:* freedom from coercion in religion, from governmental establishment of religion, and from taxation for religion; freedom of the press; the right not to be arbitrarily arrested or forced to incriminate oneself; the right to speedy trial; the right to understand the law in one's own language; equality before the law; and the right of prisoners not to be starved, tortured, or extorted; (2) *basic needs and economic rights:* the right not to be imprisoned for debt; the right to trade internationally without restrictions by monopolies; the right to a free education for everyone; the right to housing and care for poor orphans, the widowed, the aged, and the handicapped; and the right of the poor to their portion of land; and (3) *rights of participation* in choosing a government that is responsive to the people and the common good; the right to vote and participate in government regardless of one's beliefs; and the right to petition parliament for justice.

So Overton was explicit on the right of prisoners not to be starved or tortured. He describes the various instruments of torture used by the authoritarian persecutors of religious minorities in dramatic detail. He includes the following verse: "To see such millions frying in the fire / While this stern tyrant gnashed his teeth with ire, / The skins of saints, their tongues, their eyes and ears / Were at sale with floods of brinish tears."

Caring for Those Whose Voices Need Hearing. William O'Neill, S.J., writes that the language of human rights focuses our attention on atrocities and crimes against humanity, as in the unfolding tragedy of the Sudan, Somalia, and the Democratic Republic of Congo.

In victims' testimony, the rhetoric of rights becomes a mouth to tell of suffering. In South Africa, the Truth and Reconciliation Commission was charged to promote "unity and reconciliation by providing for the investigation and full disclosure of gross violations of human rights committed in the past." The first committee that began hearings was the "human rights violations committee.... Rights served not only in narratively documenting atrocity, but in interweaving 'the truth of wounded memories,' in Judge Ismail Mahomed's words, with 'social truth, the truth of experience that is established through interaction, discussion and debate.'"[200]

O'Neill helps us realize the narrative that carries the meaning of human rights for millions of persons who have struggled as victims, and other millions who have struggled to help them prevent or heal their victimhood, is no thin Enlightenment narrative; it is a narrative of caring embodied in law and custom as well as in persons and churches.

Jesus' Caring for Four Types of Injustice. David Gushee's study of those Gentiles who acted to rescue Jews from the Nazis at risk to their own lives, in his book, *Righteous Gentiles of the Holocaust*, says some described their motivation with the language of human rights, and others with the language of caring or empathy. I want to bring these motivations together, and contend that we should define human rights in terms of caring.

Jesus cared for people. He cared for lepers, for prostitutes, for tax collectors, for those who needed healing, for women, for those who were outcasts. He cared with so much compassion that he confronted the authorities over the wrongs they were doing. Many people miss this. They think the authorities were the Romans. But the day-by-day authorities were the high priests and the wealthy and the Sadducees, and their somewhat supporters, the Pharisees and scribes who taught and enforced the moral codes. In our book, *Kingdom Ethics*, David Gushee and I count thirty-seven times in the Synoptic Gospels, not including parallels, when Jesus confronted them for their injustice to the relatively powerless.[201]

Jesus confronted them because he cared for people being violated. He confronted them over four types of injustice. Each type of injustice corresponds with a basic set of human rights as they have since developed: (1) The injustice of greed that deprives the poor of basic needs of life. Human rights emphasize the positive right to life as having the basics needed to pursue a life's calling. (2) The injustice of exclusion from community. Human rights emphasize the human right to participation in community. (3) The injustice of domination by power and authoritarianism. Human rights emphasize the rights to liberty and to the means to check and balance unjust authority. (4) The injustice of violence. Human rights emphasize the right to life.

These are the same four types of injustice the prophet Isaiah focused on. They are not four arbitrary types of injustice; they are deeply grounded in the prophetic tradition of God's own caring for the powerless and the deprived and the oppressed. They are based in God's caring, and in God's own realism about who needs standing up for in a world of greed, oppression, domination, exclusion, and violence—a world of sin.

But we all sin. So do nations sin. The temptation to sin is greater the more powerful you are, and our nation is very powerful. So we badly need the check and balance of enough humility to listen to other nations, to restore international cooperation, to respect international law. It was when Cheney and Rumsfeld lifted the protection of the Geneva Convention from those defenseless prisoners that the doors were opened to all this violence and torture and terrorizing of prisoners. Torture is terrorism. It is violence against disarmed and defenseless people for the purpose of intimidation and revenge. Prisoners have been deprived of all defenses except the law. Without the protection of the treaty—the Geneva Convention, which is the law of our land—and located in Guantánamo where there is no protection of either US or Cuban law, the prisoners were in a black hole, defenseless, subject to terrible violation. I invite everyone here to go to our Web site for the Matthew5Project.org, and use it to organize discussion groups and individual signings, to spread the word of the need of this nation to return to international cooperation: www.matthew5project.org.

In response to my invitation, during the question-and-answer session, Bonnie Tamres-Moore of www.opposetorture.org gave us essential information that we all need. The Geneva Convention, a treaty the United States has ratified and therefore is the law of our land, has four sets of provisions for different categories of prisoners. The fourth category is for nonmilitary persons who have been captured, so the treaty does not apply only to soldiers. "Common article three" is repeated in all four categories. It rules out cruel and degrading treatment of any person.

As the US Supreme Court later declared, it was illegal for the president to lift the protection of the Geneva Convention from prisoners.

Incorporating Objections. An ethic is stronger and more healing if it can incorporate objections from its opponents. I will be more helpful for teaching human rights as the basis for a deeper ethic that stops torture if I deal with some objectors against human rights.

Stanley Hauerwas is in reaction against the Enlightenment, and he writes as if human rights were invented by the Enlightenment. So he sees rights as only about the ideology of possessive individualism—noninterference in others' private freedom, and insisting on my own private freedom.[202]

This misses the core of human rights as caring for persons, especially persons who need defending against violation of their rights. In defense of Stanley Hauerwas, a basically caring person, I know one place where I see him come close to affirming human rights. It is when he discusses handicapped children and mentally retarded children.[203] He writes approvingly, caringly, of their parents who definitely care for them. "Parents of handicapped children can report example after example of how they have had to struggle to secure even the most minimal of care for their children." And: "Parents of retarded or multiple-handicapped children learn from the beginning they must fight for their children.... They must learn to fight to establish and create the kind of care their children rightly deserve." He quotes Gliedman and Roth: "By failing to think through the implications of the 'civil rights lens' for the child, we had unwittingly committed ourselves to making the same kinds of mistakes about disability that were made about other groups of disadvantaged children a generation ago." Their parents know by very personal experience that their children need someone to defend their rights. They rightly speak of the rights of their children. Hauerwas notes that the US Conference of Catholic Bishops affirms "Christians' obligation to seek with handicapped people justice in a wider society." Churches "will actively work to make the rights of handicapped people real in the fabric of modern society." Yet he writes as if the battle for the rights of your child can be reduced to thinking all children should be treated alike. I have battled for the rights of my handicapped son, and believe me, I surely do not think Michael, Bill, and David should have been treated alike. Each had and still has different needs. And each has rights—including David. Hauerwas writes as if "blacks' struggle for civil rights" meant "they must forget what it means to be black." I participated very extensively in the struggle for civil rights in Virginia, North Carolina, and Kentucky, and I say with strong conviction that, in that struggle, many blacks (and whites too) learned more deeply and more meaningfully important dimensions of what it means to be black in the United States. I've been dialoging with Stanley, and he may be coming around some. He now says he does not have a problem "with rights understood as the naming of corresponding duties."

I have a handicapped son. My wife is a pediatrics nurse, and many times my son David has needed her care. I have had to intervene with authorities for his rights, but not only for the rights of our own son. I persuaded my own church to support a school of hope for retarded adults, and the school of hope has done wonderful things for them. These retarded adults, who never were given the opportunity to go to school before, have learned to do simple reading, simple arithmetic, self-care, to have a social life with other adults in the school, and earn a small income in a sheltered workshop doing repetitive work that would have bored you and me. They were overjoyed and enormously grateful. I served on the board of the county association for retarded persons. We sued the state of Kentucky for the right of handicapped children to receive the same education as other children—which Kentucky was not providing. Thousands of children who were being deprived of their right to an education now have their human right to education. This required legal action for a basic human right to education, not just individual caring for our son David. And it was an act of caring.

Now our son David, who is handicapped but definitely not retarded, translates theological books from German to English. We care for our son and for other children worldwide whose human rights are not being respected. It's not just about an ideology of possessive individualism or simple equality. It's about caring for God's children, whom God cares for. In my experiences with David's teachers at Perkins School for the Blind and Kentucky School for the Blind, and the parents and board members of Madison County Association for Retarded Persons, I have never experienced anyone talking about selfish, individual rights; it was always about rights of the relatively defenseless.

Let me incorporate objections from Joan and Oliver O'Donovan, who oppose human rights. I just lectured this weekend at Cambridge University and Monday at Exeter University. There Oliver O'Donovan forcefully objected—in fact passionately interrupted—my effort to answer his attack peacefully. I was explaining that Jesus teaches caring justice. Therefore human rights are a key practice of just peacemaking. He objected that sometimes people make war in the name of human rights. I replied, peacefully, that we who authored the just peacemaking ethic confronted that danger explicitly. That is why we advocate human rights as a practice that works patiently for peace, not an absolute ideal to make war over. Our book, *Just Peacemaking*,[204] says democracy should be spread by building a worldwide culture of human rights, not by making war. Trying to spread democracy by making war leads to violations of the right to life, to violent recriminations in the subsequent culture, and to curtailing human rights to liberty—which always happens in wartime—as we have seen. I pointed out that President Bush did not make the Iraq War in the name of human rights. His policy attacked the human rights of prisoners. In the book, *Just Peacemaking*, we point out that the worldwide pressure for human rights has prodded most Latin American countries, and many Asian and Central European countries, to change from dictatorships to democracies or democracies-in-process. And in the whole twentieth century, no democracy with human rights has made war against another democracy with human rights. The empirical evidence is as clear as social science evidence can ever be: spreading democracy by supporting human rights reduces the number of wars. That is a powerful additional reason to support human rights.

The second O'Donovan objection does have empirical grounding, and we should seriously take it into account. It is that trickle-down ideology uses human rights to focus only on property rights and freedom from interference.[205] But ideologies of greed misuse almost everything to further their power-drive. Human rights in Richard Overton, in Catholic social teaching, and in official Protestant teaching on human rights systematically include economic rights and community rights and are a protest against that distortion. Let us teach full and comprehensive human rights, including rights to basic economic needs and rights to participation in community, as we keep building the worldwide drive for human rights. Anything less would betray biblical authority and the way of Jesus.

The third objection comes from Joan Lockwood O'Donovan's contention that human rights were first advocated in germinal form by William Ockham in the fourteenth century and then by the Enlightenment, both on secular grounds. So she contends, "The modern tradition of natural rights.... is a further phase of theological naturalism."[206] She acknowledges that Pope Pius XI's *Quadragesimo Anno* speaks of "the dignity and freedom of individuals," and the rights of labor, family, and church. Catholic scholar Jacques Maritain responded to the political barbarism and tyranny of fascism and the better justice of liberal democracy by advocating "natural rights, democratic culture, and individual freedom of choice. Not only human obligations, but human rights are implied in natural law," including "the longer-standing human, civil and religious rights (to life, personal liberty, pursuit of perfection, property, freedom of association, speech, religious belief and practice and equality before the law), the 'civic' right of full political participation, and the extensive catalogue of social rights that we now take for granted (e.g., to humane employment, material security, medical care, suitable education, and cultural involvement)," and "the equal right of individuals to practice the religion of their choice." Pope John XXIII affirmed and internationalized this understanding, emphasizing that "the universal common good" requires international law and worldwide public authorities that have as their "fundamental objective the recognition, respect, safeguarding and promotion of the rights of the human person." Pope John Paul II also "retains the language of natural rights for articulating 'the common good' of civil society."[207] This would seem to be a church-based and theological affirmation of human rights.

She argues, however, that Catholic theologians shifted from an Augustinian *church*-based human good to an Aristotelian *state*-based human good and, eventually, to support for liberal democracy. This calls on civil society, and not only the church, to work for human rights.[208] It brings about what she calls an Enlightenment secularization and property-rights focus. So she sweeps Catholic developments of the last 100 years out of consideration.

Nicholas Wolterstorff has published a refutation of Joan Lockwood O'Donovan's contention that the medieval origin is Ockham in the fourteenth century. In his recent book, *Justice: Rights and Wrongs*, Wolterstorff traces the concept of human rights from the Decretists of the twelfth century back to the early church fathers, and then to the Old Testament. He concludes: "The evidence against [Lockwood O'Donovan's] narrative and this claim is as decisive as evidence in intellectual history ever gets. Ockham did not invent the idea of natural rights, nor did his nominalism have anything to do with his employment of the idea; neither did the seventeenth-century theorists of political liberalism invent the idea." It was based on theological grounds, not secular ones.[209]

If you want more extensive biblical grounding for human rights, I recommend Christopher Marshall's *Crowned with Glory and Honor*.[210] I have shown in my *Just Peacemaking: Transforming Initiatives*[211] that the full doctrine of human rights came prior to the Enlightenment in Richard Overton; it did not originate with the later Enlightenment. O'Donovan rejects this historical reality by writing that the seventeenth-century free-church movement for religious liberty and congregational church government is perfectionist and sectarian, and therefore "provides no ecclesiological model for an inclusive, democratic polity." Thus she sweeps our Baptist movement out of her history. Ironically, what that leaves is the very Enlightenment that she despises. Her statement is hardly true; Overton led the Leveller movement, was its best writer, pushing effectively for democracy, and is hardly an irrelevant sectarian. From this free-church movement we get religious liberty, human rights, separation of church and state, and democracy. An ethical position that incorporates what truth it can find in rival positions is both stronger and more healing than one that closes its ears and eyes to them, because it takes more truth into account and brings more persons together. Such respect for others is mandated by Jesus' command to love our enemies, all those on whom God shines sun and rains rain.

To respond to O'Donovan's charge, we need to recover our history that human rights are our baby, coming from the struggle for the right to religious liberty well before the Enlightenment. Each of us needs to build it on the basis of our own faith. I'm a Baptist, and I'm claiming our Baptist role in that birth through Baptist Richard Overton, and this conference at Mercer University is a terrific step in doing that!

We need to make clear that the engine pulling for human rights is not only the government, but also churches. The battle for religious liberty is surely being waged by many church groups, both historically and now. The battle for economic justice for the poor is surely being waged by Ron Sider and Jim Wallis and Sojourners and Rick Warren and thousands of local congregations, synagogues, and mosques as they work to feed the hungry, house the homeless, and advocate corrections in the enormous insensitivity and not caring of trickle-down economic ideology. The battle for human rights and against torture is being waged by the National Religious Campaign Against Torture, and Evangelicals for Human Rights, and this very conference, and its spreading influence.[212]

Twentieth-Century German Reaction against the Enlightenment and then Recovery of Human Rights. In the eighteenth and nineteenth centuries, Germany's culture was much influenced by French culture and was distant from British and American culture. Therefore, German churches overlooked the free-church Puritan and American developments of human rights, and thought human rights originated with the French Revolution a century later. This blocked churches and theologians from accepting human rights, and undermined the ability of churches to combat Adolf Hitler's violation of the human rights of Jews, as well as Poles, handicapped persons, homosexuals, and communists. By an overwhelming majority, church leaders and pastors distanced themselves from and criticized the tradition of human rights and Germany's effort to make democracy work in the Weimar Republic; this incapacitated them from resisting fascism and the Third Reich. Theologians Karl Barth and Dietrich Bonhoeffer were instructive exceptions: both wrote in support of human rights, and both led Christian opposition to Hitler.

160

After 1945, German churches realized the horrendous error of their reactionary turning away from human rights, and they have been leaders in the strong attention to human rights by world Christianity. German scholars Huber and Tödt, along with University of Virginia scholar William Lee Miller; historian of philosophy Richard Tuck[213]; Christian ethicists Michael Westmoreland White and I, Jesuit ethicist David Hollenbach; and Emory Law professor John Witte, correct the reactionary error. We all point out human rights came from Christian sources well before the Enlightenment. In the United States, human rights were formulated programmatically into law for the first time in the 1776 Virginia Bill of Rights, and then in the US Bill of Rights, with the push for the First Amendment and the Bill of Rights coming from Virginia Baptists and their fellow Puritan-influenced Virginian, James Madison.

After 1945, Germans had now experienced the injuries to human rights by the National Socialist and Stalinist regimes. They wrote human rights into the catalog of basic rights in the 1949 German Basic Law (their constitution). This change of position was also supported by identification of human rights with Western political-societal systems, in contrast with the injury to human rights in the Eastern European nations.

In the US civil rights movement, led by Baptist Martin Luther King, Jr., and others, many of us developed our deep loyalty to the struggle for human rights. We thereby learned to identify passionately with the struggle for human rights among other oppressed people worldwide. One of those who learned this lesson with passion was a Baptist Sunday-school teacher from an unlikely place, South Georgia, which had been known more for its strict enforcement of segregation in church and society alike. That Baptist Sunday-school teacher first spoke up for the dignity of all persons and especially the persecuted minorities in his own Baptist church, arguing against racial discrimination in the church's own practice. Later he worked for human rights as governor of Georgia. Only because he had learned and adopted this vision from the struggle for human rights could he have become a South Georgian elected to the Presidency of the United States. As president he translated his very specific Christian and church loyalties into the language of human rights and pushed for human rights worldwide. He was sometimes mocked by Northern realists, but he enacted human rights reviews into law as a criterion for US economic aid. That added additional support for Roman Catholics and other Christians pushing for human rights in Latin America and elsewhere. It was a major factor in moving every Latin American nation from what had mostly been national-security states and dictatorships, engaging in torture against dissenters, into now officially being democracies with human rights, although some have a distance yet to travel to embody human rights fully. That South Georgia president of the United States is now again a much-respected Sunday-school teacher, and I hope we all can express some appreciation for Sunday-school teacher Jimmy Carter.

I am a Midwesterner from the North Star State, Minnesota, but I want to say that I have an experiential preference for Southerners who have worked deeply through the process of respecting human rights for all persons over some Northern liberals whose commitment may be less deep, less warm and feeling, less born of deep struggle. I applaud Southerners and Baptists like Clarence Jordan, Martin Luther King, Jr., Harry Truman, Jimmy Carter, and Bill Clinton, who have worked this struggle for human rights through, deeply.

Baptists have played a major role in bringing us human rights and caring for them in deep struggle. I think we should give thanks to David Gushee and Mercer University for bringing us this conference, important for our nation. And I think it also important to remember that both Baptists who pioneered for the right to religious liberty, Richard Overton and Roger Williams, advocated that right not only for Catholics, Presbyterians, and Baptists, but also for Jews and "Turks," by which they meant Muslims. They advocated that farsighted vision four centuries ago, in the seventeenth century. So I think it highly appropriate that this Baptist university has welcomed the diverse participants it has attracted, including Jews and Muslims. Work on human rights for all is one of the best historical accomplishments of Baptists, and I urge us all to congratulate Mercer University for highlighting that historic contribution!

Protestant Theological Grounding for Human Rights. In her new book from Baylor University Press, *The Ethics of Human Rights: Contested Doctrinal and Moral Issues,* Esther Reed works to heal the rift I have identified above. She writes that we need to frame an ethic of rights explicitly in christological, pneumatological, and eschatological terms.[214] She pays special attention to Dietrich Bonhoeffer, Karl Barth, and also Richard Hooker's theological grounding for human rights.

Reed echoes Dietrich Bonhoeffer's criticism that Protestant ethics have lost their orientation for confronting questions of natural life because they have lost the concept of the natural. "The concept of the natural must be recovered from the gospel itself," christologically, pneumatologically, and eschatologically.[215] Some detractors of human rights, such as Hauerwas, would say duties come before rights, but that is because they are thinking from the perspective of the duties of one's individual self. When we think more deeply, from the perspective of the gospel of God's grace, rights come before duties, because "God gives before God demands." "Duties spring from the rights themselves.... They are intrinsic to rights."[216] Respecting the rights of natural life honors God the creator of created life.

Both Barth and Bonhoeffer describe the purpose of life as participation in the kingdom of God. Justice for others is essential to the kingdom of God. Therefore, participation in the kingdom of God and praying for the kingdom of God to come, as in the Lord's Prayer, involve us in duties to seek justice for others.

Bonhoeffer's ethic is strongly Christ-centered. He emphasizes the bodily incarnation of Jesus Christ. He writes: "Since by God's will human life on earth exists only as bodily life, the body has a right to be preserved for the sake of the whole person. Since all rights are extinguished at death, the preservation of bodily life is the very foundation of all natural rights and is therefore endowed with special importance. *The most primordial right of natural life is the protection of the body from killing, from intentional injury, and from bodily violation.*" That means all torture—bodily violation—is a fundamental violation of God's primordial will.[217]

The meaning of bodily life "never revolves around being a means to an end, but is fulfilled only by its intrinsic claim to joy." So there is a right to a dwelling, to eating and drinking, to clothing, relaxation, play, and sexuality. "The first right of natural life is the protection of bodily life from arbitrary killing."[218] And then immediately Bonhoeffer discusses the right to life, against the practice of euthanasia. What he has in mind is the Nazis' killing innocent life and practicing euthanasia against handicapped people, and against Jews.

Let us be very clear that Bonhoeffer's support for human life is not about asserting "my rights" individualistically and possessively, but about standing up for those whose rights are being violated. Human rights focus our attention on people who are victims of injustice; they focus our attention on compassion for the defenseless.

Reed commends Jewish scholar "[David] Novak's magnificent study *Covenantal Rights.*" He "takes us quickly to the heart of the matter from a Jewish perspective": What is central is God, God's creating all persons in the image of God, God's command to care, and not an abstract Aristotelian concept of "the good" that is then used to deny human rights. Aristotle absolutizes "the good," and makes it central instead of God. Working in a biblical and Hebraic tradition, we must do better. "MacIntyre's neo-Aristotelian naturalism is thus not reason enough for Christian ethics to shun rights discourse." Far better is to commit ourselves to the kind of rights that faith in the gospel supports.

"Personhood before the law is recognized in Christian ethics because the image of God in every living person is the personal representation of the true and living God." Every person is an addressee of divine command, and God himself has given to humankind the responsibility for the maintenance of justice. Murder and failure to respect the *imago dei* in others are an affront to the sovereignty of God, as well as an attack on human life.[219] So Reed commends a christological ethic based on God's love for all humankind revealed in Jesus Christ. She points out elsewhere that Nicholas Wolterstorff brings to speech "a biblically-informed ontology of rights characterized by the compassion implied in Christ's evangelical command.... The sheer fact of being human—which for Wolterstorff means having the relational property of being loved by

God—entitles one to certain life-goods. His account of inherent rights is a way of representing the great worth of every human person loved by God."[220]

Therefore it was an egregious violation of God's command, and of God as creator, when President George W. Bush declared in a February 2002 memorandum that "detainees had no rights under the Geneva Conventions of 1949 as prisoners of war and were not subject to human rights norms under US law because they were being held outside the territory of the United States on land leased from Cuba."[221] This was declared unconstitutional by the US Supreme Court two years later. It was "condemned by many as a monstrous failure of justice." The effect of this presidential order "was to deprive them all of any rights whatsoever."[222]

Jeanie Gushee was reading Lamentations for her morning meditation this week, and she happened upon the following verses from chapter 3: "To trample underfoot any prisoner in the land, / To deprive a person of his rights in defiance of the Most High, / To pervert justice in the courts— / Such things the Lord has never approved." Wolterstorff argues that it is better to ground human rights in persons under God, who are created by God, with basic rights than in subjective duties to respect rights, because persons have those rights regardless of whether we acknowledge our duties to them. Rights are based on God as creator, on God's caring, and on persons' basic needs, rather than on our subjective attitudes. An ethic of rights based in God's caring can raise the question about conflicts with other rights God also cares about. But the right not to be tortured does not conflict with other rights. Experts in interrogation testify that getting information by developing relationships produces much more reliable information and fuller information than torture does. The right of defenseless prisoners not to be tortured is never rightly overridden by some other alleged right.

This brings us back to Jesus' teaching that God gives rain and sun to all humankind, the just and unjust alike, and therefore we are to care for all humankind. God cares for the birds of the air and the lilies of the field; how much more does God care for all humans! Because of Jesus' compassion, Jesus confronts the injustice of greed that deprives people of basic needs of life, the injustice of exclusion from community, the injustice of domination by power and authoritarianism, the injustice of violence that deprives people of bodily life and bodily integrity. This corresponds with the right to the basics needed to pursue a life's calling: the right to community, the right to liberty, and the right to life.

And because of Jesus' justice-caring compassion, the powers and authorities nailed Jesus to a cross, causing him to die by the torture of terrible pain, gradual loss of blood, dehydration, and public shaming. Crucifixion was publicly displayed torture for the purpose of state terrorism, terrorizing people so they would give up their wish to rebel against imperialistic authority. Jesus' knowing submission to this death was a measure of the extent of his caring, and a revelation of the extent of God's caring. It is the central Christian call for us all to participate in that caring of God's. "Be ye merciful, as your Father in Heaven is merciful." Human rights are for all persons, the objects of God's caring, and therefore of our caring.

Torture is state terrorism against a people, designed to intimidate them, terrorize them, in hopes this could be an effective way to frighten them away from becoming recruits to their own terrorist organizations. But it works in the opposite way. It so angers people that it increases the numbers of recruits to terrorism. The official report of the United States Department of State on international terrorism shows the astounding increase in terrorist incidents since the Iraq War and the torture of prisoners: 208 terrorist attacks caused 625 deaths in 2003; 3,168 attacks caused 1,907 deaths in 2004; 11,111 attacks caused 14,602 deaths in 2005; 14,500 attacks caused 20,745 deaths in 2006; and approximately 14,500 attacks caused 22,605 deaths in 2007.[223]

Former Secretary Rumsfeld has mused that more terrorists are being recruited than the United States is killing or capturing. The agreed assessment by the sixteen US intelligence agencies in 2006 says US actions against Arab Muslims are increasing anger and increasing terrorist incidents and training for terrorism. Torture works: it works to cause widespread anger and to create increasing numbers of terrorists.

Caring for our Nation's Heritage of Human Rights. I began by referring to David Gushee's important book, *Righteous Gentiles of the Holocaust.*

There he shows that more of the rescuers of Jews seem to have been motivated by a patriotic sense of the identity of the nation than their specific Christian commitments. Some saw the nation as for democracy and inclusion of all persons, or for human rights, or for opposition to Hitler and his fascism, or for socialism or communism. The poll released during our conference also showed more people motivated by some political or common sense factor than by their specific faith. Admittedly, many of us are reluctant to say much about the identity of the nation because we fear jingoistic nationalism. But Gushee suggests we need to talk more about a healthy kind of national identity over against an unhealthy kind.

My grandparents and their parents emigrated from Bismarck's Germany to get away from the nationalism, authoritarianism, and militarism there. In the United States, they found religious liberty and human rights. Many of us can tell a similar family story. I suggest we should do more talking about a healthy understanding of the identity of this nation as standing for human rights and not for militarism. Muslims are saying they are finding religious liberty, jobs, and some respect, even in the midst of some prejudice, here in the United States. At the annual meeting of the Muslim Public Affairs Council, one of the speakers spoke of good experience in America with human rights, and said they should commend this to fellow Muslims in other nations. Muslims have told me that if an imam in the United States advocated violence, he would be fired by the mosque. The FBI can't find a Muslim terrorist cell anywhere in the United States. Scotland Yard, and the corresponding police in Germany, France, and Spain, cannot say the same. Maybe despite all, we do have something halfway good here—a historic experience with religious liberty, and working out how to be together as different ethnic groups and different religions as one people. Let us spread this sense of the identity of the United States.

William O'Neill writes that the "shared memory" of the Truth and Reconciliation Commission is inscribed in a greater story "conducive to human rights and democratic processes." The "real reparation we want," says Albie Sachs, "lies with the constitution, the vote, with dignity, land, jobs and education." In establishing the Truth and Reconciliation Commission, the "National Unity and Reconciliation Act" of the interim constitution looked to "a future founded on the recognition of human rights." So too for Tutu, Sachs, et al., the shared memory of the Truth and Reconciliation Commission is enacted in a new constitutional regime, which in the words of the Preamble to the Constitution seeks to heal the divisions of the past and establish a society based on democratic values, social justice, and fundamental human rights; lay the foundations for a democratic and open society in which government is based on the will of the people and every citizen is equally protected by law; improve the quality of life of all citizens and free the potential of each person; and build a united and democratic South Africa able to take its rightful place as a state in the family of nations. The new South African constitution incorporates the most comprehensive set of human rights—negative and positive—of any modern constitutional regime. Popular education by governmental and non-governmental organizations, moreover, seeks to cultivate broad-based respect for, and general compliance with, a rights regime. In a characteristically African inflection of rights, Tutu thus links final success of the Truth and Reconciliation Commission's "narrative project" to fitting redress of the vast economic "disparities between the rich, mainly the whites, and the poor, mainly the blacks." For "the huge gap between the haves and the have-nots, which was largely created and maintained by racism and apartheid, this poses the greatest threat to reconciliation and stability in our country."

Let us dedicate ourselves to furthering a United States that also stands for a comprehensive set of human rights. My sorrow yesterday, when Denise Massey and Loyd Allen got us in touch with our feelings and led us in that beautiful prayer, was especially sorrow over what this torture policy has done to corrupt the soul of this nation and many of its churches. I pray that we can make a correction. I pray that we can grow a nation that stands for human rights.

RESPONSE TO GLEN H. STASSEN BY MATTHEW NORMAN

There are places where you can drive down bombed-out roads and measure the distance by the number of roadblocks through which you pass. There are places where you can live each day surrounded by people yet still live alone. There are places where your being is determined by what you consume, where society measures your worth by your ability to respond and control. And there are places that understand war to be reality, peace to be a myth, and love to be a fetish. In these places, the individual measures humanity. The pursuit of happiness and wealth is the goal. The cost of happiness and wealth is great, for it costs nothing more than our life, which is bound to the other, and God.[224] I know these places, for it is our world, and I have lived in four of its countries, on three of its continents, and I have seen war, sickness, consumerism, loneliness, and lust. I have also seen hope.

In this place, Hope rode down a bombed-out road through the numerous roadblocks between her and her destination. At one roadblock, Hope saw the soldiers pull a young woman out of the vehicle in front of her and sit her down on the side of the road. Hope knew why they had done this. The young woman stared blankly at the ground waiting; she too knew why they had pulled her aside. Hope spoke to the soldiers through the window of the car. "She must come with me. I need her to help me." The soldier looked at the young lady, then back to Hope in the car. "Why?" he demanded." "I need her to come with me," Hope replied. The soldier turned, raising his gun to the face of Hope: "Do you want to join her?" The young woman rose to her feet, walked to the window of the car, looked into the eyes of Hope, and said, "It is okay, go." Is it okay?

Dr. Glen Stassen has done a wonderful job presenting to us the religious roots of human rights. He has shown us that the idea of human rights goes much deeper than an enlightened understanding of the individual. The biblical foundation of the idea of human rights finds its roots within our basic understanding of what it means to be human. From the

Christian perspective, our wholeness in Christ, our salvation, is bound to the other in community.

The key here hinges on what it means for humans to be "whole" or truly created by God. What does it mean when the Bible tells us we are "created in the image of God"? Christians believe that the core of God is relationship.[225] There is interrelatedness between God the father, son, and spirit. This one God, interrelated, defines love and relationship. God creates humans in God's image, meaning relationship is essential to our being, and outside of relationship with God and others, we are not "whole."[226] The story we find in scripture expresses a broken relationship. By not recognizing that our "whole identity" is bound to our dependence upon each other and God, we redefine our purpose from giving and receiving love to loving ourselves.

However, the biblical story tells us God's mission is one of healing, redeeming the relationships between creator and creation and within creation itself. Therefore, we receive the gift of new life from God so that we can give our life to the mission of reconciling others to God.[227] We see the link between the gift of salvation and our openness to each other as humanity. The opening of God to humanity occurred in Christ. Christ was "wholly" human as intended, and in this "wholeness," Christ openly embraced all that it means to be human.[228]

Our identity as human individuals is bound to the other and God. To be whole, we must enter into human relationships of mutual subordination, dependent on God, who is love. This is the core of the biblical understanding of human rights. This is the reason human rights are so important to the Cooperative Baptist Fellowship, with whom I work. The core of our understanding of God is relationship grounded in love.

Therefore, the Cooperative Baptist Fellowship emphasizes human rights as we respond to the prophetic call to care for the impoverished. We serve with and amongst, and advocate on behalf of, the billions of people who live on less than a dollar a day. From tsunamis in Asia, hurricanes and tornadoes in North America, and earthquakes across the globe, Fellowship people serve those in distress out of our common humanity. We are a people of refuge and community, embracing the diversity in God's human creation and acting as reconcilers in Christ. We welcome and love the stranger, give shelter to the alien, and offer hospitality to those who are often lonely, overwhelmed, and seeking a better life.

Christ's service to the father was borne out in ministry as reconciliation and healing. Fellowship Baptists seek to be the presence of Christ by offering spiritual and physical healing. Ministry with and among those with, and affected by, HIV and AIDS or malaria, offering opportunity for basic medical care, and training for better maternal health are among the practical methods by which we serve. Fellowship Baptists seek to educate and develop capacity with and among neglected people globally through efforts such as skills training, literacy, macro- and micro-economic and community development, and environmental sustainability.

Fellowship Baptists believe we are ambassadors of Christ in the larger societal context. We are to proclaim the good news of the kingdom of God, which is both present and to come. Such witness points to the authority of God and the opportunity to be reconciled in Christ. As ambassadors of the kingdom, we are advocates for peace, justice, and systemic transformation in Christ through such ministries as ending human trafficking, war, genocide, and child labor.

As God entered into suffering and pain through Christ, we enter into the suffering and pain of a broken world as the body of Christ.[229] Our hope stems from Christ born, crucified, risen, ascended, and present with us in his spirit. In the story I told before, the captive woman looked into the eyes of Hope and said, "It is okay, go." Is it okay?

Hope saw value in the young woman held for the pleasure of the soldiers at the roadblock; she knew the common connection they shared in their humanity. The captive young woman recognized the risk, pain, and desperation Hope was taking on her behalf. Her words of release, "It is okay, go," reflect a common sense of value and human connection between the women. Yet, herein lies the great inconsistency. We can make judgments upon this story: Should Hope drive on? Should she demand that the captive woman come with her? Yet, the fundamental question is "Should this situation exist in the first place?" Is it okay that this happens in the world we call home? If human rights are about an "enlightened" understanding of the individual, then it is okay, for we reduce humanity to the subjectivity of the self. However, if we base the foundation of our understanding of human rights upon the biblical idea that humanity is bound to the other and God, then we violate God, each other, and our self with each dehumanizing act. Therefore, I ask again, "Is it okay?"

★ ★ ★

RESPONSE TO GLEN H. STASSEN BY GRAHAM B. WALKER, JR.

My former professor and colleague Glen Stassen has identified the thick, rich Baptist heritage of human rights so often overlooked in the glib sprint to the Western Enlightenment for definitions of "human rights." Stassen has simultaneously opened other doors revealing thresholds, two of which I would like to cross. The two doorways that have captured my attention: Can there be a pluralist religious basis for engaging human rights, and what, if any, starting point for mutual religious reflection can emerge from Baptist life?

Can there be a mutuality of religious traditions for building the foundation of human rights? The motivation is no doubt evident. Since the events both on and after 11 September 2001—both the attack on the United States and the response of the American government—there is a particular kind of human suffering that calls all religions together for joint analysis and response. I refer to the suffering caused by religiously motivated violence. Peter Berger reminds us that even our so-called secular society requires religious legitimation to lay the foundation upon which the torture chambers of today are constructed. The religious traditions of humankind must give an example of united protest based on common guidelines rooted in shared religious values; this united religious protest will provide a counter-force to the way religion is being used by *all* parties in these conflicts. Rabbi Jonathan Sacks offers this eloquent call:

> Religious believers cannot stand aside when people are murdered in the name of God or a sacred cause. When religion is invoked as a justification for conflict, religious voices

must be raised in protest. We must withhold the robe of sanctity when it is sought as a cloak for violence and blood-shed. If faith is enlisted in the cause of war, there must be an equal and opposite counter-voice in the name of peace. If religion is not part of the solution, it will certainly be part of the problem.

Religion can be source of discord. It can also be a form of conflict resolution. We are familiar with the former; the second is far too little tried. Yet it is here, if anywhere, that hope must lie if we are to create a human solidarity strong enough to bear the strains that lie ahead. The great faiths must now become an active force for peace and for the justice and compassion on which peace ultimately depends.[230]

In this kind of dialogue and cooperation of religions, in which the goal is to relieve suffering, it is hopefully assumed by all that all participants can contribute, and that no single tradition has a monopoly into how suffering can be alleviated. For many evangelical Christians, not even so great a tragedy as 11 September 2001 was enough to draw them from their ensconced communities for the purpose of inter-religious prayers and services of lament for the dead and grieving.

Baptist heritage has a path to this time-sensitive inter-religious dialogue. The core value of "soul competency" has been a continuous thread through the history of Baptists. Baptists have saturated their history with appreciation for liberty of conscience.[231] Baptist historian Walter Shurden elaborates further: "How the world came together for Baptists - their inner life, their thought processes, their inner spiritual world - in the seventeenth century issued in freedom of conscience. Baptists grounded their lives in a view of the world which led inevitably to soul liberty."[232]

This Baptist core value of soul competency has consequences for society in general and for strategic inter-religious dialogue in particular. As the Baptist emphasis on freedom gives liberty to the individual, so does this affirmation give liberty to the larger community. John Freeman states this connection clearly in his 1905 address to the Baptist World

Alliance: "We did not stumble upon the doctrine. It inheres in the very essence of our belief."[233] This core liberty extends outward toward community as a whole, "including freedom *of* religion, freedom *for* religion, and freedom *from* religion."[234]

As Baptists have understood it, religious liberty offers the pluralist foundation of freedom not to believe as well as the freedom to believe and practice faith according to the dictates of one's conscience.

The revolutionary aspect of the Baptist notion of religious liberty is that Baptists promote not only their own right to believe and practice, but have been advocates for full religious liberty for all people.[235] Because of their origins as a minority group, Baptists are summoned by their history to reaffirm religious liberty for both the majority and the minority, Christian and non-Christian.[236] John Leland, Baptist proponent of religious liberty in the eighteenth century, spelled out this idea: "Let every man speak freely without fear, maintain the principles that he believes, worship according to his own faith, either one God, three Gods, no God, or twenty Gods, and let government protect him in so doing, i.e., see that he meets with no personal abuse, or loss of property, for his religious opinions..."[237]

In Southern colloquial form, Walter Shurden recounts the historic consequences of the Baptist minority appeal to freedom: "It is easy to 'holler' freedom when you are the one who does not have it. *It is a more principled position, however, to cry for freedom when you are in the majority but now lift your voice on behalf of new minorities.*"[238] The tests of 11 September 2001 and the prisons of Guantánamo Bay both give Baptists a forum to demonstrate their commitment to their cherished core value.

The current political climate extends Shurden's call to all persons of faith to lay aside their claims of superiority, recognize their mutual validity, and engage in a new kind of relationship in which all can learn from each other and work together for the benefit of all.

One of the sharpest criticisms of this mutualist model stems from the claim that mutuality between communities of faith cannot be achieved. In fact, dialogue is never constructed in a vacuum. Dialogue is a cleverly camouflaged but ultimately exploitative Western imposition.

Claims of mutuality between communities of faith ignore the reality of language. As George Lindbeck has reminded us, language both defines and confines us. Language not only expresses what we think about; it determines and therefore limits what we think about. That means when we speak about other religious perspectives, we're doing so in one particular religious vernacular. This, of course, means we are always understanding and judging other religious languages from our own. That is the problem we face with an interfaith reflection on the "religious roots of human rights," the critics say—it tries to find a common language within all religions. But in doing so it ends up imposing its own language, geography, ethnicity, and timeline on all the others.[239] There can be no mutuality, only pluralism, and that means accepting not just that religions are many but that they are different—so different that they cannot be boiled down to a system, or common essence, or common ground. This will be a challenge for the Baptist linguistic world. Baptists have a model for a plurality of faith communities; a model of mutuality will demand a new paradigm.

Secondly, the critics continue, the mutualist imposition of one religious language on all the others is seen today as the imposition of a distinctively Western language. This criticism can be verified both phenomenologically and politically. Just look at the originating, motivating ideals of human rights; whether they are rooted in the Protestant Reformation or, as others maintain, packaged in the European Enlightenment—with the language of universal truth linked to the universality of reason, evolution toward ever greater unity, *e pluribus unum*, liberal democracy; it is still Western language.

Granted, these "Western fathers of mutuality" may not have been evil-minded imperialists out to lure other cultures and religions into a Western cage. Still, in the present political context of the world, they may be doing just that, just as the persistent calls for "globalization"— that is, for a worldwide economy that will connect and gather all nations around the table of a common market—can serve, and are serving, to consolidate the dominance of those economies that built the table. So too calls for a new religious dialogue can become a tool that serves the agenda of the powerful. To call for a mutual "foundation of religious human rights" in a world in which there is no economic-political "human rights of nations and peoples" is at best naïve, and at worse dangerous. As Sheila Greeve Davaney puts it, to foster a true mutuality of religions, it is necessary to address "those dynamics of power that invest some perspectives with great legitimacy while dismissing others. It does little good to advocate a position that calls for open debate, inclusive of multiple voices, while ignoring the mechanisms by which many are rendered invisible, denied legitimacy, or so thoroughly located at the bottom of a hierarchy of values that their reality counts for little in the evaluative equation."[240]

According to John Jonsson, a Baptist model of inter-religious dialogue is rooted not in the theological commonality of different traditions; rather, mutuality is rooted in the phenomenon of common human experience:

> Scholars are divided as to whether or not we should find a common theological basis on which to agree in order to make inter-religious dialogue possible. Some are insistent that we must find some point of common theological agreement, apart from which dialogue between peoples of different religions would not be possible. I do not agree with this point of view. To find common ground in our understanding of God is neither necessary nor desirable. It would be difficult to find consensus in the realm of theological ideas…The common ground which makes dialogue with peoples of other faiths possible, is the mutual acceptance of our common humanity.[241]

These criticisms offer this interfaith community on human rights warning signs of just where the pitfalls and precipices lie. As a member of this Baptist community I do, however, believe that mutual interfaith dialogue can build a foundation for a sanctuary for human life in opposition to that of the torture chamber, Abu Ghraib, or the detention centers of Guantánamo Bay.

For persons who take religion seriously, human suffering seriously, and our fragile global context seriously, I suggest the following pathways for any contemporary reflection on human rights to flourish.

Religious truth is always concerned with universal truth. This is what we hear from and see in religious believers. The truth they have experienced, while it is certainly meant for them, is not meant only for them. It is also for others; it can also touch and transform the lives of others.[242] Minimally, we can say the meaning and power a person experiences within her own religion is also felt to be relevant for others. Some communities of faith are more missionary-based than others; Christianity, Islam, and Buddhism stand at the top of the list of those communities who have sent believers to tell others about the truth.

Bill Leonard observes that while Baptists have been committed to offering liberty in light of pluralism, Baptists have *not* been silent regarding their own faith perspectives.[243] Evangelism is at the heart of the Baptist mission, and out of this passion arises universal claims that inspire Baptist expansion and proclamation of their faith tradition.[244] Framed internally within the community, Baptists are motivated by the love of God and the commands of Christ to share in the task of taking the gospel message to the world.[245]

Hence the tension inherent in the Baptist foundation of freedom: "[O]n one hand these early Baptists were unashamed particularists, demanding conversion of all who would claim salvation in this life and the next through Jesus Christ. On the other hand they were pluralists, lobbying for a society where all religious and non-religious voices could be heard."[246]

The point is not to rank, order, and establish a missionary intensity-index; rather, it is to bring to the surface that which is at the depth of all human experience: If something is really true and important, it cannot be true just for me. If it's not also true for others, I have reason to question its claim on me. The interfaith religious community knows and understands this, and without this religious sense of commitment to universal truth, the discussion and implementation of human rights will go no further than United Nations assemblies, university libraries, and classrooms.

An important criticism must be endured for those of us who enter into religious dialogue on behalf of human rights: If a religious dialogue challenges our claim to absolutes, there may be differences between the contents of the claims that are absolute. This possibility, or probability, is often set aside.

Though talk of multiple ultimate ends and multiple ultimates may disturb the sensitivities of most, the concerns of such talk must be taken seriously by anyone working within a mutualist model. As one who grew up in multicultural Singapore, and who served for many years as a theological educator in a multi-tribal region of the Philippines, I confess that in my eagerness to bring Christians to recognize the validity of other religions, I have minimized real, deep, distinctive differences between the religions. As a Christian in the declining period of the Western hegemony of my faith community (note that the Christian community in two-thirds of the world is differently construed; see Philip Jenkins), I must learn to give a sufficient hearing to the question "Whose common ground, or whose human rights, are you talking about?"

Baptist theologian Mark Heim suggests that religions are pursuing goals genuinely different from each other. In the final analysis, the religions of the world are more different than they are similar. They have nothing to say to each other. Alan Neely observes that Baptists "have been far more concerned with their responsibility to take or proclaim the gospel to all people, including the followers of other faiths, than to study thoroughly or consider objectively what other people believe."[247] Yet, Baptist missiologist John Jonsson again reminds us that in discovering the commonality of humanity, "we are able to accept people of other faiths, and celebrate with them as human beings and co-exist together with others, without losing our distinctive identity."[248] The issue then becomes, "How should we manage our differences? How can we make genuine connections in the midst of real differences?"

In this section I want to draw on experiences that can help us grasp how persons from differing religious traditions can and do interact—how they can understand each other despite their differences. I'm talking about the experience of people who have become friends across their religious boundaries. Inter-religious friendships can tell us much about the nature of religion.

Friendships incorporate a blending of differences and commonalities. Friends recognize and affirm how genuinely different they are, but they also feel the possibility of connecting with each other despite these differences. Friends feel the need, and in their relationship find the means, to develop a language that will translate, as it were, between the two very different religious language games each lives in. Among friends, different ultimate aims, maybe even different ultimates, can connect, communicate, and clarify one another.

Friends from different religious histories and experiences discover in their conversations that no matter how different they truly are, they can talk to each other. They can communicate. What friends *do* makes it possible for them to communicate with each other. And this "something" exists between them or among them. Inter-religious friends know there is something common, something universal, some dispositional excess that surpasses our differences.

It is this something, this mystery for which we will never find the "right" name or symbol, that according to Levinas gives the "face of the other" its power and its attraction over us.[249] In the otherness of my religious friend, I find differences that I will never be able to neatly include in my limited categories, but at the same time I can talk with, learn from, and respond to this stark otherness. In the face of the religious other, I see or sense the face of the other that shines within and beyond us all.

Over the past few decades, we can detect something else going on in the world of inter-religious relations urging religious people to realize that as different and as unique as they truly are, they must set aside their claims to have the "only" or the "best" way, and cooperate and communicate between their differences. The operative word in that last sentence is "cooperate." Inter-religious friends are becoming inter-religious activists developing strategic alliances for change. Perhaps better, the shared need to act is becoming the occasion to form or deepen friendships. There are countless men and women from religious communities who seek to respond to the challenges facing the earth and all its inhabitants. And they sense that their religious response, if it is to be meaningful and effective, must be inter-religious.

To expand on Levinas's imagery, the "face of the other" that today challenges and appeals to men and women of all religious traditions is not just the face of the religious or cultural other; it is also, perhaps even primarily, the face of the suffering other. Catholic theologian Johann Baptist Metz calls this the *leidensgeschichte*.[250] A growing number of people in *all* religious communities (which does not mean *all* people in *all* communities) find themselves called to do something about the immense amount of unnecessary suffering that afflicts so many human and other sentient beings. And they feel this call precisely because they are religious. This call, I believe, is today being heard not only within the religions individually but also among them collectively. This is an agenda Baptists can and should wholeheartedly affirm.

180

8

★

HEALING THE (AMERICAN) CHRISTIAN RELATIONSHIP WITH THE MUSLIM WORLD

Rick Love

The writers of this chapter have been given a magnificent and daunting task: "Healing the (American) Christian Relationship with the Muslim World." The rift between Christians and Muslims is admittedly huge. The practice of torture and concomitant practices of human rights abuse (because of the "war on terror") exacerbate this relationship and can be compared to pouring gasoline on a raging fire. Healing the relationship between Christians and Muslims is a massive, multifaceted challenge, way beyond the scope of this summit. Nevertheless, this gathering can make a difference. A formal, unequivocal rejection of torture by Christians would be like pouring water on the fire. So let's talk about the water needed to pour on the fire. "Once upon a time, it was the United States that urged all nations to obey the letter and the spirit of international treaties and protect human rights and liberties. American leaders denounced secret prisons where people were held without charges, tortured and killed. And the people in much of the world, if not their governments, respected the United States for its values. The Bush administration has dishonored that history and squandered that respect."[251]

The "war on terror" has led the Bush administration to disregard US commitment to law and international treaties regarding torture. By defining our struggle against terrorism as "war," President Bush has used the executive powers of a wartime president to redefine torture. Ignoring definitions of torture once considered sacrosanct,[252] he now euphemistically refers to this cruel, degrading, and inhumane practice as "enhanced interrogation techniques."

In the name of national security, the Bush administration has also denied legal rights (due process and habeas corpus) to detainees accused of terrorist acts. The US government has been accused of extraordinary rendition as well (sending suspects to countries where torture is a normal part of interrogation). Thus, while promoting human rights around the world, the United States is now persistently violating them.

I was able to get a feel for how Muslims perceived this last May while attending an interfaith dialogue in Doha, Qatar. When the topic of torture was mentioned, one of the participants snarled, "We are mocked by the US. The US speaks of democracy and human rights and then violates them continually in the war on terror." The emotions were palpable as I looked around the room to see heads nodding vehemently in agreement.

These feelings are not uncommon among Muslims. A massive, multiyear study by the Gallup World Poll about Muslims[253] confirms this:

> One US diplomat who was in Egypt when the Abu Ghraib scandal broke out said she was told by the locals: "We would expect this from our own government, but not from you." Ironically, it may be because of America's idealized image as a beacon for democracy in the Muslim world that its actions elicit such passionate anger. The perception is: For you, America, to go against your own values and how you would treat your own people and to abuse Muslims in this way means you must *really* despise us and our faith.[254]

The Geneva Conventions once described the high moral ground of US policy as it relates to prisoners of war. Today the Geneva Conventions have been ignored and considered irrelevant at Guantánamo Bay and elsewhere.

Methods of war change but the "common humanity" of the people fighting the wars never changes. All people have been created in God's image. No matter how twisted, broken, or evil they may be, all people (including terrorists) remain created in God's image. Because of this, human life is sacred. As George Hunsinger notes,

> The cruel, inhumane and degrading treatment our government is inflicting on the men held at Guantánamo Bay and elsewhere goes against the core Christian conviction that all human life is sacred. Torture and abuse violates the basic dignity of the human person that all religions hold dear. It debases everyone involved—policy-makers, perpetrators, bystanders and victims. It contradicts our nation's most cherished ideals. Any laws and policies that permit torture and abuse are shocking and morally intolerable.[255]

My eyes were opened to the challenges and complexities surrounding torture during a global leaders forum in Arlington, Virginia last October (sponsored by the National Association of Evangelicals and the Micah Challenge, US). Ten working groups were structured around some of the most globally significant ethical issues facing the church today. I was part of the group addressing torture. For many of us in the working group, it was the first time we had wrestled deeply with this issue.

As I prepared to summarize the results of our working group to the larger delegation, it was clear there was no evangelical consensus. As a moral issue, torture is fairly new on the evangelical ethical agenda. It has not been processed widely or deeply—that is, until this national summit on torture. It is worth noting that, according to the president of Evangelicals for Human Rights (EHR), David Gushee, the evangelical left and center seem to be coalescing around a total rejection of torture, whereas the evangelical right continues to affirm the practice of torture in the war on terror.[256]

I would contend that one of the reasons for the lack of evangelical consensus about torture stems from the church's lack of biblical clarity about human rights in general. While the most famous human rights document—the Universal Declaration of Human Rights—is written in purely secular terms, the ethical issue of human rights is not secular.[257] In fact, there is a rich and robust theological basis of human rights. Even a quick review of "For the Health of the Nation: An Evangelical Call to Civic Responsibility" and "An Evangelical Declaration against Torture: Protecting Human Rights in an Age of Terror" would go a long way in remedying this. Christopher Marshall's *Crowned with Glory and Honor: Human Rights in the Biblical Tradition* (2001) is another excellent resource.

Walter Riggins summarizes this issue well:

> In a real sense, Christian mission is the parent of the human rights movement. There are several biblical principles that have profoundly influenced Western societies in this context: The Bible teaches that all humanity is made in God's image; the incarnation and passion of Jesus demonstrate the value of each person to God. God challenges us to work for a society characterized by righteousness, justice and peace; he commands us to care for the weak and disadvantaged in society; Jesus calls us to love even those whom we might consider enemies.[258]

Sadly, the theological foundations for human rights have not been adequately taught from our evangelical pulpits and educational institutions.

A second reason for a lack of evangelical consensus is caused by a fear-based response to terrorism that clouds our thinking regarding God's ethical norms.[259] "We move back and forth between new national color codes indicating the level of danger from terrorist attack. The Office of Homeland Security regularly moves the nation to Orange Alert—the second highest state of risk from terrorist violence."[260] The Bible teaches that "perfect love casts out fear" (1 John 4:18). In the war on terror, it seems the opposite is also true: perfect fear casts out love![261]

A third reason for a lack of evangelical consensus centers around the perceived tension between ethical interrogation practices and national security. The argument goes something like this: Torture is the best way to get the information we need to stop terrorist attacks. Therefore, we must abandon any commitment to ethical interrogation and torture terrorists for the sake of national security.[262]

It is worth noting, however, that the purpose of interrogation is to get *reliable intelligence to prevent an attack*. The goal is not vengeance or mere confession. Accuracy counts. Information from torture is inherently unreliable because people will say anything to make the pain stop. This is just one of many reasons experienced interrogators say that torture ultimately does not enhance national security.[263]

So what are our options? Can we use ethical interrogation practices ("Do unto others as you would have them do unto you?") and find good intelligence from detainees? The US Army thinks so. The 2006 US Army field manual on intelligence interrogation, in accordance with the Geneva Conventions, explicitly prohibits torture and cruel, degrading treatment. It needs to be underscored here that this manual was not written by pacifists, Sunday-school teachers, or Boy Scouts. The combat-toughened military leaders who wrote this manual are committed to "finding truth without torture."[264] And that should be the stance of every Christian—finding truth without torture.

Thus, Evangelicals for Human Rights (EHR) is promoting a "Declaration of Principles for a Presidential Executive Order on Prisoner Treatment, Torture and Cruelty." The goal of this declaration is to get the next president of the United States to sign an executive order that would affirm the US Army field manual as the one national standard for all US personnel and agencies for the interrogation and treatment of prisoners.

In summary, evangelicals have lacked consensus on torture for three reasons: lack of biblical clarity about human rights, a fear-based response to terrorism, and the tension between ethical interrogation practices and national security. This national summit on torture addresses these three points and provides an important setting to help work towards consensus. In addition, perhaps Evangelicals for Human Rights (EHR) should put on conferences similar to "justice revivals" (sponsored by Sojourners and featuring Jim Wallis) as a means to build theological awareness, to develop consensus, and to discern appropriate practices on important human rights issues such as torture.

So how does rejecting torture and standing up for the human rights of detainees in the war on terror help heal the huge rift between American Christians and Muslims?

A quote from a Christian living in the Muslim world helps give needed context. The content of this e-mail represents, I believe, the feelings of the majority of Muslims: "Our neighbor who is a fairly secular retired Muslim man, in reference to the torture, imprisonment and war in general told us that Bush is worse than Hitler. A strong statement, but one that many hold to. It's hard to explain that his views are not those of Christians when he openly claims to be a Christian."

God has raised up Evangelicals for Human Rights (EHR) to be a prophetic voice against torture. Standing for justice and love as a member of the EHR steering committee gives me credibility when I speak to Muslims about my faith. It helps me differentiate my Christian views from President Bush's. I mentioned EHR in my presentation at the Doha Interfaith Dialogue in Qatar as a positive example of a Christian organization that uses media to speak against violence. At the recent international dialogue between Muslims and Christians at Yale University, I was proud to share my role in EHR with the leader of the Common Word Initiative, Prince Ghazi bin Muhammad of Jordan. In both cases, the aroma of justice distinguishes me from the unjust policies of my "perceived Christian government" and gives people ears to hear more about Jesus—the one who came to "proclaim justice to the nations" (Matthew 12:18; cf. Matthew 23:23).

★ ★ ★

Response to Rick Love by Mahan Mirza

On 8 October 2001, when America initiated its bombing campaign in Afghanistan in response to the attacks of 11 September 2001, the Taliban held a reporter of the *Sunday Express* as prisoner. Yvonne Ridley had lost her balance while riding a donkey in a burqa while surreptitiously attempting to enter the country. The fall, witnessed by a particularly handsome green-eyed Taliban soldier, had exposed Ridley's camera that she was smuggling into Afghanistan under her loose garments. For the next ten days she remained a rebellious captive: "I was horrible to my captors. I spat at them and was rude and refused to eat."[265] She would even hang her underwear out to dry openly in view of the soldiers' quarters. Ridley's behavior prompted the intervention of the deputy foreign minister. Regarding the underwear on the clothing line, he said to her matter-of-factly: "Look, if they see those things they will have impure thoughts." Ridley remained uncooperative; oddly enough, her defiance earned her the respect, if not admiration, of her captors. She was eventually released with smiles and compliments shortly after American and coalition bombs started to rain down on Kabul.

Ridley has chronicled her encounter in some detail in her memoir, *In the Hands of the Taliban.* Ironically, she remembers the crudeness of eager reporters to get the scoop upon her release as less respectful than the behavior of the Taliban. "The reality was that the Taliban had treated me with courtesy and respect, contrary to their reputation."[266] She suggests the Taliban have been "demonized beyond recognition, because you can't drop bombs on nice people."[267]

The notion that the United States was attacked without provocation by freedom-hating, evil people has been the central narrative of the Bush administration for the past seven years. Any attempt to rationally debate this premise is marginalized, and the patriotism and allegiances of the questioner fall under suspicion and scrutiny. The prevalence of the "freedom-hating" myth prompted Osama bin Laden to address it directly in advance of President Bush's reelection in 2004:

> You, the American people, I talk to you today about the best way to avoid another catastrophe and about war, its reasons and its consequences. And in that regard, I say to you that security is an important pillar of human life, and that free people do not compromise their security. Contrary to what Bush says and claims—that we hate freedom —let him tell us then, "Why did we not attack Sweden?"…We fought with you *because* we are free…We want to reclaim our nation. As you spoil our security, we will do so to you.[268]

The purpose of this essay is to explore ways of healing the (American) Christian relationship with the Muslim world. It is not possible to do this if the causes for the rift are a figment of our imagination. So what is the nature of the conflict between Islamic terrorism and the West? Before attempting to discuss these points systematically, it would behoove us to examine some of the assumptions that are embedded in the framing of the question. Why is "American" in brackets next to "Christian"? Are the two somehow synonymous? Is America Christian? Were the 9/11 attacks an attack of Islam on Christianity? What is the status of American Muslims? Do they belong to America or the Muslim world? If there is a rift between America and the Muslim world, what does this mean for the identity of American Muslims? Are they supposed to heal a supposed rift between their American and Muslim selves? These are very important questions that are quite problematic for an oversimplified Islam-West binary.

It is also important to recognize that a conflict between "Islam" and the "West" erroneously assumes two reified and distinct entities. More problematic is the instinctive reduction of the motivations behind a perceived Islamic aggressor as "religious." It is undeniable for individuals who are engaged in activities that require ultimate sacrifices to seek ultimate explanations for their endeavors. However, there is mounting empirical evidence demonstrating that the primary motives for the conflict from the side of "Islam" are in fact political and not religious, insofar as a distinction between these two concepts is helpful. In a sweeping study of suicide bombings,[269] the political scientist Robert Pape assesses that "the presumed connection between suicide terrorism and Islamic fundamentalism is misleading."[270] In a summary piece aptly titled *Blowing Up an Assumption,* Pape concludes: "What nearly all suicide terrorist attacks actually have in common is a specific secular and strategic goal: to compel modern democracies to withdraw military forces from territory that the terrorists consider to be their homeland."[271]

Pape's research goes a long way in debunking the popular adage that "not all Muslims are terrorists, but all terrorists are Muslims." He shows that until the recent invasion and occupation of Iraq by the United States and coalition forces in 2003, the (non-Muslim) Tamil Tigers of Sri

Lanka were the lead instigators of suicide attacks between 1980 and 2003. Moreover, although it is well known that the Hezbollah of Lebanon was constituted in direct response to Israel's occupation of Beirut in 1982, what is less well known is that out of a total of thirty-eight attacks for which the names and personal data of the perpetrators are available between 1982 and 1986, "[t]wenty-seven were from leftist political groups like the Lebanese Communist Party and the Arab Socialist Union. Three were Christians, including a female high-school teacher with a college degree."[272] The research of Robert Pape is supported by the results of a Gallup poll of the Muslim world, according to which a "primary catalyst or driver of radicalism…is the threat of political domination and occupation."[273]

Contrast this analysis with the conventional wisdom surrounding the "war on terror" offered by media pundits, experts, and most tragically, politicians and policy makers. We are told that the conflict consists of the following elements:

- America was attacked unprovoked on 9/11; the attack came suddenly and without warning; our foreign policy has nothing to do with the conflict; no matter what we do, they will fight us regardless.

- We were attacked because they hate our freedom; this conflict is like none other; since the challenge is unprecedented, it requires unprecedented measures in response; this is an epic civilizational war.

- The goal of the Islamic terrorists is to kill all non-believers ("infidels"), especially Jews, and to destroy the state of Israel; this is an existential battle; if we don't stop the terrorists, there could be another holocaust.

- It is not possible to talk or negotiate with the enemy; their Islamofascist religion does not share our Judeo-Christian values.

On the first and second points, that this was an unprovoked attack having nothing to do with our policies, consider the following telling exchange during the South Carolina Republican presidential primary debate in May 2008:

> REP. PAUL: Have you ever read the reasons they attacked us? They attack us because we've been over there; we've been bombing Iraq for 10 years...right now we're building an embassy in Iraq that's bigger than the Vatican. We're building 14 permanent bases. What would we say here if China was doing this in our country or in the Gulf of Mexico? We would be objecting. We need to look at what we do from the perspective of what would happen if somebody else did it to us. (Applause.)
>
> MR. GOLER: Are you suggesting we invited the 9/11 attack, sir?
>
> REP. PAUL: I'm suggesting that we listen to the people who attacked us and the reason they did it...[Mr. Guiliani interjects]...[Rep. Paul continues]...I believe very sincerely that the CIA is correct when they teach and talk about blowback. When we went into Iran in 1953 and installed the shah, yes, there was blowback. A reaction to that was the taking of our hostages and that persists. And if we ignore that, we ignore that at our own risk. If we think that we can do what we want around the world and not incite hatred, then we have a problem. They don't come here to attack us because we're rich and we're free. They come and they attack us because we're over there.[274]

Representative Ron Paul's position, otherwise sidelined in "mainstream" circles, is courageous and accurate. It is also consistent with the opinions of Michael Scheuer, former CIA employee and chief of the station dedicated to tracking Osama bin Laden. Based on his extensive experience in counterintelligence, Scheuer has authored three books on al-Qaeda, Osama bin Laden, and the war on terror. In the first of these, *Through Our Enemies' Eyes*, Scheuer provocatively argues that "bin Laden's philosophy and actions have embodied many of the same sentiments that permeate the underpinnings of concepts on which the United

States itself is established," and that bin Laden is waging a "defensive jihad against what he has described as the onslaught of the United States and its Western and Arab allies."[275]

Incidents of torture and inhumane treatment by American forces reinforce the felt need for jihadists to double down in their "defensive" campaign. When Abu Ghraib erupted there was an outcry in the entire world, including at home in America. A CNN article published during the week when the scandal broke affirmed: "Photographs showing the apparent abuse of Iraqi prisoners by both American and British troops have been greeted with shock and outrage worldwide."[276] The same article quotes President George Bush: "I share a deep disgust that those prisoners were treated the way they were treated. Their treatment does not reflect the nature of the American people. That's not the way we do things in America." Another contemporary headline reads: "Rumsfeld twice offered to resign during Abu Ghraib scandal."[277]

The contrasting attitudes towards detention and torture at Guantánamo Bay could not be starker. Another debater in the Republican primaries, former governor of Massachusetts Mitt Romney, attempted to boost his standing with the following words about America's program in Guantánamo, to great applause: "I'm glad they're at Guantánamo. I don't want them on our soil. I want them on Guantánamo, where they don't get the access to lawyers they get when they're on our soil. I don't want them in our prisons. I want them there. Some people have said, we ought to close Guantánamo. My view is, we ought to double Guantánamo."[278] Governor of Alaska Sarah Palin, as the freshly minted running mate of Senator John McCain in 2008, mocked Barack Obama in her speech at the Republican National Convention for wanting to read the terrorists their rights.[279] So how does one explain the different approaches between Abu Ghraib and Guantánamo—one of outright condemnation and the other of straightforward advocacy? The answer to this question lies, for lack of a better explanation, in matters closely tied to politics, public image, and propaganda rather than values and human rights.

The publication of photographs depicting abuse at Abu Ghraib was an undeniable embarrassment that necessitated swift and immediate repudiation. The abuse at Guantánamo Bay, however, has been shrouded in obscure descriptions and reports. With the absence of concrete images "that speak a thousand words," people have been forced to debate whether things like waterboarding, sleep deprivation, extreme physical conditions (e.g., temperature, posture), and other forms of coercion are in fact torture or not. It is difficult, if not altogether impossible, to rally mass support for any issue in an environment of uncertainty around the facts. This is why many pressing issues seem intractable, such as the reasons for going to war, torture, Israel-Palestine, or climate change.[280] They are conveniently relegated to that which is irrevocably "controversial." Take the examples of Jimmy Carter and Al Gore. Both have achieved the pinnacle of power in the United States and received international recognition for their work. Yet, both these Nobel Laureates have become mired in controversy because of their activism on behalf of issues that have been deemed controversial. It is fascinating that it is the controversy that remains constant, unwilling to budge even when confronted with the most resourceful forms of advocacy.

Confrontation with blunt reality, whether through events or non-manipulated images, can be a powerful and immediate path towards clarity from the netherworld of controversy, which is one reason war-makers (Pentagon and administration) have encouraged the phenomenon of "embedded" journalism and restricted the display of human costs to its wars. It was Al Gore's documentary on climate change, with its dramatic narrative and images, that helped nudge the discourse on climate change along. And it was, in fact, the broadcast of images of torture at Abu Ghraib that "set the national and international media on fire."[281] It is noteworthy that accompanying the instant repudiation of the crimes at Abu Ghraib were attempts by voices in the American media to characterize the situation as aberrant, unrepresentative, and altogether un-American.[282] On the other hand, extreme right-wing voices went so far as to dismiss domestic outrage as an overblown reaction to something that might be considered as relatively harmless hazing.[283] There are a number of studies tracing the cultural forces that contribute towards the loss of clarity in the public sphere, even in the face of compelling and ample evidence.[284] Suffice it to say here that these powerful forces have collectively developed a civilizational narrative on the war on terror that is both fictional and dangerous. Edward Said's pioneering works have focused on the especially sinister, if subconscious, nature of the loss of objectivity when it comes to setting up narratives on events relating to the world of Islam in Western discourses.[285]

Turning to the third element of the mainstream imaginary narrative on the war on terror, that we can expect a holocaust if the threat is not dealt with, Osama bin Laden also addressed this allegation directly in the following excerpt from a speech delivered in September 2007:

> And among the most important items contained in Bush's speeches since the events of the 11th is...that the Americans have no choice in front of them other than to continue the war or face a holocaust...I say, refuting this unjust statement, that the morality and culture of the holocaust is your culture, not our culture... The holocaust of the Jews was carried out by your brethren in the middle of Europe, but had it been closer to our countries, most of the Jews would have been saved by taking refuge with us. And my proof for that is in what your brothers, the Spanish, did when they set up the horrible courts of the Inquisition...the blood of the Muslims will not be spilled with impunity...just a few days ago, the Japanese observed the 62nd anniversary of the annihilation of Hiroshima and Nagasaki by your nuclear weapons...and more than a million orphans in Baghdad alone, not to mention hundreds of thousands of widows... This war was entirely unnecessary, as testified to by your own reports.[286]

These words fly in the face of conventional wisdom, which states that al-Qaeda and Islamic "fundamentalists" everywhere wish to annihilate all infidels. In fact, that the exceptionally devout Muslims are somehow scripturally charged with the indiscriminate murder of non-believers is a blatant fallacy. Take the example of the Palestinian HAMAS. Alongside listing the destruction of Israel as a main objective in its founding documents, article six of its "covenant" states that "under the wing of Islam followers of all religions can coexist in security and safety where their lives, possessions and rights are concerned."[287] HAMAS, meaning "zeal," is a clever acronym for *Harakat al-Muwawamat al-Islamiyya* or "Islamic Resistance Movement." No matter how extreme one's disagreement with the positions of HAMAS, they should not be confused with insane terrorists who would initiate a holocaust if unchecked, but rather as a freedom movement that has arisen in direct response to the harsh reality of a crushing and illegal foreign occupation and settlement.

The Lebanese Hezbollah provides further evidence against the fallacy in its manifesto of 1985. Entitled "An Open Letter," it lists the following among the organization's main objectives: "(a) to expel the Americans, the French and their allies definitely from Lebanon, putting an end to any colonialist entity on our land; (b) to submit the Phalanges to a just power and bring them all to justice for the crimes they have perpetrated against *Muslims and Christians*; (c) to permit all the sons of our people to determine their future and *to choose in all the liberty the form of government they desire*."[288] In other press releases and statements of purpose, Hezbollah has explained itself as a movement that mirrors, in spirit, the struggles of the founders of the United States.[289] These stated objectives are in complete alignment with the research of Pape and analysis of Scheuer.[290]

Let us turn to the fourth and last point of the grand narrative on the war on terror, according to which it is impossible to negotiate with the enemy. The implication of this standpoint of non-negotiation is problematic in the extreme. It is tantamount to a practical negation of the full humanity of the adversary. If one considers the kinds of persons who are not negotiated with in the context of a healthy society, they are people who are certifiably mentally disabled, in an extreme emotional state of rage or grief (in other words, people who are in a hysterically "irrational" state), small children, or untrained/wild animals. These are all beings who are in some way "deficient" and must be managed/tamed or manipulated—they are not equals. We are told it is not possible to negotiate with the likes of President Ahmadinejad of Iran, the popularly elected HAMAS of Palestine, the Taliban of Afghanistan, and the Hezbollah of

Lebanon, among others, because they threaten the existence of all that is good and decent. Nothing will sway them from their destructive objectives except for their own destruction or non-negotiable submission.

The example of Iran's President Ahmadinejad provides a nice case study of the seemingly deliberate distortion-tactics at play. In a letter to President George Bush in 2006, Ahmadinejad asks how Bush reconciles his belief in Jesus Christ with his belligerent policies; voices concern over the loss of innocent life and secret detention facilities that disregard human rights; questions why Palestinian Jews, Christians, and Arabs can't all live together; calls the events of September 11 "horrendous"; suggests that the US Treasury use its funds to help alleviate poverty for American citizens rather than for waging misguided wars; inquires how long we, as a human family, can afford to manage the affairs of the world so irresponsibly; and beckons to unite in living up to the ideals and teachings of mercy and compassion preached by the prophets Muslims and Christians have in common.[291] The letter was ignored. Juan Cole, professor of Middle Eastern studies at the University of Michigan, has noted on his popular blog *Informed Comment* specific instances of how the US media has distorted the views of Iran's president.[292]

The story of the Taliban is even more compelling. After the events of September 11, Mullah Omar attempted to negotiate a truce by demanding an open investigation on the attacks, denying involvement, and offering to deliver bin Laden if evidence was provided, or permitting his trial under Islamic law under the auspices of clerics from three different Muslim countries.[293] Around the end of September, it was reported widely in the media that Rev. Jesse Jackson had been contacted by the Taliban to mediate in the conflict, and to discuss "the issue of handing over Osama Bin Laden 'in a way that preserves the dignity of all sides.'"[294] Since all other channels of communication had been cut off, as a measure of last resort the beleaguered Taliban leader even attempted to contact the White House on its public information phone line, to no avail.[295] These overtures were rejected, ignored, or mocked by the Bush administration. One is only left to wonder what might have been, as the situation in Iraq remains precarious and the situation in Afghanistan and Pakistan deteriorates, seven years, countless lives, and half a trillion dollars later. If Zalmay Khalilzad, the man who was later to be George Bush's ambassador to Afghanistan and the United Nations, could see that there were "common interests" between the Taliban and the United States when he was a lobbyist for Unocal,[296] and was willing to entertain the Taliban in Texas to negotiate oil deals,[297] how could an opportunity to talk through the crisis in the aftermath of 9/11 have been squandered so carelessly? The answer lies in *Imperial Hubris.*[298] Today we have come full circle with news of Afghanistan President Hamid Karzai's willingness to "guarantee the safety of the Taliban leader Mullah Mohammad Omar if Mr. Omar agreed to negotiate for a peaceful settlement of the worsening conflict in the country."[299]

In order to dispel any notion that this essay is nothing more than a crafty apology on behalf of terrorism, and to shatter prevailing myths about the nature of Islamist movements even further, let us note the responses of a handful of prominent Islamist leaders to the events of 11 September 2001. Charles Kurzman, professor of sociology at UNC-Chapel Hill, has compiled an impressive list of such statements entitled "Islamic statements against terrorism."[300] Even though Muslims are constantly accused of not speaking out enough against terrorism, here is a sampling that demonstrates otherwise.

The official statement of the Muslim Brotherhood: "[We] strongly condemn such activities that are against all humanist and Islamic morals.... [We] condemn and oppose all aggression on human life, freedom and dignity anywhere in the world." Muhammad Hussein Fadlallah, the spiritual guide of the Hezbollah in Lebanon, remarked, "Islamists who live according to the human values of Islam could not commit such crimes." Ali Khamene'i, the supreme jurist-ruler of Iran, published an official statement in which he condemned the killing of innocents anywhere: "It makes no difference whether such massacres happen in Hiroshima, Nagasaki, Qana, Sabra, Shatila, Deir Yassin, Bosnia, Kosovo, Iraq or in New York and Washington." The leaders of over forty Islamic groups—including Mustafa Mashhur, the general guide of the Muslim Brotherhood; Qazi Hussain Ahmed, the Ameer of the Jama'at-i Islami; and Shaykh Ahmad Yassin, the founder of the

Islamic Resistance Movement (HAMAS)—and leaders from North Africa and Malaysia published a joint statement that reads, in part:

> The undersigned, leaders of Islamic movements, are horrified by the events of Tuesday 11 September 2001 in the United States which resulted in massive killing, destruction and attack on innocent lives. We express our deepest sympathies and sorrow. We condemn, in the strongest terms, the incidents, which are against all human and Islamic norms. This is grounded in the Noble Laws of Islam which forbid all forms of attacks on innocents. God Almighty says in the Holy Qur'an: "No bearer of burdens can bear the burden of another" (Surah al-Isra 17:15).

The overwhelming and unequivocal condemnation of the events of 9/11 by people we refuse to talk to because of their apparent incapacity for rational discourse must surely be puzzling to many an observer. This is perhaps one reason the media fails to report them as headlines, or similar statements by so-called moderate Muslims—"where are the moderate Muslim voices?" These voices remain silent because they do not fit the grand narrative of the epic battle between good and evil. Sadly, this form of secondary and more insidious marginalization of potentially all Muslims has become a sub-narrative of the war on terror. The desperately sought after "moderate" Muslim becomes all the more elusive, since he or she is expected to renounce not just illegitimate, unacceptable, and deplorable forms of resistance, but resistance itself. The prevailing narrative on the war on terror, therefore, has the potential of becoming a self-fulfilling prophecy leading us all into a tragic downward spiral of unending conflict.

In his second book, *Imperial Hubris: Why the West is Losing the War on Terror*, Michael Scheuer expresses exasperation at American unwillingness to acknowledge the obvious. He calls the discourse and trajectory especially troublesome because of how easily available information is in the public sphere.[301] The tragedy, for Scheuer, is that the folly of fallacy is willful. He summarizes his conclusions in six bullet points, the first three of which are worth listing in full:

- US leaders refuse to accept the obvious: We are fighting a worldwide Islamic insurgency—not criminality or terrorism—and our policy and procedures have failed to make more than a modest dent in enemy forces.

- The military is now America's only tool and will remain so while current policies are in place. No public diplomacy, presidential praise for Islam, or politically correct debate masking the reality that many of the world's 1.3 billion Muslims hate us for actions, not values, will get us out of this war.

- Bin Laden has been precise in telling America the reasons he is waging war on us. None of the reasons have anything to do with our freedom, liberty, and democracy, but have everything to do with US policies and actions in the Muslim world.[302]

There is a reason President Bush outflanks bin Laden in the polls. In a 2006 AP/AOL celebrity poll, George Bush earned the honor of biggest villain of the year with a whopping 25 percent of the vote, beating the votes of the next five villains combined: Osama bin Laden (8 percent), Saddam Hussein (6 percent), Mahmoud Ahmadinejad (5 percent), Kim Jong Il (2 percent), and Donald Rumsfeld (2 percent).[303] Ironically, the villain of the year also earned a place as hero of the year (13 percent), eking out US troops (6 percent), Oprah Winfrey (3 percent), Barack Obama (3 percent), and Jesus Christ (3 percent). It would appear that virtue and vice both lie in the eye of the beholder. We often wonder how people could cheer in the streets when they witnessed the collapse of the Twin Towers. But we never even flinch at the cheering of Jay Leno's audience when he leads into a joke by announcing coalition bombings of Baghdad or Afghanistan. I believe that neither the people on the street nor Leno's audience would ever rejoice at the loss of innocent life. I am convinced all would weep together at the sight of human suffering, any-where. So whence the cheering and laughter? It is not at the loss and suffering of innocents, but at the perceived downfall of evil. Here I am reminded of a prayer of the prophet Muhammad: "O God! Show me the reality of things as they are."

It is perhaps an urban myth that the groundbreaking Gallup poll, conducted by the Gallup Center for Muslim Studies, was prompted by a flippant remark by Donald Rumsfeld at one of his legendary press con-ferences as secretary of defense. When asked about why they hate us, he responded by throwing up his hands in frustration: "You can't do a Gallup Poll of the Muslim world!"[304] Regardless of the prompt, what is important is that over the next few years a representative sample of a bil-lion Muslims in thirty-five countries was surveyed with striking results. Details of the study are available online, and its conclusions have been conveniently summarized and put into context in a recent book entitled *Who Speaks for Islam?*[305] On a number of questions, such as notions of progress, democracy, and human rights, Muslim responses are no dif-ferent from American responses. Most significantly, "Muslims and Americans are equally likely to reject attacks on civilians as morally unjustified." The few who justify such acts cite political reasons, not reli-gious ones. But here is the kicker. When the surveyed Muslims were asked what the one single thing was that could improve relations between Islam and the West, they answered "R.E.S.P.E.C.T."[306]

Presenting Islam as some "other" to a "Judeo-Christian" West is a fabrication that must be rectified. Imam Feisal Abdur Rauf has attempted to do just this in his book *What's Right with Islam is What's Right with America.*[307] The recent Common Word letter by over a hun-dred Muslim scholars of diverse backgrounds to the Pope and all Christian leaders affirms that Islam shares the core values of Judaism and Christianity of loving God and neighbor.[308] The West's conflict with Islam may in the end be nothing more than the West's conflict with a part of itself.

It is such a process of self-discovery, aided by dialogue, which will foster healing between "Islam" and the "West." Dialogue, however, must be accompanied by concrete steps to transform institutions in our societies that have a vested interest in breeding mistrust and conflict. Religion can be a positive force in this process towards a new and better world, and Islam need not be a rival, but rather an ally and partner with its Abrahamic siblings towards that end. This will happen only when American Muslims have been able to heal the relationship between their own American and Islamic identities.

Shaykh Hamza Yusuf has called this healing of the Muslim-American identity as one of the biggest challenges confronting American Muslims in the twenty-first century. He is also an avid advocate for the full inclusion of Islam as a legitimate member of the Abrahamic family: "The Abrahamic faiths share the sanctity of life and the Muslims must assert their Abrahamic truth. We have to reassert to the Abrahamic peoples that we are the last extension of the Abrahamic truth: that there is a God, and that He communicates with His creation, and He calls them to His unity, and He calls them to the highest morality known to humankind."[309]

Morality, however, must be exemplified in behavior. What good is a moral theory if it fails to engender action? Whereas there are countless coalitions on interfaith dialogue, the world could use more coalitions on interfaith praxis. Rabbi Michael Lerner's Network of Spiritual Progressives (NSP) is one such initiative that has proposed a Global Marshall Plan calling for a major policy shift from militarism to humanitarianism in order to make the world more secure, as well as to reclaim some of our lost humanity by transforming a world of greed into a world of generosity.[310] The NSP is actively lobbying to convert the plan into reality. Instead of being couched in an imaginary narrative of "us" vs. "them," Rabbi Lerner's philosophy is governed by a vision of "all together as one." This is the correct strategy to fight the war on terror, and to heal the relationship between America (Christian, Jewish, and other) and the Muslim world. If, however, America persists on its present path guided by a faulty imagined narrative, then we are staring into an abyss, and may all be damned into a collective "march toward hell."[311]

9

✴

Violence Finds Refuge in Falsehood

George Hunsinger

A theme needs to be lifted up that has not received the attention it deserves. It is the theme that violence finds refuge in falsehood. I myself first became aware of it through Alexander Solzhenitsyn, the great Russian novelist whose work commanded great attention some years ago and who died only recently. In accepting the Nobel Prize for Literature in 1972, Solzhenitsyn included these words:

> Violence, less and less embarrassed by the limits imposed by centuries of lawfulness, is brazenly and victoriously striding across the whole world, unconcerned that its infertility has been demonstrated and proved many times in history. What is more, it is not simply crude power that triumphs abroad, but its exultant justification. The world is being inundated by the brazen conviction that power can do anything, justice nothing....
>
> But let us not forget that violence does not live alone and is not capable of living alone: it is necessarily interwoven with falsehood. Between them lies the most intimate, the deepest of natural bonds. Violence finds its only refuge in falsehood, falsehood its only support in violence. Any man who has once acclaimed violence as his METHOD must inexorably choose falsehood as his PRINCIPLE. At its birth violence acts openly and even with pride. But no sooner does it become strong, firmly established, than it senses the rarefaction of the air around it and it cannot continue to exist

without descending into a fog of lies, clothing them in sweet talk. It does not always, not necessarily, openly throttle the throat, more often it demands from its subjects only an oath of allegiance to falsehood, only complicity in falsehood.

This connection was undoubtedly one that Solzhenitsyn had learned to make from bitter experience. But since he was a devout Christian, he would also have learned it from reading Scripture. We may see it, for example, in Psalm 5: "The Lord abhors the bloodthirsty and deceitful.... For there is no truth in their mouths; their hearts are destruction; their throats are open graves; they flatter with their tongues" (Psalm 5:6, 9). This theme is also evident in the prophets, as for example in Isaiah: "For your hands are defiled with blood;...your lips have spoken lies.... Their feet run to evil, and they rush to shed innocent blood.... The way of peace they do not know, and there is no justice in their paths.... Justice is turned back, and righteousness stands afar off; for truth has fallen in the public square, and uprightness cannot enter" (Isaiah 59:3, 7, 9, 14).

When we turn to the New Testament, we discover this theme in Romans 3, at the end of Paul's prolonged and almost unbearable indictment of human sinfulness. The apostle seals his case by quoting from the Psalms: "Their throats are opened graves; they use their tongues to deceive.... Their feet are swift to shed blood; ruin and misery are in their paths" (Romans 3:14, 16).

Allow me to give one last example. In the Gospel of John, just before Peter was again to lie by denying Jesus for the third time, we are unexpectedly reminded by the narrator that Peter had previously turned to violence by cutting off a man's ear with his sword (John 18:26). The clear implication, we might think, is that Christ himself is denied whenever lies lead his followers into violence, or whenever their crimes of violence are covered up and denied by lies, especially in the guise of pious falsehoods.

In his famous essay on "Politics and the English Language," written in 1946, George Orwell was incisive in making the same connection.

In our time, political speech and writing are largely the defense of the indefensible. Things like the continuance of British rule in India, the Russian purges and deportations, the dropping of the atom bombs on Japan, can indeed be defended, but only by arguments which are too brutal for most people to face, and which do not square with the professed aims of the political parties. Thus political language has to consist largely of euphemism, question-begging and sheer cloudy vagueness.

Orwell then gave examples of how political speech can become a cover for violence:

> Defenseless villages are bombarded from the air, the inhabitants driven out into the countryside, the cattle machine-gunned, the huts set on fire with incendiary bullets: this is called pacification. Millions of peasants are robbed of their farms and sent trudging along the roads with no more than they can carry: this is called transfer of population or rectification of frontiers. People are imprisoned for years without trial, or shot in the back of the neck or sent to die of scurvy in Arctic lumber camps: this is called elimination of unreliable elements. Such phraseology is needed if one wants to name things without calling up mental pictures of them.

And what about today? What phraseology do we need if we want to name things without calling up mental images of them? Perhaps it would run something like this:

> Suspects are swept up almost at random from places around the world; thousands are incarcerated in secret prisons; the vast majority are quietly acknowledged to be innocent; some of them are "rendered" to countries where they undergo unspeakable treatment and may never be heard from again; others are subjected to so-called "enhanced interrogation techniques" by sources closer to home; no useful information is extracted that could not be obtained by other means; those

subjected to extreme interrogation, whether guilty or innocent, are forever mentally and emotionally maimed. This is called "taking the offensive against terrorist brutality."

No charges are brought against people detained without trial for years as habeas corpus is brushed aside; outrages upon human dignity are perpetrated while Geneva conventions are abandoned as "quaint;" due process is manipulated in military tribunals behind the scenes to ensure that there will be no acquittals; evidence obtained by coercion and torture is deemed admissible in court; prisoners facing execution are denied access to lawyers and then, once they get lawyers, to the evidence against them. This is called "fighting terror while upholding the rule of law."

A generation of Arabs and Muslims is radicalized against us by graphic evidence of humiliation and abuse; some become suicide bombers; dictatorial powers are concentrated in the Executive Branch—the so-called "unitary executive"—while Congress sleeps or caves; torture regimes appeal to the tainted US example to defend their indefensible ways, while our closest allies, whose cooperation we need, are increasingly alienated and shocked. This is called "laying the foundations of peace for generations to come."

"Political language," concluded Orwell, "— and with variations this is true of all political parties—is designed to make lies sound truthful and murder respectable, and to give an appearance of solidity to pure wind."

Orwell's analysis has been carried forward by William Safire, the conservative political columnist who writes about language for the *New York Times*:

Some locutions begin as bland bureaucratic euphemisms to conceal great crimes. As their meanings become clear, these collocations gain an aura of horror. In the past century, final solution and ethnic cleansing were phrases that sent a chill through our lexicon. In this young century, the word in the news…is waterboarding.

> If the word torture, rooted in the Latin for "twist," means anything (and it means "the deliberate infliction of excruciating physical or mental pain to punish or coerce"), then waterboarding is a means of torture.[312]

Nor should it go unnoticed that the aggressive interrogation techniques used by our government can also be rationalized by religious fervor. Take, for example, the prominent boast we have recently heard that one should "always be proud of America." What exactly is being suggested? Are we to suppose that America has never done anything to be ashamed of? Do we have no sense of history? Are we expected to forget about Guantánamo, Bagram, and Abu Ghraib, which have disgraced, and continue to disgrace, our nation throughout the world? Might not lack of shame, as William Sloane Coffin has suggested, be a moral failing? "I believe the world is sustained by a kind of international solidarity of people who are ashamed by what their governments are doing. Shame is not only a deeply religious but also an intensely patriotic emotion, reflecting the determination of citizens to carry on a lover's quarrel with their country, a quarrel that is but a reflection of God's eternal lover's quarrel with the world."[313]

Are we to accept the idea that whatever America does, it can't be wrong, simply because America has done it? This view, all too familiar in the United States today, would be the essence of political idolatry.

Indeed, the idea that we must always be proud of America, no matter what it does, is inconsistent with the first commandment. That is one reason Karl Barth and Dietrich Bonhoeffer condemned religion as sin. It is why Barth insisted that the first commandment—"You shall have no other gods before me" (Exodus 20:3)—was a theological axiom with political bite. Barth and Bonhoeffer knew from painful experience that the nation is not God. They were acutely aware that it is not an idol to which we should bow down. The true vocation for people of faith today is to hold America to a standard that reaches beyond the delusions of false patriotism. "The idea that anything the nation does is right," states law professor Andrew Koppleman, "is more properly associated with Nazi Germany than with the United States."[314] Of all bad men, C. S. Lewis once remarked, religious bad men are the worst.

The CIA Exemption: A Brief History

When the Abu Ghraib photos appeared in April 2004, the Bush administration was quick to repudiate the horrific conduct that could no longer be ignored, while denying all responsibility for it. Such practices were declared to be "unAmerican," the work of a "few bad apples," the mischief of "Animal House on the night shift," etc. When I heard explanations, I felt there was room for doubt.

Darius Rejali points to a certain historical precedent. Torture, when practiced by democracies, he says, on the basis of several case studies, has inevitably led them to losses. After the practice of torture is exposed, the pattern leading to downfall runs like this: "When politicians first heard of the torture, they denied it happened, minimized the violence, and called it ill treatment. When the evidence mounted, they tried a few bad apples, disparaged the prisoners, and observed that terrorists had done worse things. They claimed torture was effective and necessary, and counterchallenged that critics were aiding the enemy. Some offered apologies, but accepted no responsibility. Others preferred not to dwell on past events."[315] The torture would continue, yielding no reliable information, while the democracies remained mired in war against weaker enemies. "Soon," states Rejali, "politicians had to choose between losing their democracy and losing their war. That is how democracies lose wars."[316] It is also, we might fear, how they lose their democracies.

Just as torture is not a new American practice, so legislative attempts to ban it are also not new. As noted by historian Alfred McCoy, the McCain Amendment of 2005 marked the third time in thirty years that Congress had voted to prohibit torture. "Twice before, in 1975 and 1994," McCoy observed, "investigations of horrific abuse, secret prisons and CIA complicity led to legislation."[317] Unfortunately, however, in each case hidden loopholes were allowed.

In 1975, according to McCoy, despite the congressional cut-off of all funds to the USAID's notorious Office of Public Safety, through which the CIA had been disseminating torture techniques through police-

210

training units throughout Asia and Latin America, a loophole was nonetheless left open for the agency to continue its operations through the Army's Military Advisor Program.[318]

Then in 1994, McCoy continues, major qualifications were introduced in ratifying the UN Convention Against Torture that "would effectively exempt the CIA's interrogation methods from international law."[319] The exemption pertained to what McCoy calls "no-touch" torture techniques. "Although seemingly less brutal than physical methods," he explains, "no-touch torture leaves deep psychological scars on both victims and interrogators."[320] There is nothing "lite," he says, about "torture lite." The so-called enhanced interrogation techniques favored by the CIA—like sleep deprivation, hooding, long-time standing, induced hypothermia, protracted isolation, self-inflicted pain, and other systematic attacks on the senses—constitute "a hammer-blow to the fundamentals of personal identity."[321] The iconic Abu Ghraib figure, hooded and standing on a box with fake electrical wires hanging from his outstretched arms, represents, according to McCoy, "key components of the CIA's psychological paradigm"—namely, sensory deprivation and self-inflicted pain.[322]

Unfortunately, the remarkable CIA exemption from established prohibitions against torture, in international and domestic law, continues right down to the present day. Three examples may be cited from our recent past. They do not bode well for the future.

The first example, as mentioned, is the McCain Amendment of 2005, officially known as the Detainee Treatment Act. Largely through the intense lobbying efforts of Vice President Cheney,[323] loopholes were again permitted for the CIA. Through a complex series of provisions, trademark psychological techniques were effectively legalized, evidence obtained under torture was made legally admissible in court for the first time in United States history, and the bedrock right of habeas corpus was denied to a class of detainees.[324] On 12 June 2008, however, the Supreme Court, in the case of *Boumedienne vs. Bush*, ruled 5-4 that detainees have the right to habeas corpus. They may now challenge their detention in conventional civilian courts, though efforts to block them from doing so are under way. The point to be stressed, however, is that despite the McCain Amendment, the CIA exemption itself remained unscathed. It effectively permitted what Jane Mayer has described as "a 'secret police,' with different rules from everyone else."[325]

Even more recently, what was long hidden in the shadows has come out into the light of day. On 8 March 2008 legislation was vetoed by President Bush (the Intelligence Authorizations Act) that would have closed all loopholes for the CIA by bringing it under the interrogation standards of the Army field manual. Torture techniques like waterboarding, sleep deprivation, and stress positions would have been ruled out. However, never before in American history has "cruel, inhuman and degrading treatment" been justified so openly. In his public statement the president claimed that the Congress had already "authorized" the CIA torture program by adopting the Military Commissions Act.[326] The ban on waterboarding was cited in particular as the reason for the president's veto.[327] In claiming the power to torture, the president not only displayed a disregard for human rights, but he also placed the authority of his office above the rule of law. Torture, as Scott Horton observed, is the measure and definition of authority with dictatorial pretense.[328]

We come to my third example. Perhaps no exemption for the CIA has been more momentous than the National Security Council "Action Memo" signed by President Bush on 7 February 2002. This early memo—adopted well ahead of the most shocking abuses that would occur in Guantánamo and Abu Ghraib—has received attention mainly because of how it abandoned the United States' obligation to abide by the Geneva Conventions. "That memorandum," wrote former CIA analyst Ray McGovern, "records the president's unilateral determination that the Geneva Convention on prisoners of war 'does not apply to either al-Qaeda or Taliban detainees.'" McGovern continued: "The determination was of dubious validity, because there is no provision in the Geneva Conventions that would countenance a unilateral decision to exempt prisoners from Geneva protections."[329]

Abandoning the Geneva Conventions, which is actually a potential war crime, was certainly troubling. Yet as Jane Mayer points out, that was not all. "There was another curious loophole in the President's February 7, 2002 order, one that took longer for the outside world to spot. A close reading of the directive…revealed that it referred only to military inter-rogators—not to CIA officials. This exemption allowed the CIA to argue that it had the full legal authority of the US government to treat pris-oners in cruel, inhumane, and degrading ways."[330]

What are we to make of this steady stream of CIA exemptions, which extends over a period of more than thirty years? At least one thing seems reasonably clear: Anxiety persists in high places about securing a viable "legality defense." The persistent unease seems to have been behind former Attorney General Ashcroft's appeal to the 1994 Senate reservations to the UN Convention Against Torture, when in April 2008, he replied testily about torture to a student critic at Tennessee's Knox College (and he was not wrong about what those reservations were intended to do).[331] This same anxiety (apparently so hard to quell) seems to lie behind that whole series of legal maneuvers that have become so depressingly familiar, but never seem to suffice. Besides the 1994 Senate reservations, think of all those 2002–2003 Office of Legal Counsel memos (some of which are still secret), the 2006 Military Commissions Act (which grants retrospective immunity to parties responsible for tor-ture), the 2008 presidential veto of the Intelligence Authorizations Act, and so on. An April 2008 *New York Times* story reported that the ever restive CIA was still seeking a "legal rationale" in certain undisclosed Department of Justice letters.[332] It would seem as though some persons feel less than assured they have the exemption from prosecution they may need.

Is There a Truth Commission in Our Future?

The issue of war crimes is moving to the front burner. In his fore-word to a recent report by Physicians for Human Rights, Major General Antonio Taguba wrote: "There is no longer any doubt as to whether the current administration has committed war crimes. The only question is whether those who ordered torture will be held to account."

The creation of a 9/11-style commission with special investigative powers has been called for by some members of Congress and organiza-tions like the American Bar Association. They hope to get to the bottom of how captured terrorist suspects have been treated by the Bush administration. The laws of war grant protections to persons who are taken as prisoners. As the Supreme Court recently upheld, no detainees in a war, even those not entitled to other protections, may be denied basic safeguards against torture and physical abuse.

The rationale for an investigative commission is clear. As explained by historians Jeremy Brecher and Brendan Smith: "The rule of law is central to our democracy. We must not allow precedents to be set that promote war crimes. We must restore the principles of democracy to our government. We must restore America's damaged reputation abroad. World peace cannot be achieved without human rights and accountability."[333] A recent article notes that:

> On the campaign trail in April, Barack Obama was asked whether, if elected, he would prosecute Bush administration officials for establishing torture as American policy. The candidate demurred. "If crimes have been committed, they should be investigated," he said. But he quickly added, "I would not want my first term consumed by what was perceived on the part of the Republicans as a partisan witch hunt, because I think we've got too many problems to solve."…
>
> The first order of business…would be learning the truth. "I think a lot of us feel that the American people are entitled to the whole truth," said [a] person who knows about the discussions. "The American people are entitled to [an investigation] from an official body that has access to the classified documents that makes as much public as it can," that person added.
>
> The commission would focus strictly on detention, torture and extraordinary rendition, or the practice of spiriting detainees to a third country for abusive interrogations. The panel would focus strictly on these abuses, leaving out any other allegedly illegal activities during the Bush administration, such as domestic spying.
>
> It would also try to confirm or debunk, once and for all, the claims of high-level Bush administration officials that the

use of abusive interrogations worked and resulted in significant intelligence gains.[334]

As the *New York Times* has noted in an editorial: "At this point it
seems that getting answers will have to wait, at least, for a new Congress
and a new president. Ideally, there would be both truth and accountability. At the very minimum the public needs the full truth."[335] There are
reasons to fear, however, that a 9/11-style commission, even without
bringing accountability, might end up delivering less than the full truth.

The Power of the CIA

Those of us who hope to abolish US-sponsored torture can ill afford
to underestimate the remarkable power of the CIA. Remember, it is primarily the CIA and related agencies such as the Special Forces that have
been perpetrating torture and abuse, past and present, on a systematic
basis for many years; and the CIA has managed to block every congressional effort to curtail these activities over a span of more than three
decades. From 1975 to 2008, no effort to close the loopholes permitting
the CIA to engage in torture has prevailed. The loopholes that could not
be removed in 1975 and 1994 have only come back to haunt us by
expanding exponentially since the events of 11 September 2001.

What are the sources of this CIA power? Anti-torture activists need
to be aware of at least two. The first source lies in media assets; the
second, in tactics of intimidation. Congressional investigations in the
1970s revealed a troubling pattern of "perception management" by
experts from CIA and Special Forces. One investigator sums up the
results:

> CIA developed covert relationships "with about 50 American
> journalists or employees of US media organizations."
> According to one CIA operative: "You could get a journalist
> cheaper than a good call girl, for a couple of hundred dollars
> a month." The agency arranged for books to be read in
> America, and for at least one of these works to be reviewed
> favorably in the *New York Times*. CIA had also developed

covert relationships with "several hundred American academics" on US campuses.[336]

In an underreported exposé on "The CIA and the Media," written in 1977, Pulitzer Prize winner Carl Bernstein revealed: "The CIA's use of the American news media has been much more extensive than Agency officials have acknowledged publicly or in closed sessions with members of Congress. By far the most valuable of these associations, according to CIA officials, have been with the *New York Times*, CBS and Time Inc."[337] Despite being based on evidence from years ago, it would be unwise to suppose that these reports are no longer relevant. The extraordinary complacency of the US media in recent years, to say nothing of tabloid triviality, has been much remarked, and no doubt multiple causes could be unearthed. When the deafening silence about torture revelations is pondered, however—a silence not only in the media but also in presidential and other campaigns—one can only wonder. Can it be entirely by accident that the agency most involved in perpetrating torture has also been known to cultivate a cadre of well-placed media assets?

Besides covert manipulation of the media, anti-torture activists need also to consider CIA tactics of political intimidation and control. Despite prohibitions on domestic activities, the CIA has been known to engage in break-ins, wiretapping, and the surreptitious inspection of mail. As revealed by past congressional investigations, it has also been known for hair-raising tactics of threats, pressure, and near blackmail, directed sometimes against members of Congress. As stated in the opening words of one congressional report, "These secret agencies have interests that inherently conflict with the open accountability of a political body, and there are many tools and tactics to block and deceive conventional Congressional checks. Added to this are the unique attributes of intelligence—notably, 'national security,' in its cloak of secrecy and mystery—to intimidate Congress and erode fragile support for sensitive inquiries."[338] No hopes in the anti-torture movement for a future truth commission should harbor any illusions about just what exactly we are up against.

The Politics of Hope and Prayer

Because God is merciful, we have every reason for hope, but none for complacency. A truth commission may finally yield less than full truth and no real accountability. Our efforts in the anti-torture movement need to be directed not toward getting a truth commission, but toward closing all the loopholes. A truth commission would mainly be important insofar as it served that overriding goal. Despite the powerful forces arrayed against us, that goal is very much within reach. People of faith, most of all, know that history is filled with surprises. "I believe," wrote William Wilberforce, "that the prayers of the faithful will prevail." Wilberforce, whom Scott Horton has called "the progenitor of the global human rights movement," struggled not only against slavery in the eighteenth century but also against torture. He learned from years of hard struggle that prayer and work were inseparable, and he believed they would finally prevail. And in the eighteenth century they did prevail. Those of us in the religious anti-torture movement today are heirs of the Wilberforce tradition.

"The hungry need bread," wrote Dietrich Bonhoeffer, "and the homeless need a roof; the oppressed need justice and the lonely need fellowship; the undisciplined need order and the slave needs freedom." Bonhoeffer continued: "To allow the hungry to remain hungry would be blasphemy against God and one's neighbor, for what is nearest to God is precisely the need of one's neighbor."[339]

That was Bonhoeffer's great insight. "What is nearest to God is precisely the need of one's neighbor." Since what is nearest to God is the need of one's neighbor, and since Christ has made himself to be one with those in dire need, Bonhoeffer drew the right conclusion. He recognized that Christians have a special obligation to those in any society who are being persecuted, humiliated, and abused. "Only those who cry out for the Jews," he wrote, "have the right to sing Gregorian chants." For the church in the Third Reich, Bonhoeffer perceived, the presence of Jesus Christ could not be separated from the plight of persecuted Jews. Whoever would serve God had to enter into solidarity with that despised and mistreated group, crying out by word and deed.

The year 2008 marks the fourth anniversary since hundreds of shocking photos were released from Abu Ghraib. These photos are difficult to look at yet impossible to forget. How can Christians view them without thinking of the plight and teachings of Christ? How can they view the wrenching scenes of nude male bodies stacked in postures of sexual humiliation without remembering the words "I was naked and you clothed me"? How can they gaze on the shackled man kneeling in an orange jumpsuit with terror in his eyes as a ferocious German shepherd strains at the leash only inches from his face without recalling "I was in prison and you visited me"? Where is the outcry? Why the silence of the churches? Can they learn what Dietrich Bonhoeffer has to teach us about what is nearest to God?

"The thought of Jesus being stripped, beaten and derided until his final agony on the cross," wrote Pope John Paul II, "should always prompt a Christian to protest against similar treatment of their fellow beings. Of their own accord, disciples of Christ will reject torture, which nothing can justify, which causes humiliation and suffering to the victim and degrades the tormentor."

The terrible stain of torture—which is not only morally wrong but also brings many harmful consequences, even from the standpoint of narrow self-interest—will not be removed from our nation until we learn to act from higher motivations than crippling fear, narrow self-regard, and ugly resentment—to say nothing of cultural racism. If torture is not evil, then nothing is evil, for torture is the very essence of evil. Only those who cry out today for the detained Muslims and Arabs have a right to sing Gregorian chants.

* ★ ★

Response 1 to George Hunsinger by Elizabeth Bounds

I am privileged to be able to respond to the powerful and impassioned statement of George Hunsinger, which emerges from his work as a scholar and activist, shaped by his reformed theological heritage. My brief reflections come from a slightly different but allied space: I probably would best characterize myself in the heritage of the Christian Social Gospel, which also called itself evangelical, but in an older sense that predates the modernist controversies and the growth of contemporary evangelicalism. And my connection with the question of torture arises from concern not so much with the violence of war, as with the violence of incarceration in this country, a situation that is as invisible as what has occurred at Guantánamo. Yet, as I think you will see, my different focus is not really very different at all.

I have no need to argue for a Christian position against torture—both Hunsinger and Gushee, among others, have presented wonderful arguments in person and in print.[340] What always interests me is why seemingly incontrovertible arguments are not accepted. And the study released at this conference shows that many do not accept these arguments, since 48 percent of the general public and 57 percent of white Southern evangelicals believe torture either sometimes or often is justified in order to obtain information from suspected terrorists. What I want to suggest is that we Americans may be shaped by our history to be more open to harsh punishment, an openness that has been supported by some strands of Christian tradition. Exploring this thread of our formation not only helps explain acceptance of torture, but helps make sense of the reality that slightly more than one in 100 Americans are confined in a jail or prison—and if we are looking only at African-American men between the ages of twenty and thirty-four, the figure shifts to one in nine, in contrast to one in thirty for all men in that age group.[341]

The core of this history is the American understanding of punishment, in both the legal and moral sense. Punishment has, generally, some element of degradation—that is, treatment that lessens or lowers someone. Good parents instinctively understand this, as they try hard not to mix needed correction of a child with this experience of being lessened. However, the US criminal justice system has consistently been the harsh parent, tolerating far greater degrees of humiliation and degradation than the European countries we have seen as allies and equals. In a fascinating comparative legal study, *Harsh Justice*, James Whitman argues that against the background of a common European heritage of status-differentiated punishment where cruel punishments were inflicted on inferiors, the Europeans developed a system that extended the forms of punishment for superiors to all citizens, while the Americans developed a system that extended the punishments for inferiors to all. For us, Whitman argues, practices of humiliation and degradation are not intrinsically inegalitarian and, relatedly, we do not generally see much need for mercy.[342]

Whitman's argument is too complex to develop here, but I want us to think about what it means to live in a culture that can accept practices of degradation. We have far fewer barriers to what Whitman terms "the intoxication of treating people as inferiors"[343]—an intoxication that is central to understanding the experience of those who carry out torture. It is this feeling that leads to the argument made elsewhere by David Gushee that torture "invites the dehumanization of the torturer,"[344] and, I would argue, not just the individual torturer but the social order that supports, or at least does not condemn, torture.

But the American impulse towards harshness and degradation also has roots in its Christian heritage. Whitman remarks on the tendency of American law to treat all criminal offenses as inherently evil,[345] something Europeans like to refer to as the Puritanical nature of US culture. The self-righteousness of our condemnation is linked to our understanding of sin, which can be seen in the ways we have shaped the criminal justice system. In Puritan America, as in pre- and early modern Europe, the punishment of the sinner was a public process that dramatized the criminal as a sinner. His or her public, physical punishment functioned to enable individual repentance for sin and also to correct disorder, or sin, in the public, who themselves were all in a state of sin. The emergence of the prison system, starting in the late eighteenth century, marked a different understanding of sin and punishment. Institutionally, punishment was privatized, removed from public view, and thus could no longer be a form of public education. Culturally, ideas of reformation emerged, focusing on the rehabilitation of the criminal/sinner whose errors were seen as more socially than morally determined. But it has always been difficult to separate the social and the moral. The prisoner was set apart from the public, requiring cleansing before re-entry was possible.

The reformative approach was always in tension with a more punitive theology. Regardless of whether the impulse toward the prisoner was fear and punishment, or pity and correction, it was clear that he or she was not "one of us," and thus able to be treated differently. Reformatory approaches were more evident in the North, since in the South, white evangelical notions of sin, purity, honor, and vengeance continued to shape the criminal justice system. Southern Presbyterians resisted the idea of a penitentiary, for example, since "the primary and chief end of punishment is to vindicate the right,"[346] a vindication justified both by the violent revenge found in the Old Testament and the suffering atonement of Christ in the New Testament. Legally justified forms of incarceration and torture shaped by these views were practiced on African Americans in the South, the paradigmatic other for US culture, well into the twentieth century.[347]

Our prison system has been shaped by punishment both as degradation and as reform, with the impulse towards degradation apparently more powerful. Until the civil rights movement, black persons knew fully that the legal system was out to degrade them, especially in the South. Our history shows that the US public, particularly the US Christian public, can tolerate—even justify—degradation and harshness if shown toward those who are not seen as part of "us." As Whitman puts it, "American punishment culture has generally rejected respect for persons" as a basic legal presupposition.[348] This is a contextual difficulty for any moral argument based, as so many religious arguments are, on the related moral concept of the dignity of the human. The increase over the past twenty-five years of retributive law (such as "three strikes and you're out" legislation) demonstrates that the punishment culture is even stronger when it is influenced by fear, whether of the criminals within or the terrorists without. Opposing torture requires work at many levels: discussions of moral principles, debates over law, pragmatic political strategizing, reflection on the nature of our military, etc. And it will also require some work on our identity as human beings, Americans, and Christians, identities that cannot be based upon fear and hatred.

★   ★   ★

Response 2 to George Hunsinger by Larry L. McSwain

We are indebted to Professor Hunsinger for providing a stimulating paper that is reflective of his tradition of scholarship—thorough research on the problem, a clear theological mandate that calls Christians to action, and a somewhat hopeful, but not overly optimistic, appraisal of moving forward on the issues of violence and deceit.

Symbols in a Human Rights Challenge

What I find most interesting is the symbolic language of the paper. Hunsinger identifies themes and images that define both the problems we face and the hopes for change for which we might pray. After all, symbols are the means by which much of reality is conveyed to persons.

These themes and images are the symbols that are at the heart of any analysis of an ethical issue. They are vivid, and let me simply identify the primary ones: the voice of truth from a specialist on the Soviet Gulags, Solzhenitsyn, who links the methods of violence with the principle of falsehood (one cannot help but be reminded that Solzhenitsyn's description of Soviet prisons is no worse than what we have heard at this conference about US detention centers); the biblical witness of the psalmist, prophet, and apostle in making the same linkage; the Orwellian imagery of language construction to cover the reality being described; and the images most representative of the problem we gather to address—abuses at Abu Ghraib, languishing detainees at Guantánamo Bay, the torture cells of Bagram military base, or the mysterious "black holes" of torture chambers in "friendly" nations less constrained by human rights considerations.

The most foreboding of all the symbols is a government agency shrouded in secrecy at Langley, Virginia, which manufactures intelligence where necessary and functions, by law, outside the bounds of legal guarantees of human rights embodied in both our Constitution and the major human rights documents of the twentieth century. Of course that dark symbol is the Central Intelligence Agency. It is truly a "principality and power" in the biblical meaning of that term (Ephesians 3:8–13).

Then there are the symbols of hope—a truth commission that might somehow transcend the politics of deceit to reveal how we really got into this mess, and the cross itself. For Christians in this conference, the cross is the ultimate symbol of the hope for resurrection and forgiveness beyond the injustices of violence, torture, and retribution because of the actions of the one we follow, Jesus himself.

But there is another set of symbols I would suggest are more powerful than these. In the backdrop of every discussion of torture is a picture of the burning World Trade Center Towers. The media and the populace of this country live in the retributive mindset of 9/11 that captures emotions of fear and translates that into votes for the candidate toughest in the "war on terror." This symbol raises the reality of idolatry Hunsinger suggests from Barth and Bonhoeffer. Most Americans reason, "How dare any opponent utilize the instruments of violence on us because we are 'Americans'?" even if the United States has perfected in global conflicts equally heinous violence in our offensives against enemies. That attitude is an idolatrous one, for it exempts the nation from the universality of moral principles that must apply to all nations.

There is also the symbol of the righteous warrior who never lives within the bounds of law or moral limits in pursuing the enemy for the sake of safety for the American people. Jack Bauer is his name. Dahlia Lithwick suggests in an analysis of the impact of the television program "24" on Bush administration policy, "The most influential legal thinker in the development of modern American interrogation policy is not a behavioral psychologist, international lawyer or counter insurgency expert." Citing evidence from Jane Mayer's *The Dark Side* and Philippe

Sands's *Torture Team,* Lithwick suggests, "…it quickly becomes plain that the prime mover of American interrogation doctrine (primarily John Yoo) is none other than the star of Fox television's '24,' Jack Bauer." This resulted in the improbable reality that "the lawyers designing interrogation techniques cited Bauer more frequently than the Constitution."[349] Even Antonia Scalia, the "strict constructionist" Supreme Court hero of the right, said, "Jack Bauer saved Los Angeles… He saved hundreds of thousands of lives. Are you going to convict Jack Bauer?"[350] It is, therefore, not surprising that one of the lines that generated the most cheers and applause at the Republican National Convention during Sarah Palin's acceptance speech was, "Al Qaeda terrorists still plot to inflict catastrophic harm on America…he's (Barack Obama) worried that someone won't read them their rights?"[351]

Strategies for the Future

This dimension of Professor Hunsinger's paper is less developed, and the one I anticipated would be more fully developed in light of his exceptional work on Barth and the Barmen Confession.[352] He recognized in his earlier work the difficulties in the American context of anything like an effective confessional community of faith. This is true of the church, the synagogue, and the mosque, given the pluralism of our religious institutions and the domination of the culture in shaping our responses. But there are hints in his address of the kind of strategies we might consider.

First, he is right with his hopeful emphasis on prayer. If the church is heir to the Wilberforce tradition that all forms of injustice in the world must be addressed by communities of faith in prayer, we must ask in what ways we can call our religious congregations to prayer around this issue. I, for one, stand judged in this regard. I have not made the torture of human beings by any government in the world the subject of my intercessions, nor has my congregation, nor has my larger community of faith. I suspect all of us could confess the same. If there is any impact of this conference event, it should become a commitment from each of us to respond to this challenge. As Karl Barth is quoted in his work, "Whenever there is theological talk, it is always implicitly or explicitly political talk as well."[353]

Our constituencies understand this. Whenever prayer is innocuous and non-specific, it is acceptable by all, regardless of political attitude or party persuasion. But let us pray for the release of Gitmo prisoners who have been held without charge or due process and see what response is forthcoming! Suddenly, the prayer is no longer patriotic or is decidedly partisan.

Second, we need to engage in social witness, however limited the response. Again, the social witness must risk the political consequences of particularity. Vague and general statements of enlightenment progressivism that call for good will and thoughtful response of political leaders are inadequate. I applaud the careful theological analysis of "An Evangelical Declaration Against Torture: Protecting Human Rights in an Age of Terror." However, it is nineteen pages of carefully reasoned analysis and four sentences of action. The actions recommended are appropriate and helpful, but unlikely to occur in the current political climate of the United States. Our social witness must commit to the ambiguity of support for specific legislation, presidential directives, and court decisions. This will be difficult without facing the charge from others of partisanship.

Third, change in the current realities that have been described well in this conference will require a commitment of well-organized persons who make known their political theology in clear and unambiguous ways across the diverse religious traditions that reside in America. Both candidates for the presidency of the United States have declared their intentions to seek justice in the treatment of prisoners in the war on terror. Will we provide the pressure, the effort, the lobbying expertise, and the political will to insist that the next administration renounce the repeated efforts of the current administration to violate constitutional and human rights promises? Will we lobby for a truth commission, so strongly advocated by this address? Will we risk the charges of "liberal," "unpatriotic," "weak," and a host of other labels if we insist on the appointment of Supreme Court justices who will apply the Constitution strictly on issues of *habeas corpus,* speedy trial, rights of access to evidence, and rejection of torture to all who are charged by our government, whether citizen or "enemy combatant"? Only if our theologies can become true political actions will I have hope that the United States of America will live up to her promise of being a nation of law and human rights.

10

Insights from the Next Generation

RELIGIOUS TORTURE IN THE WAR ON TERROR

Michael Peppard

In *Fünf Jahre meines Lebens* ("Five Years of My Life"), the most eloquent memoir yet published by a Guantánamo ex-detainee, the German Murat Kurnaz recounts the following memory from his cage in Camp X-Ray: "One time there was a long, tortured cry. I turned around. There was a second and then a third cry, but they sounded different from the cries of people being beaten. It was the long and frightening wail of death. Through the chain-link fencing I could see a guard in the cage of one of the Arab prisoners. I immediately knew what had happened."[354]

Reading these lines for the first time, your imagination might conjure, as mine did, the worst images of torture. But I never would have guessed what Murnaz saw that day. He continues:

> We were searched every day. They even searched the Korans. The guards grabbed the books by their spines and shook them to see if anything was concealed in the pages. This guard must have thrown the Koran on the ground—otherwise the prisoner wouldn't have howled like that. I saw the guard trampling on something. Some of the prisoners sprang to their feet. A terrible wailing arose. One by one, all the prisoners were losing their cool. "*Allahu akbar!*" they yelled. "Don't do that!" I screamed. The guard continued trampling on the Koran. It was as though lightning had struck in a zoo.

This story, and similar ones now trickling out of Guantánamo and other detention facilities, should highlight for us a crucial misunderstanding about the torture debate in the United States. Amid naked human pyramids, Jack Bauer hypotheticals, and a national referendum on waterboarding, we have overlooked the specific practices that tortured our Muslim detainees in their spiritual core.

The stories have often been missed because they are scattered in legal motions, government reports, or long narratives. Many come only from foreign-language media outlets. This article compiles a number of the allegations—many of them unknown to American media.[355] I will survey certain patterns of religious torture and draw historical analogies to help American readers understand its gravity. From the perspective of many detainees, religious torture has been the worst kind.

At Guantánamo, lightning strikes twice. And more. I had originally thought, like most proud Americans, that the 2005 *Newsweek* exposé—a Koran in the toilet!—was either an exaggeration or a one-time offense.[356] But Koran desecration is by far the most widely alleged form of religious torture in US detention facilities.[357] Recently the issue came to life again, when the Koran was used by a Marine in Fallujah for target practice.[358] According to allegations between 2005 and the present, the desecration has taken many forms, most of which are corroborated by multiple independent reports: the Koran has been handled with disrespect by guards and interrogators, written in, ripped or cut with scissors, squatted over, trampled, kicked, urinated and defecated upon, picked up by a dog, tossed around as a football, used to clean soldiers' boots, and yes, thrown in a bucket of excrement.[359] According to Russian ex-detainee Timur Ishmuratov, it would be laid on the back of a handcuffed, bent-over prisoner, so that it would fall to the ground if he stood up.[360] With just a Koran and a pair of handcuffs, a Muslim detainee could thus be made to torture himself.

Perhaps the word "torture" seems too strong for these offenses. It couldn't be worse than Abu Ghraib or waterboarding or sexual violation, could it? To that, one detainee responds, "We asked them to torture us physically, but not to touch the Koran."[361] But doesn't the very existence of the Koran in US detention facilities attest to our above-and-beyond respect for religious rights? Charles Krauthammer of *The Weekly Standard* argued along these lines in 2005, when we didn't have much evidence to the contrary.[362] But now Krauthammer might see how, from the detainees' perspective, the Koran was a mixed blessing. What might have begun as a symbol of the United States' respect for religious freedom became a poignant implement of religious torture.[363] When we come to understand the role of the Koran in Muslim life and to take the detainees' experiences into account, we can begin to see how this change happened.

At Guantánamo the centrality of Koran desecration to the detainee experience cannot be overstated. Deprived of circadian rhythms, several detainees seem to have marked time according to visible instances of it.[364] It was also the instigation for the collective protests of the camps—suicide attempts and hunger strikes.[365] Under Gen. Geoffrey D. Miller, desecration of the Koran and other forms of religious torture became regular—if not spelled out in the standard operating procedures (SOPs).[366] Capt. James Yee, the Muslim chaplain assigned to Guantánamo under Gen. Miller's leadership, describes the religious faith of the detainees as "Gitmo's secret weapon."[367] Though Yee was tasked with developing new SOPs for the handling and searching of the Koran, the abuse continued unabated and unpunished. At the time, British detainee Shaker Aamer told Yee, "General Miller is only playing a game with us. It's clear they hate us and our religion."[368]

The only solution the detainees envisioned was to give back all the Korans.[369] But not so fast. Religious freedom at Guantánamo did not include the freedom *not* to possess a Koran in one's cell. When the detainees tried to give them back, they were re-distributed, with the result that the Koran became a reliable and ubiquitous instrument of religious torture. There is some evidence that the power of the Koran to torment Muslims was not discovered accidentally by Gen. Miller or a clumsy guard at Guantánamo. Several sources confirm that it was part of known interrogation scenarios, and that the idea was transferred from similar abuse of the Bible used in the United States' own SERE training (Survival, Evasion, Resistance, and Escape).[370] However, the swapping of

Koran for Bible in the real-life enactment of SERE methods was an unwise substitution with drastic effects.

That is to say, the Bible/Koran analogy has been misleading. In certain contexts, the Bible is revered as a holy object. But for most American Christians, the physical Bible is not such a big deal. We see careless or even rough treatment of the Bible every week at church. (Have you ever been to youth group?) Bibles get tossed around, slid across a dirty floor, covers damaged, pages torn. The wear and tear can become paradoxically a sign of reverence—look how often we use our Bibles! My pocket Bible has been handled by TSA countless times, and I never accused them of anything but slowing me down. This line of thinking, however, is way off the mark. For Muslims, the Koran is the word of God, but not in the same way the Bible is for Christians. The best Christian analogy to the Koran is not a book at all—it is the person of Jesus Christ. For Christians, the word became flesh; in Jesus Christ, God is encountered. For Muslims, the word became text.

Historically, there is even more to this analogy. In early Christianity, a major theological debate concerned the unity of Jesus Christ with God. Was Jesus Christ eternally one with God, or was he created by God? In early Islamic thought, a striking analogy pertained concerning the Koran's divine status. Their theological controversy centered on the same point—whether the Koran was created (and thus separate from God) or uncreated (the eternal divine word). The latter, exalted view of the Koran as divine became the standard Sunni position on the matter. To most Muslims, then, Koran desecration is sacrilege of the highest order.

In the course of that controversy, the reigning Muslim caliph enacted an inquisition to force the adoption of the former, lower view of the Koran. Most prominent Muslims capitulated, but one theologian and jurist, Ahmad Ibn Hanbal (780–855 CE), is a hero to this day for refusing to recant his view of the Koran as divine. For several years, this "imam of Baghdad" was imprisoned and tortured. Though hailing from Iraq, his influence is currently most prominent in Egypt and the Arabian Peninsula, and his Hanbali school of thought has profoundly influenced Sunni Islam. These historical connections should give Americans great pause. The United States has used the Koran, whether we knew it or not, as an instrument of religious torture; at the same time, one of the most celebrated historical figures of Islam is famous for defending the Koran—under imprisonment and torture. If we wanted to inflame the enemies of the United States, we could hardly have chosen a more effective tactic.

Besides Koran desecration, the religious abuse most often described is the prevention or interruption of sacred time: the five-times-daily prayers[371] and the holidays.[372] For example, every morning and evening at Gen. Miller's Guantánamo, the "Star-Spangled Banner" blared over the loud speaker—usually drowning out those two calls to prayer.[373] But if the guards could not always succeed in separating the detainees from God through interrupting prayer, the professional interrogators could devise grotesque methods for doing so. In typical Muslim practice, as in many religious traditions, ritual impurity prevents prayer. One female interrogator, made famous in a 2005 report, used the impurity of supposedly real menstrual blood to put "a barrier" between a detainee and God.[374] Detainee Jumah Al-Dossari suffered a darker, explicitly religious adaptation of the method.[375] His female interrogator had his clothing cut off, then removed hers and stood over him. Both of them naked, she performed a similar tactic with "menstrual blood." But just before the final act of wiping it on his face, she kissed the crucifix on her necklace and said, "This is a gift from Christ for you Muslims."

Other specific instances have bolstered the detainees' perception of a religious war: at Abu Ghraib, the forced consumption of pork;[376] at Guantánamo, forced prostration within a set-up Satanic shrine, where interrogators made them repeat that "Satan" was their God, "not Allah!"[377] Others reported being draped in Israeli flags during interrogation,[378] while one interrogator explicitly told a detainee that "a holy war was occurring, between the Cross and the Star of David on the one hand, and the Crescent on the other."[379] Another bragged that he had "dressed as a Catholic priest and baptized [a] detainee in order to save him."[380] (The US law against impersonating clergy must be one of those not enforced at Guantánamo.) In sum, from the perspective of the Muslim detainees and the global audience that hears their reports, clear patterns of religious torture have emerged: the United States has desecrated the divine presence on earth (the Koran), supplanted the call to prayer with the American anthem, caused grotesque ritual impurity, and engaged in proselytism or forced apostasy.

How long can we expect the memory of religious abuse to endure? Does it qualify as torture according to John Yoo: "significant psychological harm of significant duration, e.g., lasting for months or even years"? History suggests the collective memory will last far longer than that. Centuries ago, another religious group with strict codes of ritual purity and devotion to God underwent physical and religious torture at the hands of occupying forces, prompting insurrection. Over two thousand years later, the events accompanying the revolt are still commemorated annually: the people are the Jews, and the holiday is Hanukkah.

This analogy may seem preposterous at first glance, but none less than Peter Steinfels made a similar connection in 2004.[381] Consider the history: at the end of the Hellenistic era, the inhabitants of Judea were occupied by the Seleucids and negotiating the assimilation to their Greek culture. There was internal strife between traditionalist conservatives and moderate assimilators. One Seleucid king, Antiochus IV Epiphanes (175–164 BCE), forced the issue of assimilation by interrupting or forbidding Jewish religious practices. He profaned their temple—the presence of God on earth—with an altar to a foreign god, and its courts were filled with lewd, non-Jewish women. Jews could not observe their religious holidays or even confess themselves to be Jews. The second book of Maccabees describes two martyrdom narratives from this era, in which the protagonists, later called the "Maccabean Martyrs," are compelled to eat pork. One of them replies, "What do you intend to ask and learn from us? For we are ready to die rather than transgress the laws of our ancestors."[382] When they will not capitulate, they are tortured and eventually die. Finally, Judah the Maccabee leads a band of insurgents that liberates Jerusalem.

This brings us back to Hanukkah. It is primarily the celebration of the rededicating of the temple, but behind that it recalls forced apostasy, religious torture, and guerrilla warfare. These memories resemble the stories now being told by Muslim detainees, most of which Steinfels did not know when he first made the comparison. The attitude of the

Maccabean Martyrs was echoed by ex-detainee Adil Kamil Al-Wadi in a standoff with American soldiers at Kandahar.[383] After constantly interrupting the Muslim detainees' prayers, the soldiers said, "We will teach you a lesson." But Al-Wadi responded, "If you want to do something, you will be sorry. We are not afraid to die for our religion. If you want to stop us from praying, we will fight you to the death." Meanwhile, as American forces remain in Iraq, a guerrilla insurgency in Afghanistan has had some success.[384] As in the Maccabean revolt, these insurgents are fighting against moderates of their own religion in addition to the occupying forces.

The comparisons among these stories are neither simple nor flawless. But the memory of the Maccabees offers a cautionary tale for the current situation: religious torture generates acute, determined responses and long, collective memories. What has been a mere footnote for us might be, for them, the main story.[385]

As the saying goes, a little knowledge is a dangerous thing. Personnel in US detention facilities may have learned how to manipulate Muslim beliefs and practices, but they did not learn enough to consider the long-term effects of their tactics. Religious torture inflicts communal trauma and collective memory. It might break the will of one man but turn thousands more against you. It is, in the words of one Muslim scholar, "far worse than Abu Ghraib," where individual bodies were tortured, because it affects the communal body of Islam.[386] For example, imagine how the collective memory of Islam will adopt the story of Muhammad Hamid al-Qarani. This boy was transferred to Guantánamo in 2002 at age fourteen—and is still there. In an arresting psalm of lament, titled "First Poem of My Life," he describes the place where he has finished out his childhood: "We saw such insults from them; / Not even the book of God was protected. /...Their war is against Islam and justice."[387]

Heroism in the Age of Terror:
The Dark Knight of the American Soul

Kathryn Reklis

In the immediate aftermath of September 11, the Bush administration contacted several Hollywood directors to help communicate the aims of the war on terror to the American people. Over forty television and movie executives were invited to a meeting with Karl Rove to discuss how they might respond to the terrorist crisis. The first such response issuing from Hollywood was a three-minute rapid-fire montage film, edited by legendary film-shorts editor Chuck Workman, that aired during December 2001 in a quarter of all American cinemas. The montage film, entitled *The Spirit of America*, was a tour through American cinema history, celebrating screen heroes who defined the American code of heroism, which, in the words of Workman, involves "reluctant but defiant revenge takers."[388]

The montage opened and closed with the beginning and ending scenes of John Ford's 1956 classic western, *The Searchers*. In the film, John Wayne plays Ethan Edward, a man haunted by the trauma of the Civil War who inflicts brutal violence in order to save his niece, who has been kidnapped by Comanche Indians in the Texan outback. In the final image of the film, and the final image of Workman's montage, Ethan Edward is framed in the doorway of a Texas homestead, his back to the house as he prepares to enter the barren landscape that surrounds him. While no characters in the film remain untouched by violence and an endless spiral of revenge, Edward is clearly portrayed as the only character willing and able to do whatever it takes to restore the homesteading family to something like normal domestic peace. But once his mission is complete, he is neither invited to share the fruits of his labor—to enter into the home's rest—nor does he seem capable of doing so even if asked.

Like many of the characters John Wayne played in his decades-long career, Ethan Edward is what I will call a suffering hero—a hero who bears a burden for heroism and pays a price for whatever good he (and occasionally she) achieves. The price is exclusion from, or at least marginality to, the very society the hero seeks to defend and protect. The burden is the existential awareness of the price, manifesting itself in anger, despair, sorrow, stoicism, or emotional withdrawal, and usually in some combination of these responses. Ethan Edward has many compatriots in certain kinds of cowboys, superheroes, rogue cops, and secret agents. What makes these suffering heroes heroic, and not just average men caught in tragic circumstances, is the possession of some preternatural or supernatural ability. In Edward's case, and in the cases of most of his cowboy and rogue cop peers, the preternatural ability is being "the fastest gun in the west," "a born killer," and someone who is able and willing to take the law into his own hands for the greater good. A superhero may possess all or some of these qualities in addition to obviously supernatural skills—the ability to fly, spin webs, or shoot blades out of his knuckles. Yet the social fate of the hero tends toward alienation or tragedy, since the extraordinary capacities that allow him to protect his society also exclude him from it. The dual nature of the ability—it is both a gift and a curse—gives rise to the two temptations that constantly beset the suffering hero: either to disown his ability in order to integrate into society (think of Superman in the 1980 *Superman II* or William Munny in *Unforgiven*), or to withdraw his ability completely and surrender society to whatever chaos he might otherwise have kept at bay (think of Wolverine in *X-Men 2* or Creasy in 2004's *Man on Fire*). The suffering hero must not give in to either temptation—whether integrating or withdrawing from society—but instead he must continue to pay the price of existential anguish and social exclusion.

Suffering heroes have been a mainstay of American popular culture for at least as long as there have been cowboys and frontiers in the popular imagination, but they have returned with a vengeance in the last several years. John Wayne's silhouette on the bleak frontier seems now a prescient image to herald the popular heroes who have arisen in our time of war. The increased prevalence of heroes who suffer existential anguish for their heroism is coupled with the fact that these heroes are themselves darker, more ambiguous, engaging in actions that walk a fine line between keeping chaos at bay and falling into its spiraling abyss. These two trends, in my mind, are directly related: the age of terror seems to demand a kind of heroics that is palpably distasteful and dangerous, but through the conventions of suffering heroism this danger is mitigated, and an otherwise despicable hero becomes palatable, even attractive. The suffering these heroes endure not only makes them more sympathetic, but is positively required for their heroics: if they did not suffer, they would become the very force of lawless anarchy they fight, kill, and torture to keep at bay. As a Christian theologian, I find this trend particularly worrisome because the conventions of the suffering hero

depend upon tropes of vicarious suffering drawn from a christological repertoire that have escaped the bounds of ecclesial or theological control. In other words, the suffering that makes these dark heroes attractive depends upon an idea of redemptive suffering that is especially familiar to Christians and in turn influences how Christians interpret the contours of Jesus' own suffering.

This phenomenon of dark suffering heroics is at work in three widely watched, widely admired recent heroes: Jack Bauer, Jason Bourne, and Batman. I want to briefly examine how the conventions of suffering heroism are at work in these characters, before concluding with reflections on why and how this trend in popular culture should matter to all thoughtful, engaged Christians, regardless of their vocations—and indeed to all who care about the shaping of our national moral imagination.

Perhaps no hero has stood out as a symbol of heroics in the age of terror more than Jack Bauer, the character played by Kiefer Sutherland on the Fox television show "24." Jack is clearly an heir of the cowboys and rogue cops who came before him—a mix of Josey Wales and Dirty Harry—able and willing to do what no one else will do to save America from imminent mass destruction. But the preternatural ability for which

Jack suffers, and by which he is marked as a hero, is his ability to torture. "24" has garnered attention from both the liberal and conservative press for its willingness to display graphic scenes of torture, almost all of them performed by the government-agent protagonists of the show, with Jack taking the lead. While many of the "good guys" who work for the fictional counter-terrorism unit have engaged in torture on the show, Jack is elevated above them all, both for his willingness to take the law into his own hands and for the brutality of his methods. Jack electrocutes the people he interrogates. He breaks their bones, shoots them in the leg or arm, stabs them in the shoulder or knee, suffocates them, and always threatens to do even worse. But the terror of his tactics is made palatable and even desirable as our sympathies are directed away from the body in pain to the body inflicting it. Jack suffers emotionally or existentially for the pain he causes. He is dramatically cast out of the society he defends on more than one occasion: symbolically in the death of his wife and the disintegration of his family, one time faking his own death, and another being kidnapped and tortured in an underground Chinese prison for over two years.

"24" has come under so much scrutiny for its depictions of Jack as a torturing hero that, in preparation for the seventh season (airing in 2009), the producers debated whether or not Jack should have a change of heart and repent for his brutality. Ultimately, they decided to portray him as aggressively unrepentant. We have, however, an example of the hero who suffers because of a change of heart, albeit aided by amnesia, in the character of Jason Bourne, played by Matt Damon, hero of the Bourne film trilogy that came out in increments from 2002–2007. Bourne is a black-ops secret agent, a programmed human killing machine, equipped with an arsenal of martial arts, foreign languages, and technological prowess. After a mission gone awry, Bourne has forgotten his identity, whom he worked for, and even the details of his previous missions. He has not, however, forgotten the repertoire of knowledge that makes him a walking lethal weapon. Bourne's body knows things his conscious mind does not: when confronted with danger, he responds with karate and jujitsu; when confronted with German, he finds he speaks the language fluently; when hunted by the CIA, he is a master of high-tech surveillance equipment.

We cannot help but watch with awe, and a certain amount of voyeuristic glee, as this seemingly mild-mannered young man discovers an array of near superhuman skills at, or literally in, his fingertips. But these preternatural abilities come with the price of great suffering, primarily in the form of graphic flashbacks of people he killed when following orders he no longer properly remembers. He is forced to run, abandoned, alone, with nothing but the ghosts of the lives he took as a virtuosic killer. In his anguish, he assumes the role of hero instead of assassin, seeking to find and confront the people who robbed his humanity. We are urged to overlook and forgive the violence of his past because he pays so handsomely in existential torment for the violence of his present.

In both Jack and Jason we watch heroes who do things we would find despicable, except that the suffering they bear renders them pitiable and attractive. The combination of dark and suffering heroics reached its apotheosis with the 2008 release of *The Dark Knight*, Christopher Nolan's sequel to his equally dark *Batman Begins* (2005). Hailed as an infusion of the comic book genre film with the aesthetics and sensibility of serious dramatic cinema, the new Batman movies have self-consciously played with the line between masked crusader and madman. *The Dark Knight* revels in this ambiguity, giving equal or more time to the deadly hijinks of its sadistically appealing villain, the Joker, as to its hero, the Batman himself. Rather than pitting himself against Batman, the Joker is on an elaborate, violent, high-stakes mission to persuade Batman to join his ranks, urging that they are both outcasts already, the only difference being Batman's absurd desire to play within the confines of the law while also swooping around in a mask and cape. While Batman repulses these villainous advances by allowing himself to be framed for the murder of a public servant turned madman, he ends up enacting the Joker's prophecy that he will be cast out by the society he defends. The movie ends with Batman being chased by the police as Lieutenant Gordon, an incorruptible police officer, explains to his son that this is the kind of hero the age demands: a hero the people cannot understand or accept, one they must drive out of their midst, but one who will keep protecting them from the shadowy place just outside the reach of the law.

Batman's willingness to suffer for crimes he did not commit in order to uphold a higher law of justice has drawn explicit christological parallels among cultural critics. Writing an opinion piece for the *Wall Street Journal*, mystery novelist Andrew Klavan reminds us that many heroes, like Batman, have been willing and able to do what must be done for the greater good, saying, "Many have been abhorred for it, some killed, one crucified."[389] Perhaps innocent suffering on the part of any hero is enough to earn a comparison to Jesus, but often the allusion is stronger and more visual. Jack Bauer returns from his two years in Chinese captivity with a long matted beard and a back lacerated with the scars of his torture—a visual reference, if not to standard pious images, certainly to Mel Gibson's icon of the suffering Jesus made popular less than two years earlier. At the end of *The Bourne Ultimatum* (the final movie in the series), Jason Bourne jumps to his supposed death, landing cruciform in the Hudson River. Three very symbolic days later, reports that his body cannot be found reach his last remaining ally, and in a half-smile she conveys her belief in his survival, a witness to a resurrection no one else can prove.

I do not want to suggest that these heroes are Christ figures, replete with the full allegorical equipage burdening so many of the characters I was supposed to analyze in high school English classes. I do, however, want to suggest that these characters borrow christological tropes in order to evoke the pathos that makes them properly heroic. Vicarious suffering becomes a device to make attractive what is otherwise despicable. In these movies and television shows we are being sold a vision of our world as threatened by forces worse than any we could previously imagine. These enemies do not simply want to wreck a home, take a hostage, or rob a string of banks. They are forces of mindless, irrational chaos, aimed at nothing short of mass annihilation or programmatic assassination. The heroes demanded by this kind of threat must be willing and able to fight fire with fire. They must in fact succumb to many of the same dark forces they fight: engaging in violence without respect for law, particular identity, or proven guilt or innocence. They become mirror images of the anarchy they work tirelessly to keep at bay. But anarchic heroes are hard to admire. By suffering misunderstanding, loneliness, and ultimately exclusion from the societies they defend, these heroes are rescued from the darkness that threatens to engulf them and re-enthroned in the pantheon of popular heroes.

In a national climate heavy with fear, we have been told our safety requires people willing to do "whatever it takes." It is a testament to a general uneasiness with this bravado, law-be-damned attitude that so many of our popular heroes are suffering heroes. Their suffering assures us that someone is paying the price for this bravado. They provide the fantasy that one man might bear the sins of a whole nation by suffering for the necessary evil our security seems to demand. But this is a deceptive salvation because it can never be rendered absolutely. Their final sacrifice in death would rob us of their redemptive work. There is no resurrection, no hope, no triumph over sin, despair, and injustice promised by this kind of suffering servant, only continual threat and continual suffering. This kind of hero can be the hero only of a world that imagines itself perpetually under attack.[390]

The kinds of heroes we imagine often teach us about what we fear and what we most hope to be. And when viewed by millions of Americans, they both describe and help shape our moral imagination. In a moment when we are being told to think of America as a kind of savior, willing to do whatever must be done to keep itself and the world safe for democracy, suffering heroes seem to be the heroes of our time. But they need not be. Christians in particular have the resources of a theological tradition that can reveal the false promises of violent redemptive suffering, in which there is no real redemption. We must first squarely face the assurance of salvation these heroes offer. Then, having long been taught to see in Christ's suffering a sign of God's pledge of love to the world, we can wrest our eyes from the hero's sorrowful face and the threat of endless violence he promises.

Prisons Outside the Kingdom:
A Theological Reflection on CIA Black Sites

Natalie Wigg-Stevenson

In this time of perpetual war, we encounter much to which Christians must theologically respond, to which we must herald good news. My hope here is to do this heralding. I am not going to argue that torture itself is unethical, or even that it is an ineffective, shortsighted tactic for national security, although both these points are true. Rather, I plan to tap into the resources of the Christian tradition to show why Christians must oppose not only torture, but also the legal gymnastics performed to create the extra-legal physical spaces where torture takes place.

Recent US torture practices rely on spaces like CIA black sites that exist beyond any legal jurisdiction. But a theology grounded in the Bible and Christian tradition is bound to the Christian belief that the legal rule is provisionary of God's rule. For Christians, God's kingdom fulfills the law's open-ended purpose. While a theology of God's kingdom cannot provide an easy response to torture, it does reveal hope for something Christians should perceive to be greater than individual or national security. The kingdom promises us participation in God's perfecting of the law as we now know it. And so Christians who anticipate the kingdom cannot condone black sites or governmental positioning beyond legal accountability without at the very least raising our voices in prayerful dissent.

Because descriptions of black sites are as elusive as attempts to define their legal status, a chronology from the past eight years of information pertinent to their existence can aid our understanding of them. While they function beyond the jurisdiction of international and even, for all intents and purposes, American law, the way in which they do so depends on complex and often logically incoherent divisions of power and accountability between various government agencies and departments—in particular, the Pentagon, FBI, and CIA. Black sites sit on the fringe of the places we are able to see, cordoned off by uncountable makeshift legal fences which, while fragile and crumbling, continue their labyrinthine ability to disorient our path to discovery.

As journalist Michael Otterman argues, even before 9/11 the CIA was growing impatient with FBI interrogation techniques that depended on rapport building more than psychological or physical domination.[391] Post-9/11, this gulf stretched even wider. On 17 September 2001, a mere six days after the terrorist attacks on the World Trade Center and the Pentagon, President Bush signed a presidential finding granting to the CIA, in the words of its director George Tenet, a "new robust authority to operate without restraint."[392] Cofer Black, director of the CIA's Counter-Terrorism Center, testified to the Senate and House Intelligence Committees two weeks later stating, "…there was a 'before' 9/11 and 'after' 9/11. After 9/11 the gloves come off."[393]

Empowered to act without restraint, by late 2001 the CIA was running out of places to hide their high-value detainees. They began to desire greater control over their investigations than was possible with their necessary reliance on foreign allies and were granted hundreds of millions of dollars to begin construction of their own private prison network.[394] The first known black site was built north of Kabul on an old factory site called the "Salt Pit."[395] Today they are located across the world—of particular note, in the Middle East, East Asia, Africa, and Europe.

Presidential suspensions of Geneva human rights conventions in early 2002, NGO protests against these violations and the suspected existence of black sites, and the April 2005 "60 Minutes" report breaking the story of prisoner abuse and torture at Abu Ghraib paved the way to a pivotal moment in the history of what we know about black sites. In fall 2005, journalist Dana Priest published her Pulitzer Prize-winning article in the *Washington Post*, exposing the existence of black sites and linking them to the unprecedented new powers of the CIA. Public outrage grew. But it was not until almost a year later on 6 September 2006, two months shy of the mid-term elections, that the president admitted to the existence of black sites, only hours after the Pentagon announced a new Army field manual on interrogations.

This new manual banned all coercive techniques of torture and called for a return to the more humane FBI-style interrogation practices.[396] It only applied, however, to Pentagon agents; that is, military interrogators. The CIA, in contrast, maintained and continues to maintain its own, autonomous, robust power. By admitting the existence of black site prisons, the president effectively informed the American people of a carefully constructed loophole to the national and international legal responsibilities the Pentagon had just announced. Black sites became the place where a potential national fear that obeying the rules might get us hurt could be alleviated, because they became the place where the rules simply do not count.

Many Christians in America are struggling with how to respond to this crisis. We already exhibit a conflicted understanding of the relationship between law, politics, and the kingdom of God. Rather than drawing sharp boundaries between these realms, however, we should do our theology at the places where they overlap. Towards this end, I draw on theologian Wolfhart Pannenberg's biblically-based argument that the political orders of a society play a preparatory role in the coming of God's kingdom.[397] Pannenberg theologically articulates one traditional Christian way of relating faith and culture by demonstrating how political and legal orders prepare our societies for God's redemption of all creation. In engaging this theology, we will see that Christians cannot, under any circumstances, condone the extra-legal spaces that are necessary for the existence of black sites, let alone the torture that takes place in these spaces.

Writing in post-Holocaust Germany, Pannenberg took seriously questions of God's justice as he grappled with the horrors of unchecked state power. Grounding his vision in stories of Old Testament monarchies and the prophetic calls to justice spoken in response to their failings, he argued that if we trust God is righteous, we can expect a time when God will come to rule creation directly.[398] This kingdom, God's rule, will establish an order of complete "justice, peace, and the mutual fellowship of all humanity" in a way that does not replace our attempts to construct a just society here and now, but rather perfects and exceeds them.[399]

Turning to the New Testament, Pannenberg argues that through the life, death, and resurrection of Jesus Christ, this end-of-time rule is present to us now as a promise, the fulfillment of which we anticipate with hope. It is never fully with us or known by us in a pure form until the end of time when God's rule is completed in the just and loving consummation of all of creation. But we do catch momentary glimpses of it through the life of the church, worship, and the sacraments, and in doing truly just actions. These glimpses are of something distant yet coming, of the way things will one day be. And the Christian life is lived in hopeful anticipation of this time. We seek to live, to love, as if it is already here.

Because anticipating the kingdom means anticipating just and peaceful political orders, Pannenberg argues, we construct systems that work towards that end now. Hence, our current orders, in their best— and even worst—forms, share the "task" of establishing justice and peace.[400] Whether or not the state recognizes itself as doing so, it thus always plays a role provisionally related to God's kingdom. Pannenberg assures the reader that, of course, the legal orders of a society do not necessarily reflect or embody God's righteous will.[401] Examples of unjust laws and corrupt politics abound. And yet, these systems play a preparatory role in the task of God's kingdom—that is, the task of preserving and producing peace and justice among all peoples.

In this way, Pannenberg affirms that glimpses of God's kingdom create desire in us for just social orders. While legal systems value national security by necessity, we hope the justice that transcends the law will also transcend enemy lines. A faulty law that allows abuse of another for the sake of the self is bad, but the absence of any law governing such relations is worse because it permits unmitigated caprice and reactionary fear. Christians long for the culmination of our belief in a time when global reconciliation occurs without the cost of violence. But we also know that until this is the case, all socio-political human interactions continue to require the protection of human rights law. Otherwise, the fallen human ability to wield cruel and vicious power over others simply cannot remain in check.

Therefore, for Christians to sanction black sites or any spheres of action without legal jurisdiction is not only immoral, but also contrary to our understanding of how God works in the world. God does not only judge and redeem *individuals*. This unfortunately popular vision of salvation is too narrow. Rather, God judges and redeems all of creation, a process in which the lives of individuals—to varying degrees of participation—are caught up. Twentieth-century individualism aside, this is the more accurate vision of the biblical witness. For Christians to condone banishing any apparatus by which humans are accountable for their actions in a broader community, then, is to falsely understand what we believe a human being to be before God.

And yet, of course, this is precisely what black sites do. Their extra-legal status exempts torturers from judgment by the law, while also somehow protecting the law from needing to judge the torturer. We thereby falsely imagine God turning a blind eye towards the relationship that links torture and the law to each other. But the Christian story of hope requires that God's actions not be indifferent, but be those of judgment, redemption, and reconciliation, and that these actions be performed upon both torture and the law in their relation to each other and to the rest of creation. Neither acts of torture nor legal systems are perfected or completed ends in themselves. Rather, their ends are found in God's redemption of each within the broader context of divinely created and sustained existence.

This problem is exacerbated when we consider that law does not only regulate human behavior, but also produces it. Recent philosophy, reacting against radically individualized conceptions of human beings, presents a vision in which the human ability to reason, emote, and act is created, constituted, and held together in a matrix of competing cultural systems, within which both legal and religious codes are considered to be significant players. In simple terms, in the "nature vs. nurture" debate, nurture has come to be seen as vitally important in more theoretically complex ways. Thus, to imagine we can separate the torturer from the legal context that makes torture possible is itself an erroneous belief.

Legal, religious, and other norms governing our behavior are absorbed into our self-understanding at both the conscious and unconscious level. Thus shaping our reflexes to others' behavior, they affect the complex structure of all human interactions. In terms of legal codes, then, we are constructed as people who either obey or conscientiously disobey them, or who inadvertently ignore them, but we cannot be constructed in distinction from them. For example, I can be a person who pays my taxes, who refuses to pay my taxes on moral grounds, or who forgets to pay my taxes, but I cannot act within culture without some relationship to tax law. And in each scenario, the ends of my act transcend my act. For each action there is a norm that both judges and forms it as either good or bad, and there are potential consequences in each case. I might get a refund or a fine, or I might escape the notice of the IRS. But either way, there is always the possibility that I will be held accountable for what I have done and that this potential for accountability has some bearing on the meaning of what I do to begin with.

The legal codes governing interrogation sites thus both restrict and produce the behavior of those acting within them, potentially towards the end of ethical behavior, but at least towards an end outside the activity itself. Of course people working within these systems can choose to disobey aspects of these laws. If they do so, however, they are legally accountable for their act. This distinction matters because the disobeyed law becomes embedded in the meaning of what has thus become an illegal action. Actions performed illegally are therefore qualitatively different than actions performed extra-legally. Illegal action bears the potential for a just end beyond itself; extra-legal action is its own end.

Consequently, if we continue to follow Pannenberg's idea that legal rule prepares society for God's future rule, we further note that to create spaces like black sites where people cannot be held legally accountable is to create spaces in which God's kingdom cannot be anticipated. It is to create spaces devoid of hope. And it is to create spaces that opt out of God's plan for social reconciliation and redemption. Such action wrongly imagines that we can live any aspect of our lives in isolation, apart from God's own power to observe, intercede, or judge. Thinking in this way imagines the human act, rather than God's act, to be the end of a given event. And this is idolatrous imagining for Christians. Therefore, legal and political systems take on a particular role in Christian anticipatory living for the kingdom. They construct the society from which we hope for redemption, the society that will, in fact, be redeemed. And as we see in the Old Testament narratives, they construct the society to which we are to bring prophetic speech, reforming speech, to which we must herald good news.

Let me tip my hand here for just a moment. I am a Christian theologian and minister. This is the arena in which I work and from which I speak. And the good news of the gospel is a gift that comes with a calling. Christians do not have the option of living beyond the law if we are to take seriously our role to be salt and light to the nations. To do so would be to abandon those with whom God has called us to be. And for those of us who do live under the rule of law—that is, the vast majority of us—we should refuse to receive the dubious benefit of others living extra-legally for us. The church must therefore recognize and repent of the ways in which these extra-legal practices of torture touch our lives if we are to maintain our witness as the church.

Murmurings have begun suggesting presidential pardons and the possibility of a truth and reconciliation commission so that these extra-legal actions can at least be brought to light legally. The success of the South African TRC was dependent on the involvement and wisdom of Christian leaders who could provide a deep perspective on what reconciliation truly is, with an eye towards healing for victims, and not just protection for high-level officials. Christians must begin preparing for this debate and possible action now so that our work will embody God's healing power, not merely support the status quo of the powers that be.

We have particular gifts to bring to these conversations. We must begin now to figure out what these gifts are. The theological understanding of law and God's kingdom that Christians share and can use to speak against the existence of black sites is only one starting point. My prayer is that together Christians in America will have the fortitude to seek out and articulate other aspects of our tradition that can call this nation back to a vision of justice and, one day, peace. My hope is that we will have the courage to participate in God's bringing about of that justice and peace, that we will resist a shortsighted culture of fear so that we can instead live into God's kingdom of hope.

11

National Security, Torture, and a Practical Way Forward

Rachel Laser

Back in 2003, Third Way was working on passing an amendment to close the gun show loophole. But we had some problems: Democrats were afraid of gun control. Al Gore blamed his defeat in 2000 on guns, and Democrats were scared of the issue. We didn't have the votes. We knew we couldn't pass this amendment without then-Senate majority leader Tom Daschle's commitment to bring it to the floor and support it. And Tom Daschle didn't know us from Adam.

So we decided to rub our pennies together and do a poll of South Dakota figuring that would land us a meeting. Sure enough, two months later we were in Senator Daschle's office, sitting in front of him. He had this look on his face not uncommon to politicians—a look of "I have no idea what you're doing here—you had better make it fast." So we kicked off the meeting like this: "By a margin of 88-9, South Dakotans favor closing the gun show loophole." He didn't move; he didn't smile; he just sat there, blinking at us once or twice.

Then we said this: "We're here to tell you why those poll numbers are meaningless, why the gun issue doesn't work in South Dakota and much of the country, what needs to be done to change the politics on guns, and how our strategy can help sell this amendment to people in South Dakota and across America." Now we had his attention. What we understood was that no poll would convince a seasoned politician something he thought worked poorly in his state—like gun control—actually worked well. Our task on guns was to figure out why something that seemed to poll so well sold so poorly once the debate began. If we could figure that out and develop an antidote—with message, framing, and policy—we could move forward. In the end, the message for Tom Daschle was "We're going to bring South Dakota values to Washington by supporting Second Amendment rights and making sure these rights don't extend to terrorists and criminals."

We succeeded with Senator Daschle. He changed his mind in the meeting. He bought our strategy. He brought our amendment to the floor, helped round up votes, and it passed. I tell you this story to make the point that, from our experience, Third Way understands having the moral high ground on an issue is necessary, but not sufficient. We understand issues that appear to be an easy sell have treacherous currents underneath them. We specialize in understanding these obstacles and creating a strategy to get the job done.

We've not just done this on guns. We do it on other culture issues, such as immigration, and on economic issues too—like how to speak effectively to the middle class. And we've done it on national security issues—which brings me to what I want to talk about today. I'd like to take the rest of my time to offer up to you the outlines of a strategy to make new inroads and win new allies on the issue of torture. That strategy has three components: (1) Recognize that policymakers perceive torture fundamentally as a national security issue; (2) Use the strengths and weaknesses of each party to move them in the right direction on torture; and (3) Design and pursue a game plan aimed at the executive branch—not just Congress—to win this fight.

Recognize That Policymakers in Washington Perceive Torture as a National Security Issue

When elected officials are sworn into office, the first thing they do is place their hand on a Bible. But the second thing they do is take a pledge to preserve, protect, and defend the country against enemies foreign and domestic. They don't recite the Ten Commandments, and they don't promise to act according to a moral code or religious values. They swear that above everything else, no matter what happens, they will protect the nation. It is this promise that underlies the torture debate, like so many others, in Washington. It's not that faith and values frames don't also apply; it's that torture is inseparable from the national security debate. It's just a fundamental truth that Americans, and American policymakers, see torture in this context. I am certainly not disputing the enormity of the moral implications of torture—rather I'm saying that framing opposition to torture in terms of moral or religious imperatives is important, but it does not remove torture from the national security context. In order to advocate effectively, you must address the issue in the framework where it exists in the minds of policymakers and the public.

Politicians are not ignorant of the moral implications of torture, but when they think about the torture debate, policymakers are largely focused on another imperative—securing the country against terrorist attacks. In order to convince them to oppose torture, you must first address that imperative, persuading them that torture isn't an effective way to protect our nation and giving them the tools to persuade their constituents.

The attitudes of policymakers in Washington reflect those of the American people. Even after being exposed to the abuses in Abu Ghraib and elsewhere, most Americans still do not see torture as a black-and-white issue. When asked about torture in the abstract, polls show a clear majority of Americans are opposed to torture, with 75 percent agreeing that the United States is a moral leader in the world and that we should not set a bad example by torturing or degrading people in detention. But if you dig below the surface, you find that Americans' opposition to torture is shallow. When asked about torture in a national security context, they are not so sure. In a Third Way poll last month, we asked, "Do you think the use of torture against suspected terrorists in order to gain important information can often be justified, sometimes be justified, or never be justified?"[402] Only 37 percent of people said that torture was never justified. Forty-three percent said it was sometimes justified, and 16 percent said often.

The new poll by Faith and Public Life and Mercer University focusing on white evangelicals in the South found similar attitudes. Close to six-in-ten respondents said torture can often or sometimes be justified in order to gain important information. Only 22 percent said never.[403]

When you look under the surface, public opinion on torture is not at the point that would goad policymakers to abolish its use. The American public is divided on the use of torture. Focusing on the moral implications of torture will get you on the field, but it can't bring you past the goal line. You can't convince policymakers or the public to bring an end to torture unless you confront the national security question head on. So let's move to the second part of the strategy.

Use the Strengths and Weaknesses of Each Party to Move Them in the Right Direction on Torture

Once you recognize that torture is a national security issue in the political context, you must then understand and use the strengths and weaknesses of each party on national security to persuade them to end torture. Whether we want them to or not, party labels matter. Americans hear policymakers differently depending on the politician's party. Politicians understand that reality too, and it informs their decisions. So they try not to do or say things that play into their party's perceived weaknesses.

Let me give you an example from the news recently. Barack Obama has an economic plan that would raise taxes for people making over $250,000 a year, which is the top 2 percent of earners in the country. Under that plan, everyone else gets a tax cut. But a poll released this week found that 51 percent of Americans believe Obama would raise their taxes. When people hear "Democrat," they think "higher taxes," and that association is so strong that it overcomes the reality of Obama's plan. Because policymakers are tuned into these party preconceptions, you must also be aware of them as you advocate for the abolition of torture.

On the issue of torture, policymakers come to the table carrying their party's national security baggage. Because each party has different strengths and weaknesses on national security, you must tailor your strategy by party affiliation. Democrats are generally seen as weak on national security. Historically, at least for the past few decades,

Democrats have lacked public trust on national security issues. They are overwhelmingly perceived as hesitant, indecisive, and unwilling to use force. In our poll last month, we found that Democrats were associated with the phrase "too hesitant to use force" over Republicans by a thirty-eight-point margin. The term "not decisive enough in a crisis" was associated more with Democrats over Republicans by twenty-one points.

This perception of weakness is something Democrats have struggled with for decades, and they are acutely aware of this deficiency. Their sensitivity to this perception of weakness means that even if they are opposed to torture, they may not be willing to strongly advocate for the abolition of torture until Republicans lead the way.

But Democrats have certain strengths too that are also useful to know in your efforts. Democrats are overwhelmingly perceived as sensible and willing to work with allies. According to our poll, 50 percent of Americans see Democrats as the party that "use[s] diplomacy effectively." Only 30 percent say the same about Republicans.

Now let's talk about Republicans. Republicans generally have a history of perceived strength on national security, but they are also seen as reckless. Republicans have long been dominant on security issues, and the results of our poll last month show that the party's historic advantage remains strong in the minds of Americans. When asked which party they associated with the word "tough" when it comes to national security, 55 percent of respondents picked Republicans and only 24 percent picked Democrats.

But participants also identified Republicans as the party that is "reckless" when it comes to national security—by sixteen points. Moderates pick Republicans as "reckless" by twenty-seven points. You can use these strengths and weaknesses when you design and pursue an advocacy strategy for policymakers.

To convince policymakers in Washington to put an end to torture, you must both locate the torture issue in the context of a larger national security debate and play on the strengths and weaknesses of the parties. But in order to create an effective advocacy strategy, you must first know where the parties are on the issue of torture. Democrats are largely opposed to torture as a substantive matter. It seems their hearts are already in the right place. At a debate last year during the primaries, the Democratic presidential candidates were presented with a "ticking time bomb" scenario, and every one of them emphatically denounced the use of torture.

Senator Obama gave this response: "America cannot sanction torture. It's a very straightforward principle, and one that we should abide by. Now, I will do whatever it takes to keep America safe. And there are going to be all sorts of hypotheticals and emergency situations and I will make that judgment at that time. But what we cannot do is have…a loophole or an exception where we would sanction torture. I think that diminishes us and it sends the wrong message to the world." Senator Biden also forcefully opposed the use of torture, saying, "It doesn't work. It should be no part of our policy ever—ever." Senators Clinton, Dodd, and Edwards and Representative Kucinich all wholeheartedly agreed with those sentiments. Republicans, on the other hand, appear to be not yet convinced that torture should be abolished.

Let me just be clear. No serious candidate or policymaker of either party explicitly supports "torture." But many in the Republican party have defended the use of unconscionable interrogation techniques that in reality amount to torture. They use euphemisms like "enhanced interrogation techniques" and pay lip service to ending "torture," but they have largely supported the Bush administration's use of waterboarding, stress positions, light and heat deprivation, sexual humiliation, and other torture tactics.

During the primaries, Republican presidential candidates tried to one-up each other on how "tough" they would be in using "enhanced interrogation techniques." When asked whether he would sanction torture to get information from a suspected terrorist, Rudy Giuliani said, "In the hypothetical that you gave me, which assumes that we know there's going to be another attack and these people know about it, I would tell the people who had to do the interrogation to use every method they could think of." And Mitt Romney responded, "Some people have said we ought to close Guantánamo. My view is we ought to double Guantánamo… And enhanced interrogation techniques have to be used—not torture but enhanced interrogation techniques, yes."

Representative Duncan Hunter from California said in the same debate, "I would say to the Secretary of Defense, in terms of getting information that would save American lives, even if it involves very high-pressure techniques, one sentence: Get the information." And in her acceptance speech at the Republican National Convention, vice presidential nominee Sarah Palin mocked Barack Obama's position on the issue, saying, "Al Qaeda terrorists still plot to inflict catastrophic harm on America...he's worried that someone won't read them their rights?"

The most recent vote in Congress also provides a stark illustration of the party's positions on torture.[404] In February, Congress passed a bill that included a provision to ban the use of waterboarding and other "enhanced interrogation techniques" by CIA agents. But almost every Republican in both the House and the Senate voted against it, including Senator McCain. President Bush ultimately vetoed the bill.

Obviously, based on their positions and preconceptions, both parties have deficits when it comes to leading the fight against torture. The Democrats want to end torture but are hesitant to take the lead. The Republicans aren't yet convinced that torture should be abolished. These are two very different problems—and they require different advocacy strategies.

So, what's the Democratic strategy? It's about helping them with their perception problem—not about their underlying position. It has two parts: (1) arm Democrats with the substance to show their constituents that ending torture is a show of strength and (2) convince Democrats that ending torture can also work for them politically.

Here, you need to rely on the substantive national security arguments. You know all the arguments. Torture is reckless, ineffective, and creates more enemies—not fewer. In a public letter to the troops last year, General David Petraeus, the commanding general of the multinational force in Iraq, wrote these powerful words to make sure there was no question about where the US military stands on torture, and he wove together the national security framework with the moral argument:

> Some may argue that we would be more effective if we sanctioned torture or other expedient methods to obtain

information from the enemy. They would be wrong. Beyond the basic fact that such actions are illegal, history shows that they also are frequently neither useful nor necessary. Certainly, extreme physical action can make someone "talk;" however, what the individual says may be of questionable value.... What sets us apart from our enemies in this fight, however, is how we behave. In everything we do, we must observe the standards and values that dictate that we treat noncombatants and detainees with dignity and respect.

We need more statements like this. You can help give politicians new voices—additional voices—to make this point. Your first job with Democrats is to help them convince the public that ending torture helps America fight a more effective war on terror.

Next, show Democrats that by taking a courageous stand against torture, they can gain politically. Democrats can benefit by forming coalitions with the faith community. Faith voters are an important tool in the Democrats' arsenal. They broaden their base. They demonstrate that opposition to torture isn't out of the mainstream. And public support by the religious community—perceived traditionally as part of the Republican base—can give Democrats political cover in the eyes of the moderate voter.

For Democrats, ending torture will also energize their base, for whom torture is an important issue. By stepping forward and putting their foot down, Democrats can own the moral high ground and show consistency and strength, fending off claims that they are weaklings who merely pander to public opinion.

The Republican strategy has three parts: (1) convince Republicans they will suffer in the eyes of an important part of their base if they stay the course on torture, (2) persuade them that they can compensate for their political vulnerabilities by changing their position, and (3) and convince them that torture doesn't work.

First, Republicans need to know that by staying the course on torture, they will suffer in the eyes of faith voters, who have added this to their list of top culture issues. You must persuade Republicans that faith voters aren't satisfied by legalistic answers and nominal opposition to torture. They need to hear that ending torture by any name (including enhanced interrogation techniques and cruel and degrading treatment) is a *moral imperative.*

Second, persuade Republicans that they can address their own political vulnerabilities by changing their position on torture. Americans believe Republicans are reckless on national security issues, and the Bush administration's torture policies epitomize that recklessness. So adopting anti-torture policies will do more than solidify Republicans' base of support in faith voters—it will also counteract negative perceptions held by both religious and non-religious voters around the country. And for what it's worth, opposition to torture could also help reduce distrust from the traditionally Democratic human rights movement.

Third, in addition to giving Republicans political motivation, you will also need to convince them that torture doesn't work. Republican policymakers have put a huge amount of stock in the "ticking time bomb" scenario, and many are genuinely convinced that torture is an effective interrogation technique. You can help change that assumption. Because faith voters are an important constituency to Republicans, policymakers may give substantive arguments more credence if they come from you. You are not the usual suspects, and that may open their hearts and minds to hear what you have to say.

The fact is that the ticking time bomb scenario is a comic book fantasy—not real life. Unlike the fantasy, real torture does not yield useful information. If it did, we would have caught Osama bin Laden by now.

So now we've recognized that torture is a national security issue and looked at party preconceptions as a tool for influencing Democrats and Republicans. My final piece of advice is to design a game plan that is also aimed at the executive to win this fight.

On torture, ultimately, it comes down to the president. Obviously, the strategy going forward will change drastically based on the outcome of the election. The president is the ultimate decision-maker on torture, so it is crucial to tailor your message to the executive. Congress can have an important impact on interrogation policy, but it is virtually impossible to effectively abolish torture through legislation. If the law outlines specific techniques that are prohibited, new techniques can always be developed to skirt the law. If the law lays out guidelines or standards rather than specific techniques, it can be circumvented, as demonstrated in recent years. The bottom line is that the decision to use torture is made in secret, and the decision-maker sits in the White House. When terrorism suspect Khalid Sheikh Mohammed was captured, he was brought to an undisclosed location where undisclosed things were done to him by undisclosed people. Torture takes place in the darkest of dark places. And when the moment of truth comes, it is not debated on the floor of Congress. It's up to the president.

Just as with other policymakers, the message that will move the president will be based—at least in part—on his political party. If Obama is elected president, you can use the Democratic strategy. You can address his concerns about perception by arming him with a robust and diverse coalition of support. Your coalition can provide him with new and different voices to make the point that ending torture is in the best interest of national security. Your coalition can show that opposition to torture is not weak, but mainstream. Your strength as a coalition can strengthen his political will and confidence.

In July 1862, Abraham Lincoln gathered his cabinet to discuss the possibility of abolishing slavery. He wanted to do it because it was morally right and because he thought it would enhance the war effort, but the political risks for President Lincoln were huge. The idea was deeply unpopular with the broader public.

War Democrats were strongly against ending slavery, and many Republicans were gloomy about the war, which was going badly. They viewed their struggle solely in terms of preserving the Union; they were not committed to sending their sons to die to free the slaves.

Lincoln saw that he needed a Union victory before he could issue an emancipation proclamation, so he would be acting from a position of strength. After the North's victory at Antietam, Lincoln had his opening—and he took it, issuing the preliminary Emancipation Proclamation on September 22. Emancipation went from an idea that was unpopular to one that gained broad acceptance. History has judged the issuance of the Emancipation Proclamation as one of the greatest moments in the life of this nation.

What happened? President Lincoln timed and framed the Emancipation Proclamation perfectly. He realized the moral imperative would not take root without laying the foundation of addressing people's practical concerns.

As in his day, we have the moral high ground on the torture issue. But we must not forget that to win on torture we need to address the practical concerns at play—that torture is fundamentally linked to the national security issue, and that party labels matter. We have the power and strategy to help our country take the courageous, morally right, and necessary step of abolishing the use of torture. I look forward to being in this fight with you all.

★

NOTES

Torture after 9/11—The Road to Abu Ghraib

1 Adam Zagorin et al., "Inside the Interrogation of Detainee 063," *Time Magazine* (20 June 2005): 26–33.

2 Ibid. See also Philippe Sands, *Torture Team* (New York: Palgrave Macmillan, 2008) 7–14.

3 Ibid.

4 Michael Hirsh, "Truth About Torture; A courageous soldier and a determined senator demand clear standards," *Newsweek* (7 November 2005): 57.

5 Nat Hentoff, "More torture charges; CIA must be held accountable," *Washington Times*, 12 December 2005.

6 Ian Cobain, "CIA rendition flights: Case studies: Seized, held, tortured: six tell same tale," *Guardian*, 6 December 2005.

7 Nina Bernstein, "US Defends Detentions At Airports," *New York Times*, 10 August 2005.

8 Jane Mayer, "Outsourcing Torture; The secret history of America's 'extraordinary rendition' program," *New Yorker*, 14 February 2005; Scott Shane, "Justice Dept. Amends Remark on Torture Case," *New York Times*, 21 September 2006; Testimony of Maher Arar, joint oversight hearing, "Rendition to Torture: The Case of Maher Arar," United States House of Representatives, 18 October 2007.

9 Shannon McCaffrey, "Canadian Sent to Syrian Prison Disputes US Claims Against Torture," *Knight Ridder/Tribune News Service*, 1 August 2004.

10 Doug Struck, "Canadian Was Falsely Accused, Panel Says; After Tip From Ally, US Sent Muslim to Syria for Questioning," *Washington Post*, 19 September 2006.

11 Dana Priest and Barton Gellman, "US Decries Abuse but Defends Interrogations; 'Stress and Duress' Tactics Used on Terrorism Suspects Held in Secret Overseas Facilities," *Washington Post*, 26 December 2002.

12 Ibid.

13 Military order of 13 November 2001, "Detention, Treatment, and Trial of Certain non-Citizens in the War Against Terrorism," in Karen J. Greenberg and Joshua L. Dratel, *The Torture Papers* (Cambridge: Cambridge University Press, 2005) 25–28.

14 Statements by Paul D. Wolfowitz, deputy secretary of defense, and William J. Haynes, general counsel to the Department of Defense, Senate Armed Services Committee hearing, quoted in "The President's Order on Trials by Military Tribunal," Federal News Service, 12 December 2001; Statement of Attorney General John Ashcroft, hearing of the Senate Judiciary Committee, quoted in "The Department of Justice and Terrorism," Federal News Service, 6 December 2001; Statement of Pierre-Richard Prosper, state department ambassador-at-large for war crimes issues,

Senate Judiciary Committee hearing, quoted in "Preserving Freedoms While Defending Against Terrorism," Federal News Service, 4 December 2001; Statement of Michael Chertoff, assistant attorney general, criminal division, hearing of the Senate Judiciary Committee, quoted in "Preserving Freedoms While Defending Against Terrorism," Federal News Service, 28 November 2001.

15 Memo from John C. Yoo to Patrick F. Philbin, 28 December 2001, in Greenberg and Dratel, eds., *The Torture Papers*, 29–37.

16 John Yoo and Robert Delahunty to William J. Haynes II, memo re: "Application of Treaties and Laws to al Qaeda and Taliban Detainees," in Greenberg and Dratel, *The Torture Papers*, 38–79.

17 William H. Taft, IV to John C. Yoo, "Your Draft Memorandum of January 9," 11 January 2002, in "The Torture Question," "Frontline," PBS, 18 October 2005.

18 Jay S. Bybee, "Application of Treaties and Laws to al Qaeda and Taliban Detainees," memo to Alberto R. Gonzales and William J. Haynes, 22 January 2002, in *The Torture Papers*, ed. Karen J. Greenberg and Joshua L. Dratel (Cambridge: Cambridge University Press, 2005) 86.

19 Rowan Scarborough, "Powell wants detainees to be declared POWs; Memo shows differences with White House," *Washington Times*, 26 January 2002.

20 Donald Rumsfeld, press conference, 22 January 2002.

21 Memorandum, George W. Bush for the vice president et al., 7 February 2002, in Greenberg and Dratel, *The Torture Papers*, 134–35.

22 Jay S. Bybee, "Memorandum for Alberto Gonzales Counsel to the President, 'Standards of Conduct for Interrogation under 18 USC. §§ 2340–2340A,'" 1 August 2002, in Greenberg and Dratel, *The Torture Papers*, 172–217.

23 The techniques apparently originated with a group convened in Washington that included Haynes, Gonzales, Addington, and others. Sands, *The Torture Team*, 45–48.

24 Jerald Phifer, "Memorandum for Commander, Joint Task Force 170," 11 October 2002, in Greenberg and Dratel, *The Torture Papers*, 227–28. For a legal analysis of Geneva and the way these techniques violate the conventions, see Sands, *The Torture Team*, 3–6, 220–22.

25 Diane Beaver to Commander JTF 170, "Legal Brief on Proposed Counter-Resistance Strategies," in Greenberg and Dratel, *The Torture Papers*, 229–35.

26 Sands, *The Torture Team*, 76–84.

27 Jane Dalton, Senate Armed Services Committee hearing, "Aggressive Interrogation Techniques Toward Detainees in US Custody," 17 June 2008.

28 William J. Haynes to secretary of defense, "Counter-Resistance Techniques," in Greenberg and Dratel, *The Torture Papers*, 36–37.

29 See, e.g., "The Nightmare at Abu Ghraib," editorial, *New York Times*, 3 May 2004; Gebe Martinez, "Prisoner scandal puts heat on Hill; Congress poised for deeper inquiry," *Houston Chronicle*, 9 May 2004; "Nightline, Full Disclosure," "ABC News" transcripts, 7 May 2004.

30 Maj. Gen. Antonio M. Taguba, "US Army report on Iraqi prisoner abuse: Executive summary of Article 15–6 investigation of the 800th Military Police Brigade," http://72.14.207.104/search?q=cache:txztyPh5r58J:www.msnbc.msn.com/id/4894001/+%22Taguba+report%22&hl=en (accessed 12 November 2008).

31 Jack Goldsmith, *The Terror Presidency* (New York: W.W. Norton & Company, 2007).

32 President George Bush, "President Discusses Creation of Military Commissions to Try Suspected Terrorists," White House press conference, 6 September 2006, www.whitehouse.gov/news/releases/2006/09/20060906-3.html (accessed 12 November 2008).

33 See, e.g., Mark Mazzetti, "Questions Raised About Bush's Primary Claims in Defense of Secret Detention System," *New York Times*, 8 September 2006.

34 Rosa Brooks, "In the End, Torture Hurts Us," *Los Angeles Times*, 25 November 2005.

35 www.worldpublicopinion.org/pipa/pdf/jun08/WPO_Torture_Jun08_packet.pdf (accessed 12 July 2008).

36 pewresearch.org/databank/dailynumber/?NumberID=520 (accessed 12 July 2008).

How the US Military Responded to the Drift toward Torture

37 The Army was designated the executive agent for the planned war crimes tribunals. Thomas White was fired by Secretary of Defense Donald Rumsfeld in April 2003; see Associated Press, "Rumsfeld Fired Army Secretary Thomas White," *USA Today*, 25 April 2003.

38 United Nations Convention against Torture and other Cruel, Inhuman or Degrading Treatment or Punishment, G.A. res. 39/46 [annex, 39 U.N. GAOR Supp. (No. 51) at 197, U.N. Doc. A/39/51 (1984)], entered into force 26 June 1987, Article 1.

39 United Nations Convention against Torture and other Cruel, Inhuman or Degrading Treatment or Punishment, New York, 21 October 1994, United States Declarations and Reservations; available at www2.ohchr.org/english/bodies/ratification/9.htm#N11.

40 Geneva Convention relative to the treatment of prisoners of war, entered into force 21 October 1950, Article 17.

41 Geneva Convention relative to the protection of civilian persons in time of war, entered into force 21 October 1950, Article 31.

42 President George W. Bush, memo to the vice president et al., *Subject: Humane Treatment of Al Qaeda and Taliban Detainees*, 7 February 2002.

43 Article 3 of all four Geneva Conventions.

44 Jean Pictet, ed. *Commentary: IV Geneva Convention Relative to the Protection of Civilian Persons in Time of War* (Geneva: ICRC, 1958–1994 rep. ed.) 51.

45 President George W. Bush, *Memorandum to the Vice President, et al., Subject: Humane Treatment of Al Qaeda and Taliban Detainees*, 7 February 2002.

46 Jay C. Bybee, memo to Alberto R. Gonzales, counsel to the president, *Subject: Standards of Conduct for Interrogation under 18 USC. §§ 2340–2340A*, 1 August 2002.

47 Statement of Alberto J. Mora, Senate committee on armed services hearing on the treatment of detainees in US custody, 17 June 2008.

48 Ibid.

49 Peter Rowe, "Military Medicine, Torture Examined," *San Diego Union Tribune*, 7 May 2007.

50 In an interview I held with Major General Dunlavey on 6 August 2008 in Erie, Pennsylvania, Dunlavey stated emphatically that he had never been put under pressure from anyone in the higher levels of administration. He attributed the request for harsher interrogation methods to the failure to receive intelligence from one specific detainee, even after many different "tiger teams" had interrogated the detainee. He stressed numerous times that no one in the higher levels was instructing him.

51 Major General Michael E. Dunlavey, *Memorandum for Commander, United States Southern Command, Subject: Counter-Resistance Strategies,* 11 October 2002.

52 Ibid.

53 Lieutenant Colonel James Phifer, *Memorandum for Commander, Joint Task Force 170, Subject: Request for Approval of Counter-Resistance Strategies,* 11 October 2002.

54 Lieutenant Colonel Diane Beaver, *Memorandum for Commander, Joint Task Force 170, Subject: Legal Brief on Proposed Counter-Resistance Strategies,* 11 October 2002.

55 Lieutenant Colonel Diane Beaver, *Memorandum for Commander, Joint Task Force 170, Subject: Legal Brief on Proposed Counter-Resistance Strategies,* 11 October 2002.

56 Ibid., 5.

57 Philippe Sands, "The Green Light," *Vanity Fair* (May 2008): 221.

58 Lieutenant Colonel Diane Beaver, *Memorandum for Commander, Joint Task Force 170, Subject: Legal Brief on Proposed Counter-Resistance Strategies,* 11 October 2002, 5.

59 Ibid.

60 Ibid., 7.

61 Sands, "The Green Light," 222.

62 Alberto Mora, *Memorandum for Inspector General, Department of the Navy, Subject: Statement for the Record: Office of General Counsel Involvement in Interrogation Issues,* 7 July 2004, 6.

63 Sands, "The Green Light," 222.

64 Statement by Lieutenant Colonel (retired) Diane E. Beaver, US Senate Armed Services Committee hearing, 17 June 2008.

65 Ibid.

66 Sands, "The Green Light," 224.

67 Testimony of Rear Adm. Jane Dalton, Senate Armed Services Committee hearing on the treatment of detainees in US custody, 17 June 2008.

68 William J. Haynes II, *Action Memo for Secretary of Defense, Subject: Counter-Resistance Techniques,* 27 November 2002.

69 Alberto Mora, *Memorandum for Inspector General, Department of the Navy, Subject: Statement for the Record: Office of General Counsel Involvement in Interrogation Issues,* 7 July 2004, 8.

70 Ibid., 14

71 Ibid., 17.

72 Major General Jack L. Rives, *Memorandum for SAF/GC, Subject: Final Report and Recommendations of the Working Group to Assess the Legal, Policy and Operational Issues Relating to Interrogation of Detainees Held by the US Armed Force in the War on Terrorism,* 5 February 2003.

73 Ibid.

74 Rear Admiral Michael F. Lohr, *Memorandum for General Counsel of the Air Force, Subject: Working Group Recommendations Relating to Interrogation of Detainees,* 6 February 2003.

75 Joseph Margulies, *Guantánamo and the Abuse of Presidential Power* (New York: Simon & Schuster, 2006) 82.

76 Opening statement of Senator Carl Levin, Senate Armed Services Committee hearing, "The Origins of Aggressive Interrogation Techniques," 17 June 2008.

77 Mark Benjamin, "A Timeline to Bush Government Torture," *Salon.com News* (18 June 2008) www.salon.com/news/feature/2008/06/18/interrogation/index.html.

78 Sands, "The Green Light," 224.

79 Andrew Buncombe, "US Military Tells Jack Bauer: Cut out the Torture Scenes...or else!," *The Independent* (13 February 2007) www.independent.co.uk/news/world/americas/us-military-tells-jack-bauer-cut-out-the-torture-scenes—or-else-436143.html (accessed 14 March 2008).

80 JTF GTMO "SERE" Interrogation Standard Operating Procedure, *Subject: Guidelines for Employing "SERE" Techniques During Detainee Interrogations*, 18 December 2002.

81 Timothy James, *Memorandum for JTF-GTMO/J2, Subject: JTF GTMO "SERE" Interrogation SOP DTD*, 10 December 2002.

82 In the interview held with Major General Dunlavey, he stated that during his time as commander of Guantánamo, the policy was "don't touch" the detainees. He stated that there were no violations of Geneva during his time at Guantánamo and that none of the detainees were harmed in any way.

83 Opening statement of Senator Carl Levin, Senate Armed Services Committee hearing, "The Origins of Aggressive Interrogation Techniques," 17 June 2008.

84 Josh White, "Abu Ghraib Tactics Were First Used at Guantánamo," *Washington Post*, 14 July 2005.

85 Major General Antonio Taguba, *Article 15–6 Investigation of the 800th Military Police Brigade*, 2004, 16.

86 Letter from T. J. Harrington to Major General Donald J. Ryder, *Re: Suspected Mistreatment of Detainees*, 14 July 2004.

87 US Dept. of Defense detainee directive, *Definitions, Treatment Policy, and Compliance with Laws of War*, 5 September 2006.

88 Department of the Army, Army field manual 34–52, Human Intelligence Collector Operations, September 2006, 5–21.

89 Senate Armed Services Committee hearing, 17 June 2008.

90 Ibid.

91 President George W. Bush, *Executive Order: Interpretation of the Geneva Conventions Common Article 3 as Applied to a Program of Detention and Interrogation Operated by the Central Intelligence Agency*, July 2007, 20.

92 Ibid., sec. 3 (E).

93 Common Article 3 of the Geneva Conventions.

94 Jane Mayer, *The Dark Side* (New York: Doubleday, 2008) 32–233.

95 Peter Rowe, "Military Medicine, Torture Examined," *San Diego Union Tribune*, 7 May 2007.

96 *Broken Laws Broken Lives: Medical Evidence of Torture by US Personnel and Its Impact*, a report by Physicians for Human Rights, June 2008.

97 Personal communication.

98 Lee F. Gunn, *Washington Monthly* (January–March 2008) www.washingtonmonthly.com/features/2008/0801.gunn.html (accessed 26 April 2008).

99 Ibid.

What Torture Does to Human Beings

100 *An Evangelical Declaration Against Torture: Protecting Human Rights in an Age of Terror* can be accessed at www.evangelicalsforhumanrights.org/.

269

101 *Human Intelligence Collector Operations,* Field Manual Headquarters No. 2–22.3, 5–21, Department of the Army, Washington, DC, 6 September 2006. This publication is available at Army Knowledge Online: www.us.army.mil.

102 To read the declaration and see the endorser lists, visit www.campaigntobantorture.org.

103 Jose A. Saporta, Jr. and Bessel A. van der Kolk, "Psychobiological consequences of Severe Trauma," in *Torture and its Consequences, Current Treatment Approaches,*" ed. Metin Basoğlu (Cambridge: Cambridge University Press, 1992) 151–81.

104 Ibid., 154.

105 Ibid., 155.

106 A powerful indictment of the role played by military physicians and psychologists can be found in Dr. Steven H. Miles's book, *Oath Betrayed: America's Torture Doctors* (Berkeley: University of California Press, 2009).

107 Jacobo Timmerman, *Prisoner without a Name, Cell without a Number* (Madison: University of Wisconsin Press, 2002).

108 See the HURIDOCS Web site at www.huridocs.org.

109 Grethe Skylv, "Physical Sequelae of torture," 47, in Metin Basoğlu, *Torture and Its Consequences: Current Treatment Approaches* (Cambridge; New York: Cambridge University Press, 1992).

110 Bone scintography uses the administration of a radiopharmaceutical product, then tracks its distribution in the body with a photographic recording with a gamma camera.

111 Metin Basoğlu, ed., *Torture and its Consequences: Current Treatment Approaches* (Cambridge: Cambridge University Press, 1992).

112 Metin Basoğlu, M.D., Ph.D; Maria Livanou, Ph.D; and Cvetana Crnobaric´, M.D., Torture vs Other Cruel, Inhuman, and Degrading Treatment, Is the Distinction Real or Apparent?" *Archives of General Psychiatry* 64 (March 2007): 283.

113 See, e.g., Douglas A. Johnson, "Psychological evidence of torture," in *Examining asylum seekers: A health professional's guide to medical and psychological evaluations of torture* (Boston: Physicians for Human Rights, 2001) 64–69; and M. Basoğlu, J. M. Jaranson, R. Mollica, and M. Kastrup, "Torture and mental health: A research overview," in E. Gerrity, T. M. Keane and F. Tuma, eds. *The Mental Health Consequences of Torture* (New York: Plenum, 2001) 35–62.

114 *Diagnostic and Statistical Manual of Mental Disorders, 4th edition* (Washington, DC: American Psychiatric Association, 2000).

115 Philip Zimbardo, *The Lucifer Effect: Understanding How Good People Turn Evil* (New York: Random House, 2007) 267–76.

116 Andrew D. Lester, *The Angry Christian: A Theology for Care and Counseling* (Louisville: Westminster John Knox Press, 2003) 232.

117 Karla McLaren, *Emotional Genius* (California: Laughing Tree Press, 2001) 252.

What the Torture Debate Reveals about American Christianity

118 David P. Gushee, *The Righteous Gentiles of the Holocaust,* second ed. (Minneapolis: Paragon House, 2003).

119 Reinhold Niebuhr's *Moral Man and Immoral Society* (New York: Scribner's, 1933) helps considerably here.

120 David P. Gushee, "Five Reasons Why Torture is Always Wrong," *Christianity Today* (February 2006): 33–37.

121 For an analysis of this internal struggle within evangelicalism to shape our public witness, see David P. Gushee, *The Future of Faith in American Politics: The Public Witness of the Evangelical Center* (Waco TX: Baylor University Press, 2008).

122 *Catechism of the Catholic Church* (New York: Doubleday, 1995) para. 2258. The catechism is available online at www.vatican.va/archive/catechism/ccc_toc.htm.

123 Ibid., para. 2297.

124 Whatever is opposed to life itself, such as any type of murder, genocide, abortion, euthanasia, or willful self-destruction; whatever violates the integrity of the human person, such as mutilation, torments inflicted on body or mind, attempts to coerce the will itself; whatever insults human dignity, such as subhuman living conditions, arbitrary imprisonment, deportation, slavery, prostitution, the selling of women and children, as well as disgraceful working conditions, where men are treated as mere tools for profit, rather than as free and responsible persons—all these things and others of their like are infamies indeed. They poison human society, but they do more harm to those who practice them than those who suffer from the injury. Moreover, they are a supreme dishonor to the creator. Vatican II, *Gaudium et Spes*, no. 27, available at www.vatican.va/archive/hist_councils/ii_vatican_council/documents/vat?ii_cons_19651207_gaudium?et?spes_en.html.

125 Pope John Paul II, *Veritatis Splendor*, no. 80, available online at www.vatican.va/holy_father/john_paul_ii/encyclicals/documents/hf_jp?ii_enc_06081993_veritatis?splendor_en.html. The core meaning of "intrinsically evil" finds its home in Catholic casuistry; it means that an act is wrong by virtue of its agent's immediate purpose in action, not its circumstances or motive. An intrinsically evil act is always wrong. For a primer, see M. Cathleen Kaveny, "Intrinsic Evil and Political Responsibility," *America* 199:13 (27 October 2008) 15–19.

126 United States Conference of Catholic Bishops, "Torture is a Moral Issue," 2008, www.usccb.org/sdwp/TortureIsAMoralIssueCatholicStudyGuide.pdf.

127 "Love your enemies, do good to those who hate you" (Luke 6:27).

128 Samuel Huntington, *The Clash of Civilizations and the Remaking of World Order* (New York: Simon & Schuster, 1996). The book expands upon an article Huntington wrote entitled "The Clash of Civilizations," and published in *Foreign Affairs* in 1993. The original article is republished with companion articles in Samuel Huntington, ed., *The Clash of Civilizations? The Debate* (New York: Foreign Affairs, 1996).

129 I find this mindset represented in the magazine *First Things*, an ecumenical endeavor dominated by conservative Catholics and Evangelical Protestants.

130 See, e.g., Dinesh D. Souza, *The Enemy at Home: The Cultural Left and its Responsibility for 9/11* (New York: Doubleday, 2007).

131 See, e.g., Phillip Carter, "Intel Dump, Few Bad Apples?" http://voices.washingtonpost.com/inteldump/2008/05/a_few_bad_apples.html.

132 *Catechism of the Catholic Church*, para. 2298.

133 John T. Noonan, Jr., *A Church that Can and Cannot Change* (Notre Dame IN: University of Notre Dame Press, 2005).

134 Avery Dulles, S.J., "Development or Reversal?" *First Things* (October 2005) www.firstthings.com/article.php3?id_article=234.

135 *Roe vs. Wade*, 410 US 113 (1973).

136 Much of the research and writing of this paper is credited to John Haubenreich, a student at Vanderbilt Law School in Nashville, Tennessee, who worked at Sutherland Asbill & Brennan LLP during summer 2008. My thanks to John for his fine work. The views expressed, however, are those of the author.

137 *The Dark Knight*, directed by Christopher Nolan (Warner Brothers Pictures, 2008).

138 Skyhook was a real US military program designed to rescue soldiers in trouble. See "Operation Skyhook," *Time Magazine* (4 December 1964) www.time.com/time/magazine/article/0,9171,830889,00.html.

139 The details of Shergawi's ordeal come from attorneys' interviews, on file with the author.

140 Stephen Grey, *Ghost Plane: The True Story of The CIA Torture Program* (New York: St. Martin's Press, 2006) 10–11.

141 Ibid.

142 Ibid.

143 Ibid.

144 The phrase "outsourcing" torture comes from the title of a 2005 *New Yorker* article. See Jane Mayer, "Outsourcing Torture: The Secret History of America's 'Extraordinary Rendition' Program," *New Yorker*, 14 February 2005.

145 Tony Manolatos, "CIA's Air America Finally Gets Its Due For Wartime Heroics," *Florida Today* (Melbourne), 1 July 2001.

146 Grey, *Ghost Plane*, 11–13.

147 Ibid., 13; Air America Association, "About Air America," www.air-america.orG/About/About.shtml.

148 Sometimes suspects were rendered for punishment if they had been convicted in absentia.

149 Grey, *Ghost Plane*, 38–44; Human Rights Watch, *Double Jeopardy: CIA Renditions to Jordan* (New York: Human Rights Watch, 2008) 6–9; Mayer, "Outsourcing Torture," 1–5.

150 Human Rights Watch, *Double Jeopardy*, 6; Mayer, "Outsourcing Torture," 4–5.

151 Condoleezza Rice, "Remarks Upon Her Departure for Europe," speech, Andrews Air Force Base, Maryland, 5 December 2005.

152 Grey, *Ghost Plane*.

153 Ibid., 16.

154 J. Cofer Black, unclassified testimony before the Senate Intelligence Committee, US Congress, 107th Congress, 2nd session, 26 September 2002.

155 President George W. Bush, "President Discusses Creation of Military Commissions to Try Suspected Terrorists," speech, The White House, Washington, DC, 6 September 2006.

156 Ibid.

157 Examples such as the presidential directive authorizing wiretapping without FISA approval and the USA PATRIOT Act come easily to mind.

158 "Likely" is used because the authorizing documents have not yet been made public, and so their exact contents are unknown.

159 Douglas Jehl and David Johnston, "Rule Change Lets CIA Freely Send Suspects Abroad," *New York Times*, 6 March 2005.

160 Ibid.

161 Ibid.

162 American Civil Liberties Union, "CIA Finally Acknowledges Existence of Presidential Order on Detention Facilities Abroad," press release, 14 November 2006, www.aclu.org/safefree/torture/27382prs20061114.html.

163 Ibid.

164 Ibid.; Sixth Declaration of Marilyn A. Dorn, Information Review Officer, Central Intelligence Agency at 6, 7–9, American Civil Liberties Union vs. Central Intelligence Agency, No. 04 Civ. 4151 (S.D.N.Y. 5 January 2007).

165 Convention Against Torture, G.A. Res. 39/46, Annex, 39 U.N. GAOR Supp. No. 51, U.N. Doc. A/39/51 (1984).

166 Ibid., Article 2.

167 Ibid., Article 3.

168 See, for e.g., the Jordan Section of the 2001 Country Reports on Human Rights Practices, describing torture and interrogation techniques commonly used. US Department of State, Bureau of Democracy, Human Rights, and Labor, *2001 Country Reports on Human Rights Practices*, 4 March 2002.

169 When ratifying the convention, Congress made it non-self-executing, meaning it does not come into force of its own accord, but requires implementing legislation. Thus, parties cannot claim its protection directly, but only rely on regulations passed to implement it.

170 For example, see John Yoo, deputy assistant attorney general, *Re: Military Interrogation of Alien Unlawful Combatants Held Outside the United States*, memo prepared for William J. Haynes II, General Counsel of the Department of Defense, 14 March 2003. See also Jay S. Bybee, assistant attorney general, *Re: Standards of Conduct for Interrogation Under 18 USC. §§ 2340–2340A*, memo prepared for Alberto R. Gonzales, counsel to the President, 1 August 2002.

171 Convention Against Torture, Article 3.

172 Mayer, "Outsourcing Torture," 2.

173 Council of Europe, Committee on Legal Affairs and Human Rights, *Alleged Secret Detentions and Unlawful Inter-State Transfers of Detainees Involving Council of Europe Member States*, 12 June 2006, 54; United Nations Committee Against Torture, *Summary Record of the 703rd*, 5 May 2006. Bellinger argued that pursuant to Article 3 of CAT, the "United States did not transfer persons to countries where it considered they were *more likely than not* to be tortured" (emphasis added). United Nations, *Summary Record*, 7. The Council of Europe reported that Mr. Bellinger said, "The United States does not render people to other countries for the purpose of being tortured, or in the expectation that they will be tortured," Council of Europe, *Alleged Secret Detentions*, 54.

174 Council of Europe, *Alleged Secret Detentions*, 55.

175 Yoo, "Re: Military Interrogation," 47–56, 59–74.

176 Ibid., 57–58, 74–75, 77–80.

177 Scott McClellan, "Press Briefing by Scott McClellan," press question and answer session, The White House, Washington, DC, 6 December 2005.

178 Grey, *Ghost Plane*, 231, 281–82.

179 Ibid., 29–30.

Sermons and Reflections

180 Alexander McCall Smith, *In the Company of Cheerful Ladies* (New York: Anchor Books, 2004).

181 The exception, at the very end of the century, was Kosovo.

182 Samantha Power writes in her acknowledgements that her parents are the two most extraordinary people she has ever known; obviously they must have modeled and taught empathy as Mma Ramotswe's beloved father did for her.

183 For the Armenians, it was Henry Morgenthau, Sr.; for the Jews, Raphael Lemkin (the man who coined the word "genocide"); for the Cambodians, Elizabeth Becker and Stephen Solarz; for the Rwandans, Roméo Dallaire; for the Iraqi Kurds, Peter Galbraith; and for the Bosnian Muslims, Henry McCloskey. The case of the Kosovars was somewhat different because *finally* there was intervention, in the form of NATO bombers.

184 In Kristof's column in the *New York Times* (10 July 2008), he tries to persuade people who don't think genocide is "that bad" compared to the deaths of millions from malaria and other diseases. He tries to get his readers to imagine the atrocities he has witnessed.

185 The well-known Sojourners community in Washington, through its witness and its magazine, has kept the word *sojourner* at the forefront of Christian activism, but it's a safe bet that not one in a hundred outside that community could say what it means.

186 Smith, *Cheerful Ladies*, 189.

187 The subapostolic church saw itself this way, as the second-century Epistle to Diognetus makes clear: "They [the Christians] live in their own countries, but only as aliens. They have a share in everything as citizens, and endure everything as foreigners."

188 In the New Testament the enemy is variously identified and/or personified as Satan, the devil, Hades (Revelation 20:16), Beelzebul or Beelzebub (the synoptic gospels), Sin and Death (Paul), "the ruler of this world" (John 14:30), "the father of lies" (John 8:44), "the prince of the power of the air" (Ephesians 2:2), and in the plural, "the elemental spirits of the universe" (Colossians 2:8) and "the world rulers of this present darkness" (Ephesians 6:12).

189 Martin Luther, "A Mighty Fortress Is Our God" (No. 37), in *The Baptist Hymnal* (Nashville TN: Convention Press, 1975).

190 Walker Percy, *Lancelot* (New York: Farrar Straus & Giroux, 1977) 157.

191 Donovan Webster, "The Man in the Hood," *Vanity Fair* (February 2005).

192 My husband recalls that John Opel, CEO of IBM in the 1980s, always worked standing up.

193 Orhan Pamuk, *Snow* (New York: Knopf, 2004) 334–35.

194 Jane Mayer describes all this in her new book, *The Dark Side*, and makes a point of honoring the FBI agents, military lawyers, and generals who spoke up.

195 Excerpt from address by J. K. Rowling at Harvard commencement, 2008.

The Religious Roots of Human Rights

196 Arlene Swidler, ed., *Human Rights in Religious Traditions* (New York: Pilgrim, 1982); Abdulaziz Sachedina, *The Islamic Roots of Democratic Pluralism* (New York: Oxford, 2001); and Robert A. Evans and Alice Frazer Evans, *Human Rights: A Dialogue Between the First and Third Worlds* (Maryknoll NY: Orbis, 1983).

197 Glen Stassen and Susan Thistlethwaite, *Jewish, Christian, and Muslim Scholars Reach Consensus for Just Peacemaking Practices* (Washington, DC: U. S. Institute of Peace, 2008); J.

Dudley Woodberry and Robin Basselin, eds., *Resources for Peacemaking in Muslim-Christian Relations* (Pasadena: Fuller Seminary Press, 2006).

198 Haller, Huber and Tödt, Stassen, Tuck, and Westmoreland-White.

199 I tell the story of Overton's and his wife's originating human rights in "The Christian Origin of Human Rights," in my *Just Peacemaking: Transforming Initiatives for Justice and Peace* (Louisville: Westminster John Knox, 1992). See also Michael Westmoreland White, "Setting the Record Straight: Christian Faith, Human Rights, and the Enlightenment," *Annual of the Society of Christian Ethics* (1995): 75–96.

200 William O'Neill, S.J., *A Grammar of Dissent: Rights, Religion, and the Common Good* (Washington, DC: Georgetown University, forthcoming).

201 Glen Stassen and David Gushee, *Kingdom Ethics: Following Jesus in Contemporary Context* (Downers Grove: InterVarsity, 2003) ch. 17.

202 Reed, note 28 to *Suffering Presence*, 130.

203 Stanley Hauerwas, *Suffering Presence* (Notre Dame: University of Notre Dame, 1986) 161, 182, 187, 189, 193, 196, 198, 200, 207.

204 Glen Stassen, ed., *Just Peacemaking: The New Paradigm for the Ethics of Peace and War* (Cleveland: Pilgrim Press, 2008).

205 Mark Tushnet has shown that on the one hand the US Supreme Court has given significant impetus to the civil rights struggle by its 1954 *Brown vs. Board of Education* decision for integration of the schools, and has consistently defended freedom of speech. But it has blocked serious campaign spending reform by identifying spending of millions of dollars by wealthy donors for political campaigns as an issue of freedom of speech rather than an issue of distorting the processes of democracy—by contrast with England and Germany. He argues that the US Supreme Court is not as effective as it could be in enforcing human rights because it most often defends property rights, its decisions are "rarely out of line for an extended period with the policies supported by the nation's governing coalitions," and courts are structured so their pace of change will be slow. "All institutions inevitably make mistakes," and they do not listen enough to criticisms from the people, which should be heard so they can call for corrections of mistakes. But this is a criticism of the Supreme Court and its appointees, not a criticism of human rights. Tushnet sees the guardian-force bringing correction to these problems to be a worldwide culture of human rights. He writes: "A worldwide culture of human rights has begun to emerge, penetrating all countries but some more than others. This culture suggests that there might be what we could call a pent-up demand for enforcement of human rights. In its simplest form, this demand seeks the elimination of egregious violations of human rights that for one reason or another—legislative inertia, indifference, or inattention [and the O'Donovans and I add, greed, powerful money interests, and ideologies driven by greed and power]—have remained on the books." Mark Tushnet, "Scepticism about Judicial Review: A Perspective from the United States," in Tom Campbell, K. D. Ewing, and Adam Tomkins, eds., *Sceptical Essays on Human Rights* (Oxford: Oxford University 2001) 360–63, 365, 367, 369, 372–74. See also Tushnet, *Taking the Constitution Away from the Courts* (Princeton: Princeton University, 1999) 153.

206 Joan Lockwood O'Donovan, in her and Oliver O'Donovan's *Bonds of Imperfection: Christian Politics, Past and Present* (Grand Rapids MI: Eerdmans, 2004) 96.

207 Ibid., 229–38.

208 Ibid., 95, 243–44. "Consequently, instead of allowing civil society to be opened by the Holy Spirit to the demands and reality of evangelical community, this concept closes civil society to those demands and that reality, enveloping it in sinful complacency."

209 Ibid., 62–64.

210 Christopher Marshall, *Crowned with Glory & Honor: Human Rights in the Biblical Tradition* (Scottsdale PA: Pandora, Herald, and Lime Grove House, 2001).

211 Glen Stassen, "Chapter 6: The Christian Origin of Human Rights," *Just Peacemaking: Transforming Initiatives* (Louisville: Transforming Initiatives for Justice and Peace, 1992).

212 Similarly, Alisdair MacIntyre (*After Virtue*, 68–69) reacts against human rights because he sees them as based in Enlightenment claims that they have universal reason as their source. But none of us possesses universal reason; we are all influenced by where we come from, historically and socially. Advocates of human rights respond that this commits the fallacy of confusing the source with the intention. Human rights originated in a free-church tradition, not in an Enlightenment claim to possess universal reason. They have multiple historical sources, carried by diverse faiths and contextualized narratives. But these particular historical traditions each have universal intent; they intend to affirm the dignity and human rights of all persons, universally. For example, the biblical claim that all humankind is created in the image of God is a *particular* biblical claim, and it affirms the *universal* dignity of all humankind. Universal intent can be affirmed from particular ground. What was a particular struggle for religious liberty, and then for economic justice and participation in community, led by Richard Overton, has become a worldwide affirmation, an "almost universal language of moral debate," as Christopher Marshall says. "It would appear then, that if Christians are to engage meaningfully with the great moral issues of our day, they will need to master the rhetoric of rights, and to use it sensitively to articulate key Christian insights and perspectives." Or, as Esther Reed puts it, "Human rights provide the language and conceptuality around which theorists and politicians unite, even if they do not agree about their reasons for unity." Affirmation of the inalienable dignity of all persons does not require one exclusive, universal, rationalistic grounding.

213 Richard Tuck, *Natural Rights Theories: Their Origin and Development* (Cambridge, England: Cambridge University Press, 1979).

214 Esther D. Reed, *The Ethics of Human Rights: Contested Doctrinal and Moral Issues* (Waco TX: Baylor University Press, 2007) 83.

215 Reed, *The Ethics of Human Rights*, 69–80; Dietrich Bonhoeffer, *Ethics* (Minneapolis: Fortress, 2005) 173.

216 Bonhoeffer, *Ethics*, 180.

217 Ibid., 185–86.

218 Ibid., 187–89.

219 Reed, *The Ethics of Human Rights*, 165.

220 Reed, review of Wolterstorff's *Justice: Rights and Wrongs*, forthcoming.

221 Reed, *The Ethics of Human Rights*, 147–48.

222 Ibid.

223 "Global Acts of Terrorism on the Rise," *Los Angeles Times*, 29 April 2006, A.7, and updated from news reports subsequently.

224 Ultimately, sin is about choosing our selves rather than relationship. "But in the biblical perspective sin is a much more serious problem than this [legal-moral definition of justice]. The problem is not simply a broken law but a broken relationship." Norman Kraus, *Jesus Christ our Lord: Christology from a Disciple's Perspective* (Eugene OR: Wipf and Stock, 2004) 166.

225 Newbigin explains the implications of interpersonal relatedness by writing, "Interpersonal relatedness belongs to the very being of God. Therefore, there can be no salvation for human beings except in relatedness. No one can be made whole except by being restored to the wholeness of that being-in-relatedness for which God made us and the world and which is the image of that being-in relatedness which is the being of God himself." Leslie Newbigin, *The Open Secret: An Introduction to the Theology of Mission*, rev. ed. (Grand Rapids MI: W.B. Eerdmans, 1995) 70.

226 The ability to respond to God and others intrinsically connects with God creating us in God's image. Sin distorts this response, placing our self-interest in the place of the other. "God's ideal is that human beings enjoy positive social interaction and ongoing cooperation with one another in spontaneous obedience to the will of God." Arthur F Glasser and Charles Edward van Engen, *Announcing the Kingdom: the Story of God's Mission in the Bible* (Grand Rapids MI: Baker Academic, 2003) 35. Anderson writes, "Quite clearly the image is not totally present in the form of individual humanity but more completely as co-humanity." Ray Sherman Anderson, *On being Human: Essays in Theological Anthropology* (Pasadena CA: Fuller Seminary Press, 1982) 73. He goes on to write about the I-Thou relationship within God and also found within humanity. The implication of the image of God in humanity existing more completely in "co-humanity" is that the pursuit of individualism and autonomy takes us further from the encounter that is "fundamental to the image of God." Ray Sherman Anderson, *On Being Human*, 73–74.

227 As Newbigin states: "But if the truly human is the shared reality of mutual and collective responsibility that the Bible envisages, then salvation must be an action that binds us together and restores for us the true mutual relation to each other and the true shared relation to the world of nature. This means that the gift of salvation would be bound up with our openness to one another." Leslie Newbigin, *Open Secret*, 70.

228 When we look at God through the lens of Christ, we begin to get some sense of the faithfulness of the God we worship (Romans 3). We start to see a self-giving God of love. This good news allows us to forfeit our understanding of an angry, bloodthirsty, wrath-filled God as the reason we need reconciliation and redemption. The incarnation, life, death, and resurrection of Christ reveal to us a God of love that reconciles us not out of anger at sinful humanity, but out of love for a humanity bound by sin. Through Christ, the bonds of sin are broken; a human response to God's love is possible. This response is the reason for reconciliation and redemption. The ability to respond to God and others intrinsically connects with God creating us in God's image. Sin distorts this response, placing our self-interest in the place of the other. It is Christ, fully God and fully human, who succeeds in his response to God's love. Christ who issues a perfect response on behalf of all nations takes up the imperfect response of sinful people. His perfect response replaces the imperfect response, as Jesus is the mediator between God and humanity. This is the point, as Thomas Torrance writes, "…God has drawn so near to man and drawn man so near to himself in Jesus that they are perfectly at one." Thomas Torrance, *The Mediation of Christ* (Colorado Springs: Helmers & Howard, 1992) 29. God has entered into this world of pain and has borne the responsibility. Moreover, this gives us a glimpse as to why John tells us that "God is love" (cf. 1 John 4:7–20).

229 "The transcendence of God is therefore revealed through the self-abnegation of God. There is within the very being of God a 'divine humility,' or 'downward movement' as Barth puts it. This is the divine kenosis which is proper to God's being in relation of the Son to the Father and which became the inner logic of the incarnation." Ray Sherman Anderson, ST514 Expanded Lecture: 22. Kraus writes, "Love finds its vindication in unhesitating faithfulness to its purpose. Love is ultimately its own justification." Norman C. Kraus, *Jesus Christ our Lord*, 168. This is a christological view that places the life and death of Christ at the center of our view of God. Through Christ, God is self-communicating. Michael Jenkins writes, "God reveals who God is, Luther says, in complete vulnerability by placing himself in the hands of humanity, in surrendering to suffering and death." Michael Jenkins, *Invitation to Theology* (Downers Grove IL: Intervarsity Press, 2001) 128. He also writes, "God meets us in Christ, and in Christ God calls us to follow through the cross in which we die to the world and through which the world is given its life." Michael Jenkins, *Invitation to Theology*, 129.

NOTES

230 Jonathan Sacks, *The Dignity of Difference: How to Avoid the Clash of Civilizations* (New York: Continuum, 2002) 9, 4–5.

231 Charles W. Deweese, "Doing Freedom Baptist Style: Liberty of Conscience," *The Baptist Style for a New Century* (Nashville TN: Baptist History and Heritage Society and William H. Whitsitt Baptist Heritage Society, 2001).

232 Walter B. Shurden, "How We Got That Way: Baptists on Religious Liberty and Separation of Church and State," address for Baptist Joint Committee's 60th Anniversary Religious Liberty Conference, 6–8 October 1996, Washington, DC: Baptist Joint Committee on Public Affairs, 9.

233 John Freeman, cited in Walter B. Shurden, *The Baptist Identity: Four Fragile Freedoms* (Macon GA: Smyth & Helwys Publishing, 1993) 47.

234 Walter Shurden, "Introduction," in Roger Williams, *The Bloudy Tenent of Persecution*, ed. Richard Groves (Macon GA: Mercer University Press, 2001) xv.

235 James Dunn, "The Baptist Vision of Religious Liberty," in *Proclaiming the Baptist Vision: Religious Liberty*, ed. Walter B. Shurden (Macon GA: Smyth and Helwys, 1997) 34.

236 Alan Neely, "Religious Pluralism in the United States and Other Lands: A Challenge for Baptists and Other Christians in the 21st Century," *Baptist History and Heritage* 36 (Winter/Spring 2001): 90.

237 John Leland, *The Rights of Conscience Inalienable* (1791), in *A Sourcebook for Baptist Heritage*, ed. H. Leon McBeth (Nashville: Broadman Press, 1990) 180.

238 Shurden, "How We Got That Way," 9–10.

239 See George Lindbeck, *The Nature of Doctrine: Religion and Theology in a Postliberal Age* (Philadelphia: Westminster Press, 1984); William Placher, *Unapologetic Theology: A Christian Voice in a Pluralistic Conversation* (Louisville: Westminster/John Knox Press, 1989); and J. A. DiNoia, "Pluralist Theology of Religions: Pluralistic or Non-Pluralistic?" in *Christian Uniqueness Reconsidered: The Myth of a Pluralistic Theology of Religions*, ed. Gavin D'Costa (Maryknoll: Orbis Books, 1990).

240 Sheila Greeve Davaney, *Pragmatic Historicism: A Theology for the Twenty-First Century* (Albany: SUNY, 2000) 162.

241 John N. Jonsson, *Incarnation Mission Twenty-one* (Charlotte: A Nilses Publication, 1998) 100–101.

242 Paul Knitter, unpublished lecture, Union Theological Seminary, May 2005.

243 Bill J. Leonard, "Changing a Theology: Baptists, Salvation, and Globalism Then and Now," *Perspectives in Religious Studies*, issue 3 (Fall 2004): 254.

244 David S. Russell, "The Ecumenical Role of Baptists," in *Growth of Interreligious Dialogue 1939–1989*, ed. Franklin H. Littell and George Estreich (Lewiston NY: Edwin Mellen Press, 1989) 121.

245 Claude L. Howe, Sr., "The Missions Impulse Propels the Baptist Experience," in *Defining Baptist Convictions: Guidelines for the Twenty-First Century*, **ed. Charles W. DeWeese** (Franklin TN: Providence House Publishers, 1996) 148.

246 Leonard, "Changing a Theology," 253.

247 Neely, "Religious Pluralism," 82.

248 John N. Jonsson, *Incarnation Mission Twenty-one* (Charlotte: A Nilses Publication, 1998) 98.

249 For an insightful review of Levinas's thought and its implications for Christian theology of religions, see Mervyn Fredrick Bendle, "The Postmetaphysics of Religious Difference," *Pacifica* 11 (1998): 1–26.

250 Johann Baptist Metz, *Faith in History and Society: Toward a Practical Fundamental Theology* (New York: Crossroad Books, 1980).

Healing the (American) Christian Relationship with the Muslim World

251 "On Torture and American Values," *New York Times*, 7 Oct 2007; also at http://query.nytimes.comgstfullpage.htmlres=9C02EFD91238F934A35753C1A9619C8B63&sec =&spon=&pagewanted=1 (accessed 9 September 2008).

252 Article 5 of *The Universal Declaration of Human Rights*, "No one shall be subjected to torture or to cruel, inhuman or degrading treatment or punishment," www.un.org/Overview/rights.html.

253 This study resulted in the brilliant book *Who Speaks for Islam? What a Billion Muslims Really Think*, ed. John L. Esposito and Dalia Mogahed (New York: Gallup Press, 2007).

254 Ibid., 165.

255 George Hunsinger, "A Moral Imperative," *Huffington Post*, 18 January 2008.

256 Gushee, *The Future of Faith*, 122–23.

257 "For the church to apply the principles of human rights in its mission is not to follow a 'secular religion,' but to make basic commitments emerging directly from core Christian beliefs. It follows that evangelism which ignores human rights abuses in the context of its activity lacks both authority and credibility" (Wieland, 174).

258 A. Moreau, *Evangelical Dictionary of World Missions* (Grand Rapids: Baker Academic & Brazos Press, 2000) 462.

259 See Jane Mayer's *The Dark Side* for a detailed and disturbing chronicle of how fear has impacted the American response to terrorism and torture.

260 Jim Wallis, *God's Politics* (New York: HarperCollins, 2005) 88.

261 A bumper sticker reads: "Who Would Jesus Torture?" The obvious answer: No one. Perfect love (found in Jesus) casts out fear and doesn't torture!

262 The strongest argument for this is called the "ticking bomb scenario." The argument is that the torture of one terrorist at a pivotal moment could in turn save thousands of lives, and thus it must be permitted. See the EHR Web site for a cogent refutation of this argument: www.evangelicalsforhumanrights.org/index.php?option=com_content&task=view&id=58&Itemid=44.

263 See www.humanrightsfirst.info/pdf/080624-ETN-principles-bios–15-signers.pdf. In addition, there are other excellent materials about interrogation techniques at www.torturesnotus.net on the page labeled "Interrogation Techniques."

264 See Dennis Wagner's brilliant article, "Finding Truth without Torture," in the *Arizona Republic*, 6 January 2008, azcentral.com. Wagner describes the kind of training given by the US Army to ensure good fact-finding interrogation without torture.

265 Hannah Bayman, "Yvonne Ridley: From Captive to Convert," "BBC News," 21 September 2004, http://news.bbc.co.uk/2/hi/uk_news/england/3673730.stm.

266 Yvonne Ridley, *In the Hands of the Taliban* (London: Robson Books, 2001) 172.

267 Bayman, "From Captive to Convert."

268 Osama bin Laden, "Your Security is in Your Own Hands," CNN, 29 October 2004, www.cnn.com/2004/WORLD/meast/10/29/bin.laden.transcript/.

269 Robert Pape, *Dying to Win: The Strategic Logic of Suicide Terrorism* (New York: Random House, 2005).

270 Robert Pape, "Blowing Up an Assumption," *New York Times*, 18 May 2005, www.nytimes.com/2005/05/18/opinion/18pape.html.

271 Ibid.

272 Robert Pape, "Ground to a Halt," *New York Times*, 3 August 2006, www.nytimes.com/2006/08/03/opinion/03pape.html.

273 John Esposito and Dalia Mogahed, eds. *Who Speaks for Islam? What a Billion Muslims Really Think* (New York: Gallup Press, 2007) 91. See below for more on the poll.

274 Council on Foreign Relations Republican debate transcript, South Carolina, 15 May 2008, www.cfr.org/publication/13338/republican_debate_transcript_south_carolina.html.

275 Michael Scheuer, *Through Our Enemies' Eyes: Osama bin Laden, Radical Islam, and the Future of America*, rev. ed. (Washington, DC: Potomac Books, Inc., 2006) 3f.

276 "Shock, outrage over prison photos," CNN, 1 May 2004, www.cnn.com/2004/WORLD/meast/04/30/iraq.photos/.

277 Jamie McIntyre, "Rumsfeld twice offered to resign during Abu Ghraib Scandal," CNN, 5 February 2005, www.cnn.com/2005/ALLPOLITICS/02/03/rumsfeld.resign/.

278 Council on Foreign Relations debate transcript.

279 Sarah Palin, "Sarah Palin's Speech at the Republican National Convention," *New York Times*, 2008, http://elections.nytimes.com/2008/president/conventions/videos/20080903_PALIN_SPEECH.html.

280 Cf. Jimmy Carter, *Palestine: Peace Not Apartheid* (New York: Simon & Schuster, 2006); and Al Gore's work on the documentary *An Inconvenient Truth*, www.climatecrisis.net/.

281 Lila Rajiva, *The Language of Empire: Abu Ghraib and the American Media* (New York: Monthly Review Press, 2005) 10.

282 See Susan Sontag's brilliant piece on the limitations and manipulation of images in the context of the Abu Ghraib scandal: "Regarding the Torture of Others," *New York Times Magazine* (23 May 2004); also available at www.nytimes.com/2004/05/23/magazine/23PRISONS.html?ex=1400644800&en=a2cb6ea6bd297c8f&ei=5007&partner=USERLAND.

283 Cf. Camine Sarracino and Kevin Scott, "Chapter 6: The Nexus of Porn and Violence: Abu Ghraib and Beyond," *The Porning of America* (Boston: Beacon Press, 2008) 137–67.

284 For example, Amy Goodman and David Goodman, *Static: Government Liars, Media Cheerleaders, and the People Who Fight Back* (New York: Hyperion Press, 2006); W. Lance Bennet et al., *When the Press Fails: Political Power and the News Media from Iraq to Katrina* (Chicago: University of Chicago Press, 2007); and Danny Schechter, *Embedded: Weapons of Mass Deception* (New York: Prometheus Books, 2003).

285 See in particular Edward Said's trilogy: *Orientalism* (New York: Pantheon Books, 1978); *The Question of Palestine* (New York: Times Books, 1979); and *Covering Islam* (New York: Pantheon Books, 1981).

286 Osama bin Laden, transcript of speech in 2007, http://counterterrorismblog.org/2007/09/obl_transcript.php.

287 *The Covenant of the Islamic Resistance Movement*, 18 August 1988, http://avalon.law.yale.edu/20th_century/hamas.asp.

288 [Emphasis added] *An Open Letter: The Hizballah Program*, www.standwithus.com/pdfs/flyers/hezbollah_program.pdf; according to the reference, this is a "slightly" abridged translation of the original that was published on 16 February 1985 in *al-Safir* (Beirut).

289 For easily accessible material online, cf. the documents on the server of *Al Mashriq: The Levant, Cultural Riches from the Countries of the Eastern Mediterranean,* http://almashriq.hiof.no/lebanon/300/320/324/324.2/hizballah/.

290 A conflation of purported or actual "Islamist" movements in the analysis presented here is not to detract from their diverse, complex, and unique histories. It is, rather, only to highlight what is shared: that the incorporation of terrorist tactics is predicated on a defensive, not offensive, posture.

291 Mahmoud Ahmadinejad, "Ahmadinejad's letter to Bush," CNN, 9 May 2006, http://edition.cnn.com/interactive/world/0605/transcript.lemonde.letter/index.html.

292 Juan Cole, "Ahmadinejad Censored, Distorted in US Media," *Informed Comment* (20 September 2008): np; also available at www.juancole.com/2008/09/ahmadinejad-censored-distorted-in-us.html.

293 Cf. Mullah Mohammad Omar, "Speech by Taliban's Leader to Clerics," *Associated Press,* 19 September 2001. Two translations of the speech can be found on the Robert Fisk Web site: www.robert-fisk.com/speech_mullah_umar_sept19_2001.htm.

294 "Jesse Jackson Considers Taliban Meeting; US Reaction Cool," *Los Angeles Times,* 28 September 2001; also available at http://articles.latimes.com/2001/sep/28/news/mn–50948. Note that there were conflicting reports on whether the offer was initiated by Jackson or the Taliban, but regardless, even in the conflicting report Mullah Omar was reported to have accepted Jackson's offer.

295 Cf. Greg Mortenson and David Oliver Relin, *Three Cups of Tea: One Man's Mission to Promote Peace…One School at a time* (New York: Penguin Books, 2006) 267.

296 Cf. Zalmay Khalilzad, "Afghanistan: A Time to Reengage," *Washington Post,* 7 October 1996; reference lifted from "Introduction," in *The Taliban and the Crisis of Afghanistan,* ed. Robert Crews and Amin Tarzi (Cambridge: Harvard University Press, 2008) 51; and endnote no. 91 on 368.

297 Cf. *Taliban and the Crisis of Afghanistan,* 51; also "Taleban in Texas for talks on gas pipeline," "BBC News," 4 December 1996, http://news.bbc.co.uk/1/hi/world/west_asia/37021.stm.

298 See below.

299 John F. Burns, "Karzai Offers Passage to Taliban Leader for Talks," *New York Times,* 17 November 2001; also available at www.nytimes.com/2008/11/17/world/asia/17afghan.html ?partner=rss&emc=rss.

300 Charles Kurzman, ed. *Islamic Statements Against Terrorism,* www.unc.edu/~kurzman/terror.htm.

301 In addition to the availability of everything that is required to understand the situation online, the statements of Osama bin Laden have been published by Bruce Lawrence, ed., *Messages to the World: The Statements of Osama bin Laden* (London & New York: Verso, 2005).

302 Michael Scheuer, *Imperial Hubris: Why the West is Losing the War on Terror* (Virginia: Brassy's, Inc., 2004) 10.

303 Associated Press/AOL, "Celebrity Rankings Study," 19–21 December 2006, http://surveys.ap.org/data/Ipsos/national/2006/2006–12–19%20AP-AOL%20Celebrities%20 ranking%20topline.pdf.

304 Cf. Imad-ad-Dean Ahmad, "Gallup Poll Lets Muslims Speak for Themselves," *Minaret of Freedom,* 27 February 2008, http://blog.minaret.org/index.php?s=gallup+poll+lets+muslims+speak+for+themselves.

305 Ibid.

306 Cf. *Who Speaks for Islam,* xiii.

307 Feisal Abdur Rauf, *What's Right with Islam is What's Right with America* (New York: HarperCollins, 2005).

308 Visit www.acommonword.com/.

309 Hamza Yusuf, "A Message to Humanity," keynote address to the annual ISNA convention, September 2004.

310 Visit www.spiritualprogressives.org/ to access the Global Marshall Plan and learn more about NSP. Rabbi Lerner has elaborated his vision in *The Left Hand of God* (New York: HarperCollins, 2006). Others have proposed similar plans from slightly different perspectives. A prominent approach from the point of view of sustainability is Lester Brown's *Plan B*, now in its third edition (Washington, DC: Earth Policy Institute, 2008).

311 A reference to the title of Michael Scheuer's latest book, which also captures its sentiment: *Marching Toward Hell: America and Islam after Iraq* (New York: Free Press, 2008).

Violence Finds Refuge in Falsehood

312 William Safire, "On Language: Waterboarding," *New York Times*, 8 March 2008.

313 William Sloane Coffin, *The Collected Sermons of William Sloane Coffin* (Louisville: Westminster John Knox, 2008) 8.

314 Andrew Koppleman, "Always Proud of America," *Balkinization*, 4 September 2008, http://balkin.blogspot.com/2008/09/always-proud-of-america.html.

315 Darius Rejali, *Torture and Democracy* (Princeton: Princeton University Press, 2007) 536.

316 Ibid.

317 McCoy, "New Loopholes May Exist for Abuse," *San Francisco Chronicle*, 8 January 2006.

318 McCoy, "Question of Torture," 11, 73–74. Senator Alan Cranston explained that Congress banned police training in 1974 after learning that police trained and equipped by the US "in Iran, Vietnam, Brazil, and other countries were involved in torture, murder, and the suppression of legitimate political activity." Statement to the United States Senate, 5 March 1992, www.fas.org/irp/gao/920300-train.htm.

319 Ibid., 101.

320 Ibid., 9.

321 Ibid., 8

322 McCoy, "Invisible in Plain Sight," *Amnesty International Magazine* (4 May 2006); also available at www.amnestyusa.org/magazine/invisible_in_plain_sight.html.

323 See Jane Mayer, *The Dark Side*, 319–22.

324 McCoy, *Question of Torture*, 223–24.

325 Mayer, *The Dark Side*, 320.

326 "President's Radio Address," 8 March 2008, www.whitehouse.gov/news/releases/2008/03/20080308.html.

327 Dan Eggen, "Bush Announces Veto of Waterboarding Ban," *Washington Post*, 8 March 2008.

328 Scott Horton, "Another Milestone on the Road to Serfdom," No Comment/Harper's online, 8 March 2008, www.harpers.org/archive/2008/03/hbc–90002574.

329 Ray McGovern, "Torture in Our Name," *truthout* (4 November 2005): np.

330 Mayer, *The Dark Side*, 125.

331 "John Ashcroft Yelled at Me Tonight," DailyKos (Knox College), 22 April 2008, www.dailykos.com/storyonly/2008/4/23/04046/3938.

ASHCROFT: No. No it doesn't violate the Geneva Conventions. As for other laws, well, the US is a party to the United Nations Convention against Torture. And that convention, well, when we join a treaty like that we send it to the Senate to be ratified, and when the Senate ratifies they often add qualifiers, reservations, to the treaty which affect what exactly we follow. ...

STUDENT: I have here in my hand two documents. One of them, you know, is the text of the United Nations Convention against Torture, which, point of interest, says nothing about "lasting physical damage"...

ASHCROFT: (interrupting) Do you have the Senate reservations to it?

STUDENT: No, I don't. Do you happen to know what they are?

ASHCROFT: (angrily) I don't have them memorized, no. I don't have time to go around memorizing random legal facts. I just don't want these people in the audience to go away saying, "He was wrong, she had the proof right in her hand!" Because that's not true. It's a lie. *If you don't have the reservations, you don't have anything.* Now, if you want to bring them another time, we can talk, but... [italics added].

332 Mark Mazzetti, "Letters Give C.I.A. Tactics a Legal Rationale," *New York Times,* 27 April 2008. "The Justice Department has told Congress that American intelligence operatives...can legally use interrogation methods that might otherwise be prohibited under international law.... The administration is arguing that the boundaries for interrogations should be subject to some latitude, even under an executive order issued last summer that President Bush said meant that the C.I.A. would comply with international strictures against harsh treatment of detainees."

333 Jeremy Brecher and Brendan Smith, "Nine Reasons to Investigate War Crimes Now," *The Nation* (20 July 2008) www.thenation.com/doc/20080804/brecher_smith (accessed 20 July 2008).

334 Mark Benjamin, "Would Obama prosecute the Bush administration for torture?" *Salon.com* (4 August 2008) www.salon.com/news/feature/2008/08/04/obama/ (accessed 5 August 2008).

335 "The Torture Sessions," editorial, *New York Times,* 20 April 2008.

336 Peter Dale Scott, *The Road to 9/11: Wealth, Empire and the Future of America* (Berkeley: University of California Press, 2007) 19.

337 Carl Bernstein, "The CIA and the Media," *Rolling Stone,* October 1977, http://carlbernstein.com/magazine_cia_and_media.php.

338 The Pike Committee Report (1976); quoted by Lisa Pease, "History Repeats Itself with Spy Scandals," *Real History* (25 December 2005). Also available at http://realhistoryarchives.blogspot.com/2005/12/history-repeats-with-spy-scandals.html. See CIA, *The Pike Report* (Nottingham, England: Spokesman Books, 1977).

339 Dietrich Bonhoeffer, *Ethics,* 137.

340 See George Hunsinger, "Torture Is the Ticking Time Bomb: Why the Necessity Defense Fails"; and David Gushee, "Six Reasons Why Torture is Always Wrong," in Hunsinger, ed., *Torture Is a Moral Issue,* 51–72, 73–91.

341 *One in One Hundred: Behind Bars in America 2008,* Pew Center on the States 2008. I note also that the UN Convention Against Torture has been used in this country to support prison reform. Indeed, when the US ratified the convention in 1994, it was stated that the interpretation of the convention had to conform to the history of interpretation of the Eighth Amendment banning cruel and unusual punishment.

342 James Whitman, *Harsh Justice: Criminal Punishment and the Widening Divide between America and Europe* (New York: Oxford University Press, 2003).

283

343 Ibid., 23.

344 Gushee, *The Future of Faith*, 85.

345 Whitman, *Harsh Justice*, 14.

346 Edward Ayers, *Vengeance and Justice: Crime and Punishment in the 19th Century American South* (New York: Oxford University Press, 1984) 56.

347 For discussion of the continuation of slavery in the South through forced labor and incarceration, see Douglas Blackmon, *Slavery by Another Name: The Re-Enslavement of Black Americans from the Civil War to World War II* (New York: Doubleday, 2008).

348 Whitman, *Harsh Justice*, 43.

349 Dahlia Lithwick, "The Fiction Behind Torture Policy," *Newsweek* (4 August 2008): 11.

350 Ibid.

351 Sarah Palin, "Sarah Palin's Speech to the RNC," 9 September 2008, www.johnmccain.com/Informing/News/Speeches/c1af6c79-f5bf–42ed–9fb9–9e83b0c580e1.htm.

352 George Hunsinger, *Disruptive Grace: Studies in the Theology of Karl Barth* (Grand Rapids MI: William B. Eerdmans Publishing Company, 2000), esp. his section on "Political Theology," 21–128.

353 Ibid., 114, from Eberhard Busch, *Karl Barth* (Philadelphia: Fortress Press, 1976) 185.

Insights from the Next Generation

354 Murat Kurnaz, *Fünf Jahre meines Lebens* (Berlin: Rowohlt, 2007); quotation from English version, *Five Years of My Life*, trans. Jefferson Chase (New York: Palgrave Macmillan, 2008) 149.

355 In a longer version of my research, published in *Commonweal* magazine (5 December 2008, 11–18), there are more examples and further analysis. Thanks to *Commonweal* for permitting portions of that text to be included here.

356 Michael Isikoff and John Barry, "SouthCom Showdown," *Newsweek* 145/19 (9 May 2005): 10.

357 In addition to allegations made by ex-detainees, there is also the recent report of the US inspector general, in which thirty-one FBI agents claimed awareness of such allegations while working at Guantánamo. US Dept. of Justice, Oversight and Review Division, and Office of the Inspector General, "A Review of the FBI's Involvement in and Observations of Detainee Interrogations in Guantánamo Bay, Afghanistan, and Iraq," May 2008, unclassified, 187–88, available at www.usdoj.gov/oig/special/s0805/final.pdf.

358 "US Soldier Uses Quran for Target Practice; Military Apologizes," www.cnn.com/2008/WORLD/meast/05/17/iraq.quran.

359 Almost all of these claims are multiply attested. The most common are rough handling, throwing, squatting over, trampling, and kicking. For the rest of the list, here is at least one source for each: written on: James Yee, *For God and Country* (New York: Public Affairs, 2005) 112; ripped or cut: Kurnaz, *Five Years*, 212; urinated or defecated on: interview of Mohamed Mazouz in "Les Américains pissaient sur le Coran et abusaient de nous sexuellement," *La Gazette du Maroc*, 11 April 2005, also available at www.lagazettedumaroc.com/articles.php?id_artl=6272&n=415&sr=852&r=2; picked up by dog: Gösta Hultén and Mehdi Ghezali, *Fånge På Guantánamo* (Stockholm: Leopard Förlag, 2005) 7, 32, and US State Department cable concerning an interview in the Jordanian newspaper *Al-Sabil*, available at http://humanrights.ucdavis.edu/projects/the-Guantánamo-testimonials-project/testimonies/prisoner-testimonies/statedept_cable_2004.pdf; tossed and used to clean boots: Mahvish Rukhsana Khan, *My Guantánamo Diary* (New York:

Public Affairs, 2008) 217; thrown in bucket of excrement: interview of Khalid al-Asmr in Roger Willemsen, *Hier Spricht Guantánamo* (Frankfurt: Zweitausendeins, 2006) 45, and the "Tipton Report," 72, 74, also available at http://humanrights.ucdavis.edu/projects/the-Guantánamo-testimonials-project/testimonies/prisoner-testimonies/the-tipton-report.

360 Interview of Timur Ishmuratov in Willemsen, *Hier Spricht*, 121.

361 Interview of Mazouz, "Les Américains."

362 He wrote, "Our scrupulousness extends even to providing them with their own Korans, which is the only reason alleged abuses of the Koran at Guantánamo ever became an issue. That we should have provided those who kill innocents in the name of Islam with precisely the document that inspires their barbarism is a sign of the absurd lengths to which we often go in extending undeserved humanity to terrorist prisoners." Charles Krauthammer, "The Truth About Torture," *The Weekly Standard* 11/12 (5 December 2005) www.weeklystandard.com/content/public/articles/000/000/006/400rhqav.asp (accessed 10 August 2008).

363 Only a week after its publication, Krauthammer's argument was deftly rebutted in this way by Pierre Tristam, "Iraq's Undivine Comedy," *Daytona Beach News-Journal*, 13 December 2005.

364 Kurnaz, *Five Years*, 148, 188; interview of al-Asmr in Willemsen, *Hier Spricht*, 64; "Tipton Report," 114.

365 Kurnaz, *Five Years*, 148, 188; interview of al-Asmr in Willemsen, *Hier Spricht*, 65; Hultén and Ghezali, *Fånge På Guantánamo*, 32; according to Marc Falkoff, lawyer for several Yemeni detainees, the mass suicide attempts of August 2003 were also sparked by Koran abuse.

366 Kurnaz, *Five Years*, 154; interviews of Ishmuratov and Abdul Salam Zaeef in Willemsen, *Hier Spricht*, 122, 227; "Tipton Report," 72.

367 Yee, *For God and Country*, 110.

368 Ibid., 121.

369 Kurnaz, *Five Years*, 151; Hultén and Ghezali, *Fånge På Guantánamo*, 36; interview of Ishmuratov in Willemsen, *Hier Spricht*, 121.

370 Bill Dedman, "Battle Over Tactics Raged at Gitmo," MSNBC.com, 23 October 2006, http://humanrights.ucdavis.edu/projects/the-Guantánamo-testimonials-project/testimonies/testimonies-of-the-defense-department/battle-over-tactics-raged-at-gitmo/?searchterm=koran; Juan Cole, "Guantánamo Controversies: Bible and Koran," from his "Informed Comment" blog, 16 May 2005, available at www.juancole.com/2005/05/Guantánamo-controversies-bible-and.html; Jane Mayer, *The Dark Side*, 157–64, 196–97.

371 The most common complaint was that the guards made noise on the cages or played loud rock music during prayer. Kurnaz, *Five Years*, 98, 116, 146, 181; interview of al-Asmr in Willemsen, *Hier Spricht*, 47; "Tipton Report," 63, 71; Hultén and Ghezali, *Fånge På Guantánamo*, 32; interview of Adel Hassan Hamad in Scott Baldauf, "Former Guantánamo Prisoner Asks US to Review Its Founding Ideals," *Christian Science Monitor* (6 February 2008).

372 The prayerful season of Ramadan was respected, in a sense, since the entire ordeal was really a fast. (The meals shown to the media were fake, according to the detainees.) But the joyful Muslim holidays were not to be celebrated. Eid is the Muslim holiday that concludes Ramadan. It is a festive time of gift-giving, unity, and abundance. Abdullah Wazir Zadran, an ex-detainee from Afghanistan, reports that guards put up two posters around the camp to mark the holiday. One showed "beautiful, happy, Muslim children" who were "laughing, wearing new clothes, and holding gifts and money." The other one showed Muslim children "wearing tattered, dirty clothing, crying, with no gifts or money." It contained the caption, "These are your children on Eid day." Reported by Abdullah Wazir Zadran in Khan, *My Guantánamo Diary*, 259.

NOTES

373 Kurnaz, *Five Years*, 98; interview of Ishmuratov in Willemsen, *Hier Spricht*, 124; interview of Airat Vahitov in Valentinas Mite, "Former Guantánamo Detainees Meet To Share Experiences," *Radio Free Europe/Radio Liberty* (19 November 2005).

374 Erik Saar and Viveca Novak, *Inside the Wire* (New York: Penguin, 2005) 221–29.

375 Seth B. Waxman et al., "Memorandum of Law in Support of Motion for Temporary Restraining Order and Preliminary Injunction," filed in the US District Court for the District of Columbia, for *Isa Ali Abdulla Almurbati, et al. v. George Walker Bush, et al.*, Civil Action No. 04–1127 (RBW) 31 October 2005, 9–10.

376 Amin al-Sheikh, during the trial of Spc. Charles Graner, http://news.bbc.co.uk/1/hi/world/americas/4165627.stm.

377 Yee, *For God and Country*, 113.

378 Waxman et al., "Memorandum," 8–9, corroborated by the FBI; interview of al-Asmr in Willemsen, *Hier Spricht*, 65.

379 Waxman et al., "Memorandum," 8.

380 Federal Bureau of Investigation, "GTMO, Counterterrorism Division, Special Inquiry," 44–46, available at http://foia.fbi.gov/foiaindex/Guantánamo.htm.

381 Peter Steinfels, "The Truth About Torture," *New York Times*, 4 December 2004.

382 2 Maccabees 7:2, trans. NRSV.

383 Interview with Tom Lasseter of *McClatchy Newspapers*, available at http://detainees.mcclatchydc.com/detainees/9.

384 For example, the prison break in Kandahar on 13 June 2008; see Carlotta Gall, "Taliban Free 1,200 Inmates in Attack on Afghan Prison," *New York Times*, 14 June 2008.

385 We can also learn from the ways that Jews and Christians read themselves into the story of the Maccabees. Empathy lies undoubtedly with the protagonist heroes. Perhaps a reader identifies with one of the martyrs, who would rather die nobly than be forced to religious apostasy. Perhaps another is inspired by the chief insurgent, Judah the Maccabee, who would rather retaliate with force than accept the religious humiliation of his people. The question then becomes, where do we read ourselves into the stories of Afghanistan, Iraq, and Guantánamo?

386 M. A. Muqtedar Khan, "Quran Desecration: Far Worse than Abu Ghraib," published 19 May 2005 at commondreams.org, www.commondreams.org/views05/0519–23.htm.

387 Mohammed El Gharani, "First Poem of My Life," in *Poems from Guantánamo*, ed. Marc Falkoff (Iowa City: University of Iowa Press, 2007) 39.

388 Rick Lyman, "White House Takes Steps to Renew Ties to Hollywood," *New York Times*, 11 November 2001; Gregg Kilday, "H'wood Meets White House at War Summit," *Hollywood Reporter* (12 November 2001); Dana Calvo, "Hollywood Signs on to Assist War Effort," *Los Angeles Times*, 12 November 2001; Megan Garvey, "Studios to Put on a Show of Support, Patriotism," *Los Angeles Times*, 7 December 2001; Jill Feiwell and Pamela McClintock, "White House Sez H'W'D True Blue," *Daily Variety*, 7 December 2001; Rick Lyman, "3 Minutes of Patriotism on Film," *New York Times*, 20 December 2001. For a detailed analysis of the film in relation to larger cultural effects of the September 11 attacks, see Susan Faludi, *The Terror Dream: Fear and Fantasy in Post-9/11 America* (New York: Metropolitan, 2007) 6–7.

389 Andrew Klavan, "What Bush and Batman Have in Common," *Wall Street Journal*, 25 July 2008. For an even more extended comparison between Batman and Jesus, see Margaret Stahl and Daniel Cosacchi, "God and 'The Dark Knight,'" *America* (18 August 2008).

390 *The Dark Knight* goes further than either "24" or the Bourne series to suggest the causal connection between vigilante justice and increased threat: it repeatedly suggests that when Batman took the law into his own hands to make the world a safer place, he unleashed a force of anarchy, represented in the Joker, that to be fought will require him to step even further out of the bounds of law.

391 Michael Otterman, *American Torture: From the Cold War to Abu Ghraib and Beyond* (Ann Arbor MI: Pluto Press, 2007) 119–21.

392 Ibid., 118.

393 Ibid.

394 Ibid., 122.

395 Ibid.

396 Ibid., 181.

397 Wolfhart Pannenberg, *Systematic Theology (Vol. 3)*, trans. Geoffrey W. Bromiley (Grand Rapids MI: Eerdmans, 1993) 49.

398 Ibid., 51.

399 Ibid., 49.

400 Ibid.

401 Ibid.

National Security, Torture, and a Practical Way Forward

402 Third Way's National Security Poll was conducted by Greenberg Quinlan Rosner Research and sampled 800 registered voters from 21–24 July 2008.

403 Faith in Public Life and Mercer University poll was conducted by Public Religion Research and sampled 600 participants from 14–22 August 2008.

404 The Intelligence Authorization Bill passed 222-199 in the House in December 2007 and 51-45 in February 2008. Both votes were almost exactly along party lines. Bush vetoed the bill in March 2008.

✳

APPENDIX

New Poll of White Evangelicals Shows Faith, Golden Rule Influence Attitudes on Torture

EMBARGOED FOR RELEASE until September 11, 2008 at 10:45 a.m. Contact: Katie Paris, Faith in Public Life, 202-243-8289

A new poll commissioned by Faith in Public Life and Mercer University and conducted by Public Religion Research demonstrates the conflicted attitudes on torture among white evangelical Christians in the South.

Close to six-in-ten white evangelicals in the South say that torture can be often (20%) or sometimes (37%) justified in order to gain important information. This compares to roughly half (48%) of the general public who believe that torture can be justified, according to a recent Pew Research Center poll (02/2008).

Despite high levels of religiosity, white evangelicals in the South are significantly more likely to rely on life experiences

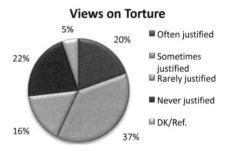

Views on Torture

- Often justified
- Sometimes justified
- Rarely justified
- Never justified
- DK/Ref.

20%
5%
22%
16%
37%

and common sense (44%) than Christian teachings or beliefs (28%) when thinking about the acceptability of torture. And only about one-in-twenty white evangelicals rely on the advice of government leaders when it comes to torture. These different sources of moral thinking lead to strikingly different attitudes.

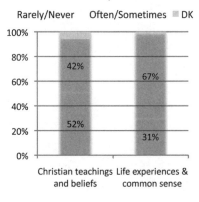

Different Sources, Different Attitudes on Torture

Torture can be justified...

Rarely/Never Often/Sometimes ▒ DK

Among those influenced by Christian teachings, a majority (52%) oppose torture—14 points higher than white evangelicals in the South overall. In contrast, among those who rely most on life experiences and common sense, less than one-in-three (31%) oppose torture.

A majority (52%) agree with the Golden Rule argument against torture—that the U.S. government should not use methods against our enemies that we would not want used on American soldiers. This movement represents a 14-point increase from the 38% of white evangelicals who initially said that torture is rarely or never justified. Appeals to three other moral and theological frames did not significantly influence views on torture.

An appeal to the Golden Rule increases opposition to torture among every subgroup of white evangelicals. For example, only about one third (34%) of white evangelicals who attend worship services more than once a week say torture is never or rarely justified, but a majority (50%) of this group was persuaded by the Golden Rule argument against torture. This represents a 16-point shift in opinion among the most frequent attending white evangelicals in the South.

Other Findings

A majority (53%) of white evangelicals in the South believe that the government uses torture as part of the campaign against terrorism, despite repeated claims made by government officials that the U.S. does not engage in torture. Only about one third (32%) say that the U.S. does not use torture as a matter of policy.

Among white evangelicals in the South who are registered voters, 65% support Republican John McCain, 14% support Democrat Barack Obama, and 21% remain undecided. These findings are consistent with the recent Time Magazine poll (08/04/2008) that showed 66% supporting McCain, 17% supporting Obama, and 17% undecided among white evangelicals nationwide.

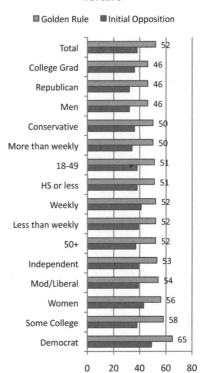

Difference in Opposition to Torture

■ Golden Rule   ■ Initial Opposition

Total	52
College Grad	46
Republican	46
Men	46
Conservative	50
More than weekly	50
18-49	51
HS or less	51
Weekly	52
Less than weekly	52
50+	52
Independent	53
Mod/Liberal	54
Women	56
Some College	58
Democrat	65

0   20   40   60   80

Two thirds of John McCain's supporters say torture can often or sometimes be justified, compared to only 46% of Obama supporters and undecided voters.

About the Survey

This survey was commissioned by Mercer University and Faith in Public Life and conducted by Public Religion Research. Results for this survey were based on telephone interviews conducted under the direction of Opinion Access Corporation among a sample of 600 white evangelical Christian adults, age 18 years or older in the southeastern United States.

This region includes the following states: Alabama, Arkansas, Florida, Georgia, Kentucky, Louisiana, Mississippi, North Carolina, Oklahoma, South Carolina, Tennessee, Texas, Virginia and West Virginia. The survey was fielded from August 14-22, 2008. The margin of error for the total sample is +/- 4.5% at the 95% confidence interval. In addition to sampling error surveys may also be subject to error or bias due to question wording, context and order effects. The data was weighted using demographic weighting parameters derived from the Religious Landscape Survey. Conducted by the Pew Forum on Religion & Public Life from May 8 – August 13, 2007, the Religious Landscape Survey is a national survey of 35,000 adults with detailed information on religious affiliation and identity.

Faith in Public Life is a communications and organizing resource center dedicated to helping faith leaders reclaim the values debate in America for justice, compassion, and the common good. Faith in Public Life is a nonpartisan 501(c) (3) organization. For more information, visit www.faithinpubliclife.org.

292

Founded in 1833 by Georgia Baptists, Mercer University is a comprehensive, faith-based university enrolling more than 7,600 undergraduate, graduate and professional students in 11 schools and colleges on major campuses in Macon, Atlanta and Savannah. For more information, visit www.mercer.edu.

✲

A Bibliography on Religious Faith and Torture

Compiled by Peter Otto, Mercer University Librarian

Amnesty International. *Optional Protocol to the Convention Against Torture: Time to Take a Stand on the Prevention of Torture.* London: Amnesty International, International Secretariat, 2001.

Amnesty International. *Preventing Torture at Home: A Guide to the Establishment of National Preventive Mechanisms.* London: Amnesty International, International Secretariat, 2004.

Annas, G. J. "Unspeakably Cruel—Torture, Medical Ethics, and the Law." *The New England Journal of Medicine, 352*(20): 2127.

Athey, S. "Rethinking Torture's Dark Chamber." *Peace Review, 20*(1): 13–21.

Avram, W. *Anxious about Empire: Theological Essays on the New Global Realities.* Grand Rapids MI: Brazos Press, 2004.

Basoglu, M. *Torture and Its Consequences: Current Treatment Approaches.* Cambridge NY: Cambridge University Press, 1998.

Bassiouni, M. C. "The Institutionalization of Torture under the Bush Administration." *Case Western Reserve Journal of International Law, 37*(2): 389–425.

Betz, J. "The Definition of Torture." *Social Philosophy Today, 22* (2006): 127–35.

Beverley, J. "The Question of Torture, the Spanish Decadence, and Our Own." *Boundary 2, 34*(3): 189–205.

Bilder, R. B., and D. F. Vagts. "Speaking Law to Power: Lawyers and Torture." *The American Journal of International Law, 98*(4): 689.

Bovard, J. "Breaking Bush's Resistance." *American Conservative, 6*(15): 25–27.

———. "Sins of Commission." *American Conservative, 5*(24): 16–18.

———. "We Have Ways…." *American Conservative, 6*(21): 24–25.

Burgers, J. H., and H. Danelius. *The United Nations Convention Against Torture: A Handbook on the Convention Against Torture and Other Cruel, Inhuman, or Degrading Treatment or Punishment.* Dordrecht; Boston: M. Nijhoff, sold and distributed in the USA and Canada by Kluwer Academic Publishers, 1988.

Bybee, J. S., United States Dept. of Justice and Office of Legal Counsel. *Standards of Conduct for Interrogation under 18 USC. 2340–2340A, Memorandum from the Justice Department's Office of Legal Counsel for Alberto R. Gonzales, Counsel to the President.* Washington, DC: Office of the Assistant Attorney General, 2002.

Carnes, T. "Front Line Dilemmas: Christians in Intelligence Services Are Conflicted over the Use of Torture." *Christianity Today, 50*(2): 38–41.

Carson, C. R. "The Military Commissions Act of 2006: How Its Inability to Curb Abusive Interrogations Threatens the Future Treatment of Detainees and the United States' Reputation." *Emory Law Journal, 57*(3): 695–733.

Cavanaugh, W. T. "Liturgy as Politics: An Interview with William Cavanaugh." *Christian Century, 122*(25): 28–32.

———. "Taking Exception: When Torture Becomes Thinkable." *Christian Century, 122*(2): 9–10.

———. *Theopolitical Imagination.* London; New York: T & T Clark, 2002.

———. *Torture and Eucharist: Theology, Politics, and the Body of Christ.* Oxford UK; Malden MA: Blackwell Publishers, 1998.

Celermajer, D. "If Islam Is Our 'Other,' Who Are 'We'?" *Australian Journal of Social Issues, 42*(1): 103.

Chung, E. Y. "A Double-Edged Sword: Reconciling the United States' International Obligations under the Convention Against Torture." *Emory Law Journal, 51*(1): 355.

Cobb, J. B., and Progressive Christians Uniting. *Progressive Christians Speak: A Different Voice on Faith and Politics.* Louisville KY: Westminster John Knox Press, 2003.

Crook, J. R. "Contemporary Practice of the United States Relating to International Law: US Report to Committee Against Torture Expresses US Opposition to Torture." *American Journal of International Law, 99*(3): 719.

———, editor. "International Human Rights and International Criminal Law." *American Journal of International Law, 102*(1): 177–87.

Cutler, L. "Human Rights Guarantees, Constitutional Law, and the Military Commissions Act of 2006." *Peace & Change, 33*(1): 31–59.

Danner, M. *Torture and Truth: America, Abu Ghraib, and the War on Terror.* New York: New York Review of Books, 2004.

Davis, M. "Three Fallacies of Torture." *Free Inquiry, 26*(1): 49–50.

Decker, J. A. "Is the United States Bound by the Customary International Law of Torture?" A proposal for ATS litigation in the war on terror. *Chicago Journal of International Law, 6*(2): 803.

Doris, J. M., and D. Murphy. "From My Lai to Abu Ghraib: The Moral Psychology of Atrocity." *Midwest Studies in Philosophy, 31*(1): 25–55.

Elsea, J., Library of Congress and Congressional Research Service. *US Treatment of Prisoners in Iraq: Selected Legal Issues.* Washington DC: Congressional Research Services, the Library of Congress, 2005.

Farer, T. J. "The Two Faces of Terror." *American Journal of International Law, 101*(2): 363–81.

Feld, E. "Developing a Jewish Theology Regarding Torture." *Theology Today, 63*(3): 324–29.

Foster, G. D. "America's Strategically Debilitating Torture Posture." *The Humanist, 67*(4): 10.

Glancy, J. A. "Torture: Flesh, Truth, and the Fourth Gospel." *Biblical Interpretation, 13*(2): 107–36.

Goldberg, J. "The Torture Question." *National Review, 57*(23): 12.

Goldstone, R. "Combating Terrorism: Zero Tolerance for Torture." *Case Western Reserve Journal of International Law, 37*(2/3): 343.

Gross, O. "Torture and an Ethics of Responsibility." *Law, Culture and the Humanities, 3*(1): 35.

Gushee, D. P. "5 Reasons Torture Is Always Wrong." *Christianity Today, 50*(2): 32–37.

————. "Against Torture: An Evangelical Perspective." *Theology Today, 63*(3): 349–64.

————. *Christians and Politics beyond the Culture Wars: An Agenda for Engagement.* Grand Rapids MI: Baker Books, 2000.

————. *The Future of Faith in American Politics: The Public Witness of the Evangelical Center.* Waco TX: Baylor University Press, 2008.

Gutierrez, D. "The Extraordinary Cruelty of 'Extraordinary Rendition.'" *Humanist, 66*(1): 11–15.

Hakimi, M. "The Council of Europe Addresses CIA Rendition and Detention Program." *American Journal of International Law, 101*(2): 442–52.

Harbury, J. *Truth, Torture, and the American Way: The History and Consequences of US Involvement in Torture.* Boston: Beacon Press, 2005.

Heffernan, J. "US Health Professionals' Call to Prevent Torture and Abuse of Detainees in US Custody." *Journal of Ambulatory Care Management, 28*(4): 366–67.

Henderson, S. W. "Disregarding the Suffering of Others: Narrative, Comedy, and Torture." *Literature & Medicine, 24*(2): 181–208.

Herron, R., and D. Taylor. *How Can a Christian Be in Politics: A Guide toward Faithful Politics.* Wheaton IL: Tyndale House Publishers, 2005.

Hersh, S. M. *Chain of Command: The Road from 9/11 to Abu Ghraib.* New York: HarperCollins, 2004.

Hodgson, G. "The US-European Torture Dispute: An Autopsy." *World Policy Journal, 22*(4): 7–14.

Holmes, D., and A. Perron. "Violating Ethics: Unlawful Combatants, National Security and Health Professionals." *Journal of Medical Ethics, 33*(3): 143–45.

Hooks, G., and C. Mosher. "Outrages against Personal Dignity: Rationalizing Abuse and Torture in the War on Terror." *Social Forces, 83*(4): 1627–45.

Hron, M. "Torture Goes Pop!" *Peace Review, 20*(1): 22–30.

Huggins, M. K. "Torture 101: Lessons from the Brazilian Case." *Journal of Third World Studies, 22*(2): 161–73.

Hunsinger, G. "Torture, Common Morality, and the Golden Rule: A Conversation with Michael Perry." *Theology Today, 63*(3): 375–79.

Johnson, K. D. "Inhuman Behavior: A Chaplain's View of Torture." *Christian Century, 123*(8): 26–27.

————. *Theology, Political Theory, and Pluralism: Beyond Tolerance and Difference.* Cambridge: Cambridge University Press, 2006.

Kira, I. A., T. Templin, L. Lewandowski, D. Clifford, P. Wiencek, A. Hammad, et al. "The Effects of Torture: Two Community Studies." *Peace & Conflict, 12*(3): 205.

Krause, J. "The Architects." *ABA Journal, 93*(9): 27–29.

Lamy, S. L. "The Mighty and the Almighty: Reflections on America, God, and World Affairs." *Journal of Church and State, 49*(4): 779.

Levinson, S. *Torture: A Collection.* Oxford; New York: Oxford University Press, 2004.

Limon, J. *The Shame of Abu Ghraib.* Chicago: University of Chicago Press, 2007.

Lomas, L. "'The War Cut out My Tongue': Domestic Violence, Foreign Wars, and Translation in Demetria Martínez." *American Literature, 78*(2): 357–87.

Luban, D. "Torture and the Professions." *Criminal Justice Ethics, 26*(2): 2–66.

Lukes, S. "Liberal Democratic Torture." *British Journal of Political Science, 36*(1): 1.

Margulies, J. *Guantánamo and the Abuse of Presidential Power.* New York: Simon & Schuster, 2006.

Margulies, P. "The Military Commissions Act, Coerced Confessions, and the Role of the Courts." *Criminal Justice Ethics, 25*(2): 2.

Marks, J. H. "Doctors of Interrogation." *The Hastings Center Report, 35*(4): 17.

Marshall, P. A. *God and the Constitution: Christianity and American Politics.* Lanham MD: Rowman & Littlefield, 2002.

McCoy, A. W. *A Question of Torture: CIA Interrogation, from the Cold War to the War on Terror.* New York: Metropolitan Books/Henry Holt and Co., 2006.

McMahan, J. "Torture, Morality, and Law." *Case Western Reserve Journal of International Law, 37*(2/3): 241.

Mesle, C. R. "What Shall We Say to the Torturer? Moral Realism, Conscience, and Human Nature." *American Journal of Theology & Philosophy, 26*(1–2): 129–45.

Methods of Combating Torture. Geneva: United Nations Center for Human Rights, 1989.

Midgley, J. "Advocacy, Politics, and the Responsibilities of Professional Associations: The Curious Case of the Guest Editorial." *Journal of Progressive Human Services, 18*(2): 1–5.

Miles, S. H. *Oath Betrayed: Torture, Medical Complicity, and the War on Terror.* New York: Random House, 2006.

Mitka, M. "Physicians Condemn Torture." *JAMA: Journal of the American Medical Association, 294*(22): 2833.

Monahan, T. "Securing the Homeland: Torture, Preparedness, and the Right to Let Die." *Social Justice, 33*(1): 95–105.

Nelson-Pallmeyer, J. *Saving Christianity from Empire.* New York: Continuum, 2005.

Nowak, M., E. McArthur and K. Buchinger. *The United Nations Convention Against Torture: A Commentary.* Oxford; New York: Oxford University Press, 2008.

Ogletree, T. W. *The World Calling: The Church's Witness in Politics and Society.* Louisville KY: Westminster John Knox Press, 2004.

Okie, S. "Glimpses of Guantánamo: Medical Ethics and the War on Terror." *The New England Journal of Medicine, 353*(24): 2529.

Ortiz, D. "Theology, International Law, and Torture: A Survivor's View." *Theology Today, 63*(3): 344–48.

Osofsky, H. M. "Domesticating International Criminal Law: Bringing Human Rights Violators to Justice." *The Yale Law Journal, 107*(1): 191.

Pahl, R. H. "Gitmo! Reviews of Four Recent Books about Guantánamo Bay and the Conduct of the United States in Its War on Terrorism." *Social Studies, 98*(2): 78–79.

Paust, J. J. "Above the Law: Unlawful Executive Authorizations Regarding Detainee Treatment, Secret Renditions, Domestic Spying, and Claims to Unchecked Executive Power." *Utah Law Review, 2007*(2): 345–419.

Pfiffner, J. P. "Torture and Public Policy." *Public Integrity, 7*(4): 313–29.

Ratner, M., and E. Ray. *Guantánamo: What the World Should Know.* White River Junction VT: Chelsea Green Publishing, 2004.

Ratner, S. R. "Geneva Conventions." *Foreign Policy,* (165): 26–32.

Reis, C., A. T. Ahmed, L. L. Amowitz, and A. L. Kushner. "Physician Participation in Human Rights Abuses in Southern Iraq." *JAMA: The Journal of the American Medical Association, 291*(12): 1480.

Roth, K., M. Worden, A. D. Bernstein, and Human Rights Watch. *Torture: Does It Make Us Safer? Is It Ever OK?: A Human Rights Perspective.* New York: New Press, distributed by W.W. Norton, 2005.

Rothchild, J. "Moral Consensus, the Rule of Law, and the Practice of Torture." *Journal of the Society of Christian Ethics, 26*(2): 125–56.

Rothchild, J., M. M. Boulton and K. Jung. *Doing Justice to Mercy: Religion, Law, and Criminal Justice.* Charlottesville VA: University of Virginia Press, 2007.

Rubenstein, L., C. Pross, F. Davidoff, and V. Iacopino. "Coercive US Interrogation Policies: A Challenge to Medical Ethics." *JAMA: The Journal of the American Medical Association, 294*(12): 1544.

Rychlak, R. J. "Interrogating Terrorists: From Miranda Warnings to 'Enhanced Interrogation Techniques.'" *San Diego Law Review, 44*(3): 451–75.

Sands, P. "Lawless World: The Cultures of International Law." *Texas International Law Journal, 41*(3): 387–97.

Scott, P., and W. T. Cavanaugh. *The Blackwell Companion to Political Theology.* Malden MA: Blackwell Publishing, 2008.

Seidman, L. M. "Torture's Truth." *The University of Chicago Law Review, 72*(3): 881.

Shoemaker, H. S. *Being Christian in an Almost Chosen Nation: Thinking about Faith and Politics.* Nashville TN: Abingdon Press, 2006.

Sider, R. J., and D. Knippers. *Toward an Evangelical Public Policy: Political Strategies for the Health of the Nation.* Grand Rapids MI: Baker Books, 2005.

Skillen, J. W. *The Scattered Voice: Christians at Odds in the Public Square.* Grand Rapids MI: Zondervan, 1990.

Skoll, G. R. "Torture and the Fifth Amendment: Torture, the Global War on Terror, and Constitutional Values." *Criminal Justice Review, 33*(1): 29–47.

Smith, H. F., and M. Freeman. "The Mandatory Reporting of Torture by Detention Center Officials: An Original Proposal." *Human Rights Quarterly, 27*(1): 327.

Sundstrom, R. "Torture and Legitimacy." *Peace Review, 18*(4): 439–46.

Taylor, D. "Double-Blind: The Torture Case." *Critical Inquiry, 33*(4): 710–33.

Taylor, M. L. "American Torture and the Body of Christ: Making and Remaking Worlds." In *Cross Examinations: Readings on the Meaning of the Cross,* edited by M. Trelstad, 264. Minneapolis: Fortress, 2006.

Tétreault, M. A. "The Sexual Politics of Abu Ghraib: Hegemony, Spectacle, and the Global War on Terror." *NWSA Journal, 18*(3): 33–50.

United Nations, and Office of the High Commissioner for Human Rights. *Combating Torture* (revised 1st edition). Geneva: United Nations High Commissioner for Human Rights, 2002.

Utter, G. H. *Mainline Christians and US Public Policy: A Reference Handbook.* Santa Barbara CA: ABC-CLIO, 2007.

Waldron, J. "What Can Christian Teaching Add to the Debate about Torture?" *Theology Today,* 63(3): 330–43.

Wallis, J. "The Theology of Torture." *Sojourners Magazine, 33*(8): 5–6.

Wantchekon, L., and A. Healy. "The 'Game' of Torture." *The Journal of Conflict Resolution,* 43(5): 596–609.

Wendland, L., and Association for the Prevention of Torture. *A Handbook on State Obligations under the UN Convention Against Torture.* Geneva: Association for the Prevention of Torture, 2002.

Wisnewski, J. J. "Unwarranted Torture Warrants: A Critique of the Dershowitz Proposal." *Journal of Social Philosophy,* 39(2): 308–21.

Wittes, B. "Terrorism, the Military, and the Courts." *Policy Review,* (143): 21–42.

Wogaman, J. P. *Christian Perspectives on Politics* (revised edition). Louisville KY: Westminster John Knox Press, 2000.

Wynia, M. K. "Laying the Groundwork for a Defense against Participation in Torture?" *The Hastings Center Report,* 38(1): 11.

★

Contributors[*]

Dr. Elizabeth M. Bounds is an associate professor of Christian ethics, the director of the graduate division of religion, and the coordinator of the Initiative in Religious Practices and Practices Theology at Emory University. She is the author of *Coming Together/Coming Apart: Religion, Modernity, and Community* and coeditor of *Welfare Policy: Feminist Critiques*. She attended Harvard, Cambridge, and Union Theological Seminary.

John Chandler is a partner at Sutherland Asbill & Brennan LLP and is currently representing seven men from Yemen who have been detained by our government at Guantánamo without being charged, some for five years now. John graduated with a B.S. from the University of Tennessee in 1966, served two years in the Army, and then graduated from Vanderbilt University Law School in 1972.

Mark P. Denbeaux is a professor of law at Seton Hall Law School, as well as the director of the Seton Hall Law School Center for Policy and Research, which is best known for its dissemination of the internationally recognized series of reports on the Guantánamo Bay detention camp. Denbeaux's interest in the conditions of detainment arose from his representation of two detainees there. He graduated from the College of Wooster and the New York University School of Law.

Mohamed Elsanousi is the director of communications and community outreach for the Islamic Society of North America. He also serves on the board of directors for several interfaith organizations, including the board of governors of the Religious Communicators Council, the Interfaith Broadcasting Commission, and the National Religious Campaign Against Torture. He is currently a doctoral candidate in law and society at Indiana University School of Law.

Dr. Karen J. Greenberg is the executive director of the Center on Law and Security at New York University School of Law. She is the editor of the NYU Review of Law and Security, co-editor of *The Torture Papers: The Road to Abu Ghraib*, and editor of the books *Al Qaeda Now* and *The Torture Debate in America*. She is also a former vice president of the Soros Foundation/Open Society Institute and the founding director of the Program in International Education.

*As of 09/11/08

Dr. David P. Gushee is the distinguished university professor of Christian ethics at Mercer University and the president of Evangelicals for Human Rights. He has authored eleven books; over seventy-five scholarly essays, book chapters, articles, and reviews; and hundreds of magazine articles and opinion pieces. His most recent book is *The Future of Faith in American Politics*, and he is currently researching and writing a book about the theological and ethical roots and implications of belief in the sanctity of human life.

Don Guter is the dean of Duquesne University School of Law, his alma mater, and a former Navy judge advocate general. He retired from the Navy as a rear admiral in June 2002. His military decorations include the Defense Distinguished Service Medal, the Legion of Merit with two gold stars, the Meritorious Service Medal with two gold stars, and the Navy Commendation Medal. He also serves as president of the Judge Advocates Association Foundation.

Gita Gutierrez is an attorney with the Center for Constitutional Rights, a New York-based human rights organization litigating extensive challenges to the executive's post-9/11 anti-terrorism policies. She conducted the first visit by a habeas attorney to Guantánamo in September 2004 and is representing Saudi Guantánamo detainee Mohammed Al-Qatani, who has been held since January 2002 and was subjected to the "first special interrogation plan," a regime of torture and inhuman treatment authorized by the secretary of defense.

Dr. George Hunsinger is the founder of the National Religious Campaign Against Torture and serves as the Hazel Thompson McCord professor of systematic theology at Princeton Seminary. There he served as the director of the seminary's Center for Barth Studies for four years. Before founding NRCAT, he coordinated an open letter on torture to Alberto Gonzales at the time of his confirmation as attorney general of the United States signed by over 225 prominent religious leaders.

Dr. Cheryl Bridges Johns is the professor of Christian formation and discipline at the Church of God Theological Seminary. She has published two books and numerous articles in scholarly and professional journals and has served on the executive committee for the Association of Theological Schools in the United States and Canada. Her areas of interest include Pentecostal theology and the practices of ministry.

Doug Johnson has been a committed advocate of human rights since the 1970s and is currently the executive director of the Center for Victims of Torture. He has led the organization through an important period of growth, as offices and treatment centers opened in St. Paul, Washington, DC, Guinea, and Sierra Leone. He has also pioneered the New Tactics in Human Rights project and the Tactical Mapping methodology. He also serves as a consultant to UNICEF and the World Health Organization.

Dr. Cathleen Kaveny is the John P. Murphy Foundation professor of law and professor of theology at the University of Notre Dame. She has published many articles on issues lying at the intersection of law, morality, and religion, in journals such as *The Hastings Center Report, Theological Studies,* and the *Wake Forrest Law Review*. She has served on the editorial boards of the *Journal of Law and Religion, The Annual of the Society of Christian Ethics,* and the *American Journal of Jurisprudence.*

Rachel Laser is the director of the culture program at Third Way, a Washington, DC think tank dedicated to advancing a twenty-first century progressive agenda. She handles issues such as abortion, finding a common ground culture agenda with centrist Evangelicals, and crime. Prior to joining Third Way, Rachel was senior counsel in the health and reproductive rights group at the National Women's Law Center. Rachel graduated from Harvard University and the University of Chicago Law School.

Dr. Rick Love is currently a postdoctoral fellow in the reconciliation program at the Yale Center for Faith and Culture at the Yale University Divinity School. The goal of Yale's reconciliation program is to promote reconciliation between Muslims and Christians and between Muslim nations and the West. Love has worked to promote reconciliation between Christians and Muslims for twenty-five years, specializing in coaching faith-based organizations in cross-cultural communication and Christian-Muslim relationships.

Dr. Ron Mahurin is the academic vice president and dean of Houghton College. He previously served as the vice president for professional development and research for the Council for Christian Colleges & Universities. He is also the co-author of *Saints as Citizens: A Guide to Political Responsibilities for Christians.* He attended Gordon College and Miami University of Ohio.

Dr. Denise Massey is the associate professor of pastoral care and counseling at the McAfee School of Theology at Mercer University. She is also a certified supervisor with the Association of Clinical Pastoral Education, a life and professional coach, and an affiliate member of the International Coaching Federation. She has lectured extensively in organizations affiliated with the Association for Clinical Pastoral Education.

Dr. Larry McSwain is professor of ethics and leadership at the McAfee School of Theology at Mercer University where he holds the Watkins Christian Foundation-endowed chair in ministry. He is a graduate of Oklahoma State University, Southwestern Baptist Theological Seminary, and the Southern Baptist Theological Seminary. He was at Southern Seminary twenty-three years where he served as a professor and a dean and then served as the president of Shorter College for seven years.

Professor Mahan Mirza is an assistant professor at California State University, Chico. He has an M.A. in Islamic studies and Christian-Muslim relations from Hartford Seminary and is currently completing a Ph.D. in Islamic studies from Yale University in religious studies. Mahan's dissertation is on the confluence of reason and revelation in the eleventh-century Muslim polymath al-Biruni (ca. 1048). He is also currently serving as assistant editor of a forthcoming *Encyclopedia of Islamic Political Thought* from Princeton University Press.

Rev. Matt Norman is working with the Cooperative Baptist Fellowship Global Missions Department based in Atlanta as missiologist and personnel selection manager.

His responsibilities include mentoring candidates interested in mission service through the CBF appointment process, as well as research on mission practice and theology. He is a graduate of Gardner-Webb University with a B.A. in communications. Prior to joining the CBF staff, he held advertising and marketing positions in North Carolina.

Sister Dianna Ortiz is a Catholic nun who was abducted and tortured while working with indigenous people in Guatemala. She is now the executive director of TASSC International, Torture Abolition and Survivors Coalition International, the only organization founded by torture survivors. The mission of TASSC is to abolish torture wherever it occurs. She tells her story in *The Blindfold's Eye: My Journey from Torture to Truth.*

Michael Peppard is a Ph.D. candidate in religious studies at Yale University. His areas of specialization include the New Testament, Judaism and Christianity in antiquity, Greco-Roman religions, and contemporary Jewish-Christian relations. He holds degrees from Yale Divinity School and the University of Notre Dame. His writings have appeared in scholarly books and journals such as *Journal for the Study of the New Testament, Judaism,* and *Commonweal.*

Kathryn Reklis is a Ph.D. candidate in religious studies at Yale University, concentrating in Christian theology. Her areas of interest include theological aesthetics, feminist theology, the relationship between theology and popular culture, and the way that political, cultural, and religious practices mutually inform each other in the creation of modern subjectivities. She is also special assistant to the president at Union Theological Seminary in New York.

Rev. Fleming Rutledge is a preacher and teacher known throughout the mainline Protestant denominations of the United States, Canada, and parts of the UK. She is the author of seven books and has received a grant from the Louisville Foundation to complete a book about the meaning of the crucifixion. Her three sermon collections, *The Bible and The New York Times, Help My Unbelief,* and *The Undoing of Death* (Eerdmans) have met with wide acclaim across denominational lines. Her most recent book is *Not Ashamed of the Gospel: Sermons from Romans.* She is also author of *The Battle for Middle-earth: Tolkien's Divine Design in The Lord of the Rings* and *The Seven Last Words.*

Dr. Glen H. Stassen is the Lewis B. Smedes professor of Christian ethics at Fuller Theological Seminary. He is the author of several books, including two on just peacemaking, and he co-authored the award-winning *Kingdom Ethics: Following Christ in Contemporary Context.* He serves as the president of the Council of the Societies for the Study of Religion, the North American Baptist Professors of Religion, and the Pacific Coast Section of the Society of Christian Ethics.

Dr. Graham B. Walker, Jr. is associate dean for the master of divinity degree program and professor of theology at the McAfee School of Theology at Mercer University. He came to McAfee from the Asia Baptist Graduate Theological Seminary in Baguio City, Philippines, where he served as academic dean. He has published numerous articles in various religious journals and has authored *Elie Wiesel: A Challenge to Theology.*

Rabbi Brian Walt is the founder and executive director for Rabbis for Human Rights, North American. He was born in South Africa where he was active as a Jewish student in the struggle against apartheid. He is also Rabbi Emeritus of Congregation Mishkan Shalom, an activist congregation he founded in Philadelphia in 1988.

Natalie Wigg-Stevenson is a Ph.D. student in the graduate department of religion at Vanderbilt University, focusing on theological studies. She is also a fellow in the Vanderbilt program in theology and practice and holds previous degrees from Yale Divinity School (M.Div., magna cum laude) and McMaster University (combined honors B.A. in art history and religious studies). Prior to coming to Vanderbilt, she lived in her native England for a year, where she worked in the charity sector for a health care organization.

Rev. Tyler Wigg Stevenson is the founder of Two Futures Project (twofuturesproject.org), a confessional Christian initiative seeking a world free of nuclear weapons. An author and ordained Baptist preacher with nearly a decade of experience in nuclear weapons issues, he also directs policy for Faithful Security, a national multi-faith coalition working to reduce the nuclear threat, and sits on the board of directors for the Global Security Institute and the steering committee for Evangelicals for Human Rights. He is the guest contributing editor of the Spring 2009 Yale Divinity School journal, *Reflections*.

Thomas Wilner is the managing partner of the international trade and government relations practice at Shearman and Sterling LLP. He recently served as the counsel of record to Guantánamo detainees in *Rasul vs. Bush* and *Boumediene vs. Bush*. He is a graduate of Yale University and the University of Pennsylvania, where he was the editor of the University of Pennsylvania Law Review.

Steve N. Xenakis, M.D. is retired from the US Army as a brigadier general and is a leading critic of the US torture policy. Since the June 2006 press release of the Pentagon's new guidelines affirming the involvement of psychologists in interrogations, he has been traveling across the country speaking out against torture and abuse of detainees in US custody. He believes this violates the basic code of medical ethics: "first do no harm." He also works with Physicians for Human Rights on this issue.

Drew Zimmer is an intern for Evangelicals for Human Rights. He graduated from Union University with a B.A. in Christian ethics. He is currently pursuing an M.Div. at the McAfee School of Theology at Mercer University and studying Islam at Emory University. He is a research assistant to Dr. David P. Gushee and did the research for the *Christianity Today* article, *5 Reasons Torture is Always Wrong*. He is also a veteran of the US Army Reserves.

Jill Zimmer is an intern for Evangelicals for Human Rights and administrative assistant to Dr. David P. Gushee. She graduated from Union University with a B.A. in Christian ethics and received the Academic Excellence in Christian Ethics Award. She is currently pursuing an M.Div. with an emphasis in academic research from the McAfee School of Theology at Mercer University, including writing a thesis on the use and ethics of memory in Lamentations.